LOST FILMS

LOST FILMS
Important Movies
That Disappeared

Frank Thompson

A Citadel Press Book
Published by Carol Publishing Group

A Citadel Press Book
Published by Carol Publishing Group
Citadel Press is a registered trademark of Carol Communications, Inc.
Editorial Offices: 600 Madison Avenue, New York, N.Y. 10022
Sales and Distribution Offices: 120 Enterprise Avenue, Secaucus, N.J. 07094
In Canada: Canadian Manda Group, One Atlantic Avenue,
Suite 105, Toronto, Ontario M6K 3E7
Queries regarding rights and permissions should be addressed to Carol Publishing
Group, 600 Madison Avenue, New York, N.Y. 10022
Carol Publishing Group books are available at special discounts for bulk
purchases, sales promotion, fund-raising, or educational purposes. Special editions
can be created to specifications. For details, contact: Special Sales Department,
Carol Publishing Group, 120 Enterprise Avenue, Secaucus, N.J. 07094
Manufactured in the United States of America
10 9 8 7 6 5 4 3 2 1

Library of Congress Cataloging-in-Publication Data
Thompson, Frank T., 1952–
Lost films: important movies that disappeared / Frank Thompson.
p.   cm.
"A Citadel Press book."
ISBN 0-8065-1604-6 (pbk.)
1. Silent films—History and criticism.   I. Title.
PN1995.75.T56   1995
791.43'75—dc20   95-19250
                                                          CIP

To
Thomas W. Holland
My friend

CONTENTS

INTRODUCTION*

In 1900, the legendary actress Sarah Bernhardt, then fifty-six years old, was lured before the early motion picture camera to enact a three-minute-long dueling scene from William Shakespeare's *Hamlet*. Over the next two decades, she repeated the cinematic experiment a few times, dying with a thudding fall into an ornate cushion in *La Dame aux Camélias* (1911), emoting imperiously in the successful four-reel production of *Queen Elizabeth* (1912), aiding the war effort in *Mères Françaises* (*Mothers of France*, 1917).

Bernhardt didn't care much for the experience of making movies, nor did she like seeing herself projected, bigger than life, onto a screen; she was reportedly so disgusted by *Tosca* (1908), she demanded that the negative be destroyed.

Nevertheless, she valued the cinema's potential for creating a permanent record of at least some aspect of her genius. She said, "I rely upon these films to make me immortal."

If the Divine Sarah is indeed immortal, it is not her films that make her so; most of her motion pictures have disappeared, consigned to memory and legend no less so than her stage performances.

Many thousands of artists have shared Bernhardt's dream of cinematic immortality, and most of them were just as wrong about the medium's permanence. The cinema gives every promise of living forever; but in fact, it is among the most fragile of art forms. It is commonly believed that of the twenty-one thousand features and shorts produced before 1950, over half have vanished forever. For the silent period—roughly 1893 to 1930—the ratio of lost films may be anywhere from 80 to 90 percent.

The reasons for these dreadful statistics are numerous, but one of

---

*Part of this introduction appeared in a different form as "Fade Out: What's Being Done to Save Our Motion Picture Heritage?" in *American Film Magazine*, August 1991.

the most important is the unstable nature of the film on which all pre-1951 movies were made. The film stock was composed of nitrocellulose (generally called "nitrate"), a highly flammable material that can eventually deteriorate into a bubbling goo, then dry to a powder or a black mass of unprojectable material. Nitrate can last for a very long time if stored in perfect conditions, but decomposition, once begun, progresses rapidly. The challenge to film preservationists is to transfer prints and negatives from nitrate to safety acetate stock as quickly as possible, before more films are lost.

Today, more than ever, studios are supporting preservation efforts, but a film's commercial potential has a lot to do with whether or not it is protected. For non-studio-owned nitrate, held by archives, funding is grossly inadequate to the task.

At this writing, the archives of the world hold about 150 million feet of uncopied nitrate film. Of that, it is estimated over 100 million feet is "unique or best-surviving footage" that, once gone, is irretrievable. With current lab costs at about two dollars per foot for transferring nitrate to safety stock — and this doesn't even count problem pictures that require more time and effort to restore — it doesn't take a math whiz to see that the National Endowment for the Arts/American Film Institute Preservation budget — $355,600 a year in 1994 and slashed to half that in 1995 — cannot do much to erode that $200-million backlog.

Here is just one example: at current budgets, it would take 150 years for the International Museum of Photography at George Eastman House in Rochester, New York, to transfer all the nitrate footage it holds. Of course, most of the nitrate won't survive that long, anyway. Similar budgetary problems afflict every motion picture archive in the world.

Nitrate, however, isn't the only problem. The very nature of film distribution has a great deal to do with how films disappear. When a film is released it is not unusual for dozens, perhaps even hundreds, of prints to be struck and circulated around the world. When the release is over, the great majority of these prints are destroyed. This is only common sense; there isn't much reason to pay for storage of prints that have already been projected many times and that probably bear scratches, scars, and torn sprockets. In the age before video, some films were popular enough to be rereleased, but most were not. Mass audiences, past and present, prefer the latest big picture to one they consider old and out of date.

Because nitrate stock is highly flammable, some studios devised a novel way to get a little more use out of obsolete prints: often, if a film in production needed a large bonfire or other conflagration, the flames were fueled by volatile nitrate footage. Very probably prints—perhaps even negatives—of some of the films discussed in this book were lost this way, or were simply thoughtlessly thrown away by people who could have saved them, but saw no reason to do so.

Junking old release prints is standard operating procedure and is a perfectly reasonable business decision—*if* the negative is kept in good enough condition to reprint the title, when and if it should become desirable to do so. But when the negative is also lost, there is nothing to return to, and the film is gone forever.

To be fair to the studios of the past, few people believed there was any lasting worth to motion pictures. Cinema was a disposable art form, enjoyed this week, forgotten the next, in much the same way we think of a newspaper or, perhaps, a television situation comedy. Audiences didn't notice that these frivolous entertainments also contained a record of the times in which they were made, capturing people, places, styles, and attitudes in a truer, more vivid way than could any history book. As Jean Firstenberg, director of the American Film Institute, has put it, "The people who first made movies, the pioneers, ran a movie in a theater and thought that was the end of its life. They didn't know that it was as much a historic record as an artistic achievement. You need perspective to know that. We know it now."[1]

Saving a single print of an endangered film is obviously important, but saving or restoring the original camera negative, or creating a new duplicate negative from which more prints can be struck, is even more vital. The condition of those negatives—if they exist at all—depends in large part on how popular the film was. The original camera negatives for classics like *Casablanca* were used to print reissue copies for decades and were eventually worn out. Ironically, this practice means that a genuine masterpiece might exist today only as a shadow of its former self, while there are minor films from the thirties, with no rerelease potential, whose negatives are in pristine condition.

Even those studies that kept negatives and prints on hand realized that filling warehouses with highly flammable nitrate stock was probably not such a good idea. They each dealt with the problem in varying ways. Metro-Goldwyn-Mayer deposited all of its nitrate, three-strip Technicolor negatives with Eastman House in the 1970's, ensuring that at least most of M-G-M's three-strip Technicolor films can be preserved or restored to something close to their original condition; in fact, since 1988, an aggressive and successful restoration program has been in place.

Twentieth Century-Fox, on the other hand, quickly (and, some say, carelessly) transferred all of its original nitrate negatives—both black-and-white and Technicolor—to safety acetate and then destroyed the nitrate originals (a devastating vault fire in the thirties had already taken a terrible toll on the Fox library).

The camera negatives of Fox classics like *How Green Was My Valley* (1941), *The Ox-Bow Incident* (1943), the features of Shirley Temple, Will Rogers, Betty Grable—gone. Nitrate 35mm studio prints of many Fox films were donated to the University of California Los Angeles, so duplicate negatives, at least, can be made. However, lacking pristine original negatives, the great Fox films of the twenties, thirties, and forties will never again look quite as good as they did upon first release.

The past few years have seen a dramatic increase in awareness of preservation issues, among studios, filmmakers, and the moviegoing public. In fact, most archivists, despite the discouraging numbers against which they constantly struggle, have begun to feel a guarded optimism about the fight to preserve America's film heritage. And the unexpected savior has been video.

Robert Gitt, of the UCLA Film and Television Archives, admits that "in the bad old days," most of the studios "had a pretty bad record, unfortunately," regarding film preservation. "On the other hand, starting in the fifties and sixties, there have been studios that have tried to be more responsible. Certainly M-G-M [now owned by Turner Entertainment] had a major program to copy everything they had on nitrate over to safety. They weren't able to save everything, but they rescued an awful lot of it. Disney was also quite conscientious. Universal, today, seems to be doing quite a lot. [The studios] are working with archives like ours, and they're also working on their own.

"Admittedly, this is all just good economic sense," Gitt continues, "because of the video revolution and because they can sell these restored films. Also, I think there may be more of a general interest in film history. In each company, I think you will find a few people, somewhere in the executive echelon, who have been to film school, who went to film societies, who saw these movies and care about them. And that dovetails with the fact that these films are economically viable again."[2]

With the birth of home video and the hungry presence of cable television, studios have been forced to dig deeper and deeper into their vaults in search of more and more product. It may be dollars and cents to them, but it's a welcome turn of events for movie lovers who now have greater access to more films than at any time in history. Ted Turner, widely reviled by movie buffs for his enthusiastic support of colorization has, oddly, been at the forefront of preservation, restoring films and showing them on his cable channels Turner Network Television and Turner Classic Movies. Rare early talkies, unseen on television—or anywhere else—in decades, have suddenly become available in pristine, shimmering prints.

Other cable channels, most notably American Movie Classics (which each year hosts a Film Preservation Festival, airing significant movie restorations) regularly present cinematic rarities and treasures, including the UCLA restorations of classics like *Becky Sharp* (1935), the first three-strip Technicolor feature; *Hell's Angels* (1930), Howard Hughes's air spectacle; and William A. Wellman's Technicolor Hollywood tragedy *A Star Is Born* (1937).

There is, however, a certain irony in the fact that film preservation is progressing at full speed at a time when there are virtually no venues left in which to see films in their original forms. Except for the rare big-screen rereleases of restored epics like *Spartacus* (1960), *Lawrence of Arabia* (1963), and *My Fair Lady* (1964), all of the CinemaScope and 70mm blockbusters of the Fifties and Sixties can only be seen on the unfriendly confines of the television screen. John Wayne's *The Alamo* was shorn of about a half hour just weeks after its premiere in the autumn of 1960. That footage was presumed lost until a faded Todd–AO print of the original version was discovered in Toronto in 1990. MGM/UA reinstated this lost footage into both its videocassette and laser disc versions of *The Alamo* but the 70mm film itself remains unrestored. Consequently we are faced with the dilemma of acknowledging that we can now see the film in its "director's cut," but may never again be able to experience its full, visceral, Todd–AO power. By some definitions *The Alamo* has been "restored," but in the strictest sense it has not.

New technology, such as improved laser discs and the long-promised high-definition television, may someday make it possible to present a movie on video with the same tonal range and clarity of film, but that day has not yet come. Systems are being developed that would allow archivists to store entire feature films onto digitally recorded computer files, but this technology is costly (about twelve dollars a frame or almost three hundred dollars per foot of film!), and quite unwieldy—a single 35mm frame requires an entire personal computer's worth of memory to store. Most crucially, the technology is not developing quickly enough to meet the preservation demands of an archive filled with deteriorating motion pictures. For now, the archives must chip away at the mountain of endangered film material and hope that enough can be saved to be enjoyed in whatever format eventually comes down the pike.

In 1980, The American Film Institute released their "Ten Most Wanted List" of lost films. This list included *Cleopatra*, starring Theda Bara (1917); D. W. Griffith's *"That Royle Girl"* (1926); *The Kaiser, Beast of Berlin* (1918); *The Rogue Song*, with Lawrence Tibbett and Laurel and Hardy, photographed in two-color Technicolor (1930); the complete, forty-reel version of Erich von Stroheim's *Greed* (1923); Walt Disney's *Little Red Riding Hood* (1922); Edison's one-reel version of *Frankenstein* (1910); Tod Browning's *London After Midnight*, starring Lon Chaney (1927); *Camille*, starring Norma Talmadge (1927); and the Greta Garbo feature *The Divine Woman* (1927).

In the years since 1980, a reel from *Divine Woman* has been discovered, as has a minute or two from *Rogue Song*. *Frankenstein* is known to exist in a private collection, but attempts to have it preserved in an archive have so far failed. Rumors persist that *London After Midnight* exists and that the collector who owns it is holding it ransom for some astronomical sum. However, these same rumors have floated around for years—with nothing to substantiate them.

Three years after the "most wanted" list was issued, the AFI inaugurated a "Decade of Preservation," in an attempt to bring the issue to the studios, politicians, and moviegoers who could help fund preservation efforts. On May 1, 1990, another blow was struck for the cause. Filmmakers Martin Scorsese, Steven Spielberg, George Lucas, Woody Allen, Sidney Pollack, Francis Coppola, Stanley Kubrick, and Robert Redford joined together to form the Film Foundation, an organization meant to promote and coordinate restoration and preservation projects.

Whereas the studios once viewed archives with distrust, they now seem to be working harmoniously with them in an attempt to save America's film heritage. When New York's Museum of Modern Art began collecting films in 1935, says archivist Eileen Bowser, "it wasn't easy for our founders to convince the studios to deposit their films with us. There was a lot of time winning their confidence. Today, we have it. They know that we have saved many films that were lost by the studios. They appreciate and take advantage of what the film archives have done."[3]

The problems of film preservation, however, extend far beyond copying nitrate onto safety stock and the restoring of endangered films. Susan Dalton of the Library of Congress comments that "all educational, industrial, and documentary films produced on 16mm are in danger. Acetate film also deteriorates [at just about the same rate as nitrate] if not stored properly. We also have the problem of all the local television news footage; it presents great problems in selection and organization and access to the material. Then, of course, we come to the problem of videotape," which has an estimated shelf life of ten to twenty years, "and an even bigger problem with the longevity of the hardware."[4]

Even films that seem perfectly safe may have problems. An alarming number of acknowledged classics no longer have original negatives from which new prints can be struck. The camera negative for *Citizen Kane* (1941) was lost in a fire in the 1970s. Director Robert Wise, *Kane*'s original film editor, supervised the film's "restoration" in 1991, working with a duplicate negative struck from a worn fine-grain print. The result is a compromise: *Citizen Kane* isn't lost, but neither will it ever again look as good as it should. Nor has it been restored; its visual and aural degradation has just been slowed down.

Even a relatively recent film like *Spartacus* (1960) had to be meticulously restored from the black-and-white separation masters and various other preprint sources because its original negative was unusable.

There has never been so much public interest and support for the cause of film restoration and preservation ("They used to tell us it wasn't glamorous," says Eileen Bowser[5]), but the harried archivists all tell the same tale: There is too much to do and not enough money or time to do it. Even if there were, time has run out for thousands and thousands of films. Sarah Bernhardt's wish was granted: the negative to *Tosca* was indeed destroyed—not by design, but by time or by neglect.

Perhaps Bernhardt's other wish might also come true. The day may yet come when the images captured on film will last, when the lucky citizens of the future may know not only the facts of history but the sights, sounds, colors, ideas, attitudes, and tastes of the past. When that day comes, not only Sarah Bernhardt but everyone and everything ever committed to film will be, in a sense, immortal.

Working on this book has been alternately exhilarating and sobering. I have from time to time felt apprehensive about its effect on the reader. I hope I can convey my fascination with these tantalizing motion pictures and can communicate some of the excitement and drama and fun that I have found in them. But *Lost Films* is suffused with sadness, too. These films are gone. No matter how interesting or amazing they seem on paper, we can never, ever experience them as audiences once could. We can read their plot synopses, listen to what the critics had to say, gaze longingly at their surviving photographs. But we can never have the opportunity to evaluate them for ourselves.

A plot synopsis is a fairly dangerous thing. It can tell us what happened in a film but not how it happened. Like the bones of an extinct animal, the synopsis can offer us clues to how the original work moved, lived, breathed. But a synopsis, no matter how thorough or expressive, cannot communicate the artistry, the beauty, the subtlety, the nuance of those privileged moments in film when actors, writers, directors, cinematographers, music composers, and set designers work together to create a mood that simply cannot be adequately described in words. The plot synopses for each film in this book may sound trite or silly or dull. "The story," wrote Peter Milne of *Cleopatra*, "will naturally lose practically all its color in the mere telling."[6] Alone, synopses can't show us how the artists who brought these stories to the screen transformed them from something prosaic into something magical.

All the plot synopses printed in this book come from original sources: pressbooks, magazine articles, studio story departments. I decided not to change a word of any of them, except to silently correct spellings here and there. I made this decision because, obviously, I had no way of examining the films themselves in order to come up with better descriptions, and I wanted to keep the feeling of the period alive, to anchor these movies firmly in the language and expression of their own times. Some films are timeless works of art. The motion pictures in this book are not: Their time has literally come and gone.

In a few cases I decided to combine two, even three, synopses to provide the reader with as much detail as possible. In those cases, always noted, the language has sometimes been slightly altered in order to accommodate the various versions.

Naturally I had to rely very heavily on contemporary reviews. No one who has seriously studied film can doubt how dangerous it is to believe the opinions of critics. Too many films, now acknowledged as classics of their kind, were ignored or ill-treated by reviewers—only to be reevaluated later. Obviously such reevaluation is impossible with these films, so we must use reviews carefully as important, if flawed, reports from the front. In the very earliest days of the cinema, motion picture reviews often consisted of little more than a plot synopsis—a practice that now seems quite valuable, since so many of the films reviewed have vanished. Later in the twenties, when film criticism had reached a certain maturity, a film's artistic merits became a more important topic of discussion than its plot. As a result, each review became more subjective and, for my purposes here, less useful. I have tried to use only those review excerpts that describe scenes in some detail or say something specific about cinematic technique or quality. The aim, after all, is to reclaim as much as possible of the motion picture we can no longer see.

When it came time to decide which titles were to be discussed in *Lost Films* it became tragically clear just how many important, tempting films there were to choose from. Literally thousands of motion pictures have vanished from the face of the earth. I have already prepared myself for the inevitable avalanche of "Why didn't you cover . . . ?" demands. I knew from the first that I could not hope to be comprehensive in my choices. Many major artists—directors and actors alike—are not even mentioned in these pages; entire genres remain undiscussed. I can't help that. Only so much space was available to me here. There was no way to be objective about this project, so the only option was to be subjective. In its simplest form, this book represents a catalogue of films I would dearly love to see. However, since my first list contained about three hundred titles, I realized I had to establish some kind of criteria, just to keep the project manageable.

First, I determined that only lost American films would be included. The subject is so vast that my colleagues in other countries will have no problem coming up with similar lists, and they know their turf better than I do.

Next, I rather randomly decided I would deal mainly with feature films, with only a couple of exceptions from the period before features began to dominate the market.

While many students of the period will be shocked to find I have omitted discussion of such notable lost films as the complete *Greed* (1923), *London After Midnight* (1927), and *The Rogue Song* (1930), it seems to me that these motion pictures have been adequately covered elsewhere, and my limited space would be better filled with less familiar titles. Is *Pied Piper Malone* (1924) as important to the history of cinema as Erich von Stroheim's *The Honeymoon* (1928; part two of *The Wedding March*)? Probably not. But the interested reader can find plenty of background material on the latter in other books on von Stroheim while the former is forgotten, and shouldn't be. At the end of *Lost Films* is a bibliography of publications in which information on some of the more prominent lost movies can be found.

My list of films changed constantly over the many months I spent on this project. I repeatedly sent it around to a group of the world's leading film historians, asking for suggestions, additions, omissions. A few titles on my original roster—*Snow White* (1917), *The Cradle Snatchers* (1928)—turned out to exist after all, and so their places were taken by other deserving movies. Kevin Brownlow suggested adding *A Daughter of the Gods* (1916) and *The Miracle Man* (1919) to the roster, which I did. *Titanic* maven Don Lynch brought *Saved From the Titanic* (1912) to my attention. Robert Birchard told me about *Damaged Goods* (1914) and *Purity* (1916); they made it into the book, too.

Other titles are here simply because of my own enthusiasms; anyone who knows me will recognize the impulse behind the selection of: an Alamo movie (*The Immortal Alamo*, 1911); a *Titanic* movie (*Saved From the Titanic*); a Custer movie (*The Flaming Frontier*, 1927); a Foreign Legion picture (*Beau Sabreur*, 1928); and *three* William A. Wellman movies: one as actor (*The Knickerbocker Buckaroo*, 1919) and two as director (*Ladies of the Mob* and *Legion of the Condemned*, both 1928).

Finally, even though there are many lost sound films—notably the mouthwatering risqué pre–Production Code comedy *Convention City* (1933)—I elected to stick to the silent period here. We must, after all, leave something for the sequel. . . .

One could, in fact, write ten books, just on the lost American movies from the years 1927 and 1928. The last days of the silent era were tragic for so many motion pictures. Hastily released to the last theaters not wired for sound, many late silents had terribly short lives. In small towns, silent films flourished well into the thirties, but for the big markets like Los Angeles, Chicago, and New York, sound films were a fact of life by 1928. It is a bitter irony that the years that arguably represent the pinnacle of the art of the silent cinema have been so ravaged by loss. Part-talkies fared even worse—absolutely no one saw any additional commercial potential in these stopgap motion pictures.

When George Loane Tucker died in 1921, *Photoplay* magazine called him "the first of the immortals whose name is engraved on the great silent tablets of motion picture history."[7] The acclaimed director of *Traffic in Souls* (1915), *The Miracle Man* (1919), and other motion pictures highly prized by his contemporaries, barely reached the age of forty. In mourning his passing, *Photoplay* sought solace in the fact that "although he has passed on, yet the art of the screen remains, richer and finer for his gifts. And we now realize that those who follow in his steps will also pass; and still there will remain the art they helped create."[8]

The art of the motion picture certainly remains and, in some ways, even continues to advance and thrive. But if that *Photoplay* writer could step forward nearly eight decades, how could we explain to him what terrible caretakers we have proved to be of the cinematic art of his day? The films of George Loane Tucker, considered one of the greatest directors of his time, have disappeared, with the single exception of *Traffic in Souls*.

The work of thousands upon thousands of other film artists—good, awful, mediocre, brilliant—has also vanished. How many moments of intense drama, side-splitting comedy, searing truth, or heartbreaking beauty are we now missing? How many precious documentary images are gone, pictures that illuminated a unique moment in time, recorded a vanished society, images that might have brought us a step closer to the past?

Lost Films, then, is not simply a nostalgic look backward but an indictment of the ignorance and neglect that led to the destruction of so much irreplaceable treasure. I hope this book is a warning, too: We still have time to save a great deal of our motion picture heritage, but time is running out. We have lost so much, but we don't have to lose any more.

Finally, to quote an anonymous writer from 1921, I hope *Lost Films* "also makes vivid for us the knowledge that the art of motion pictures is not only of our short day and generation, but of the long tomorrows and the generations yet to come."[9]

ACKNOWLEDGMENTS

If you'll listen carefully, you'll hear sighs of relief from scores of people around the country and across the seas, delighted that I have completed this book and will stop making such a nuisance of myself.

For the time being.

In a normal film book, the author has the luxury of studying the films themselves and drawing conclusions from them. In the case of *Lost Films*, I had to rely entirely on source materials, much of which was impossibly arcane. Left to my own pitiful devices, I never would have found most of it. Happily, I have been blessed with a coterie of knowledgeable and generous friends and colleagues who answered my incessant questions, reviewed my text, checked my facts, made suggestions, and generally made my path immeasurably easier and more comfortable than it might have been.

Although everyone listed below assisted me in innumerable vital ways, I must especially thank Bob Birchard for his endless help, support, and advice. He knows as much about motion pictures in the early decades of this century as anyone I have ever met and is more willing than most to share that knowledge. Bob is responsible for so much of this book; he gets all of my gratitude—but none of my royalties.

Sam Gill, of the Margaret Herrick Library, was also an invaluable source of information and inspiration, as well as being a consistently gracious and generous friend. Sam brought several items to my attention that I could have discovered in no other way. I am particularly thankful to Sam for showing me the detailed notes on many films of the twenties left by some anonymous theater musician. What these writings lack in style, they most certainly make up for in detail. My synopses of *Gentlemen Prefer Blondes* (1927) and *The Last Moment* (1927) come from this fascinating source. I have Sam Gill to thank for this, and for much, much more.

In fact, the entire staff of the Herrick Library proved, once again, to be unfailingly generous and helpful. I've said it before: I don't know how anybody can write a book on film history without the aid of the Herrick Library. I know I wouldn't want to try it.

Deep and humble thanks also go to Leith Adams, Warner Bros.; Richard Bann; Jeanine Basinger, Wesleyan University; Trudy Bazemore, Georgetown County Library, Georgetown, S. C.; the Robert S. Birchard Collection; Edna Bodian, who took the *Pied Piper Malone* snapshots in 1923; Michael and Nancy Boldt; Q. David Bowers, Bowers and Merena Galleries, Inc.; Eileen Bowser, The Museum of Modern Art, New York; Claire Brandt, *Eddie Brandt's Saturday Matinee*; Kevin Brownlow; Quince Buteau; Pete Comandini, YCM Labs; Craig Covner; Susan Dalton, The American Film Institute; Dennis Doros, Milestone Film and Video; Donna and Mike Durrett; Scott Eyman, the *Palm Beach Post*; Jean Firstenberg, The American Film Institute; Dan Gagliasso; John Andrew Gallagher; Robert Gitt, UCLA Film and Television Archives; Dan Goddard, *San Antonio Express-News*; Mary Elizabeth Sue Goldman; Karen Morley Gough; Howard Green, Walt Disney Company; Randy Habercamp; Hank Harrison, Witte Museum of Art, San Antonio; Thomas W. Holland, Holland Entertainment Group; Jan-Christopher Horak, International Museum of Photography at George Eastman House; Brian Huberman, Rice University; Paul Andrew Hutton, University of New Mexico, Albuquerque; Richard T. Jameson, *Film Comment*; Don Lynch, Titanic Historical Society; Scott MacQueen, Walt Disney Company; Tony Malanowski; Leonard Maltin; Ken Marschall, Titanic Historical Society; Richard May, Turner Entertainment; Kay McCauley; Patrick McInroy; Marge Meyer; Simon Mills; Dean Mora; Josie Neal; Sheryl O'Connell; David Parker, the Library of Congress; Harry Ringel; Nina Rosenstand; Kay Scheer; Wolf Schneider; Martin Scorsese; David Shepard; Susannah Shields; Anthony Slide; Patrick Stanbury, Photoplay Productions; Brian Taves, the Library of Congress; John Tibbetts; Tom Trusky, Boise State University; Lee Tsiantis, 20th Century–Fox; Jesse Tullos, the *Georgetown Times*, Georgetown, S. C.; Marc Wanamaker, Bison Archives; William A. Wellman, Jr.; Allan J. Wilson, Citadel Press; Kevin Young; and Pete, Jake, and Molly, the dogs as volatile as nitrate.

Finally, I am most grateful to my wife, Claire McCulloch Thompson, for her love, patience, and inspiration.

LOST FILMS

1

THE IMMORTAL ALAMO

Star Film Company. G. Méliès. Filmed on location in San Antonio, Texas. Released May 25, 1911. One reel; 1,000 feet. Also known as *Fall of the Alamo.*

CREDITS

Producer: G. Méliès; *Company Chairman:* Henry Stanley; *Director:* William F. Haddock; *Cinematographer:* William "Daddy" Paley; *Scenic Artist:* Horace Young; *Utility Car Man:* Archie Stuart.

CAST

Francis Ford (*Navarre*); Gaston Méliès (*Padre*); William Carroll (*Lieutenant Dickenson*); Edith Storey (*Lucy Dickenson*); Donald Peacock (*baby*); William Clifford (*Travis*); Cadets from the Peacock Military Academy (*Mexican Army*); Anna Nichols.

Note: Complete credits for this film have not been found. The following performers were Méliès players at the time. Because of the size of the production and the number of players needed, it must be assumed that most, if not all, of them appeared in *The Immortal Alamo*: Henry Stanley (*Orlando Pegram*); Mildred Brachen; Bert Brachen; Sam Weil; Joseph Karle; Richard Stanton; Fannie Midgely; Evelyn "Jet" Selbie.

Real San Antonio cowboys who doubled as performers and stuntmen in Star Films include: Otto Meyer; "Big Bill" Giddingar; Joe Flores; Eugene Flournoy; Harry Knight; Ben and Sep Cooper; Frank Fernandez, Jr.; John Ortega.

SYNOPSIS

The Alamo is a historic building in San Antonio, Texas, erected in 1744 for a mission used for religious purposes until 1793 when, on account of the great strength of its walls, it was converted into a fort in the struggle

Colonel Travis's last stand

by Texas for independence. The most sanguinary and heroic conflict of
the border warfare which merged into the Mexican War occurred there.
The conflict which for years was familiar to Americans as the Thermop-
ylae of Texas. A body of Texans under the command of William Barret
Travis took refuge in the mission in 1836 when attacked by the Mexican
forces under General Santa Anna, sent to force the Texans back to al-
legiance or kill them on the spot. The Texans numbered only 140 men
while the Mexican army was 4000 strong. The enemy took possession
of the town and finally stormed the mission, and after a siege of eleven
days, the historic house of worship fell and such well-known braves as
William Barret Travis, James Bowie, and Davy Crockett met their
death.

The romance follows: Lieutenant Dickenson had with him at the mission his pretty wife, Lucy, for whom Señor Navarre, a Mexican spy, feels a tender regard. When the Mexicans besiege the mission and Colonel Travis calls upon his men to deliver a message to Gen. Sam Houston, Lieutenant Dickenson volunteers.

He is no sooner gone than the spy cunningly presses his suit, much to the disgust of Lucy Dickenson. Despite her repulses, he would have overpowered her save for the timely intervention of Colonel Travis. The spy is forced to leave the mission. He goes to the Mexican army with information of the mission, which he gives to General Santa Anna on the condition that when the Alamo falls, he may choose whomever he desires of the survivors for his bride.

In the great scene, the mission falls and the only survivors are a few

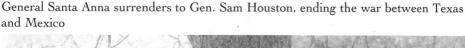

General Santa Anna surrenders to Gen. Sam Houston, ending the war between Texas and Mexico

women, among whom is Mrs. Dickenson. The spy holds Santa Anna to his promise, and the next day the marriage is about to be performed when the reinforcements arrive under the command of Lieutenant Dickenson. The Mexican spy is captured. Lieutenant Dickenson avenges his wife's honor with the sword.

—*Film Index*, May 20, 1911

....

THE PRODUCTION

Georges Méliès (1861–1938), the French illusionist and filmmaker, was one of the cinema's founding fathers. He began making films to show with his stage magic act as early as 1896 and soon learned that the camera was capable of trickery undreamed of by stagecraft. His marvelously imaginative films, such as *A Trip to the Moon* (1902), had a profound influence on generations of filmmakers; his movies were also enormously popular with the public.

Méliès's success bred problems. In America, where copyright laws were lax, his films were widely copied by unscrupulous distributors and pirated.

In 1902 Georges sent his brother Gaston (1852–1915) to New York to oversee the distribution of Méliès's Star Films. Setting up shop at 204 East 38th Street, Gaston proclaimed, "In opening a factory and office in New York we are prepared and determined energetically to pursue all counterfeiters and pirates. We will not speak twice, we will act!"[1]

Between 1902 and 1908, Gaston primarily acted as an administrator. Now and again he produced a newsreel like *The Yacht Race* (1903), but he was generally content to stick to the books and let Georges make the movies. Georges's trick films began losing popularity in the United States by 1910, and Gaston was stuck with a well-oiled distribution machine and no product to send through it. He had only one option: make the movies himself.

Gaston moved his company down to San Antonio in January 1910 and leased a ranch house and several acres of land near Hot Wells Hotel, a sulphur springs resort. Gaston did not share his brother's innovative attitudes about movies and was not concerned with stretching the artistic boundaries of the medium. He wanted only to crank out profitable movies. Audiences loved Westerns, Gaston reasoned, and for Westerns, Texas had everything that was required.

The *Moving Picture World* told exhibitors:

"People may have seen moving pictures of the 'Wild West' taken in 'Hohocus' [*sic*] or some other irrelevant place, and they haven't seen the wild West at all. If you want to show them the real, genuine article of the wild and wooly; the native cowboy and rancheros, with chaperajos, sombreros and lariat; wild Indians in war paint and feathers, wait for these . . . 'record busters' from Texas."[2]

With Hot Wells as headquarters, the troupe had access to a wide range of scenic settings, from deserts to foothills to the San Antonio River to the surrounding Franciscan missions, particularly Mission San Jose just a few hundred yards away.

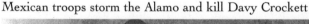

Mexican troops storm the Alamo and kill Davy Crockett

Given the location, a production based on the battle of the Alamo was inevitable. An Alamo movie, in fact, was in the works almost from the day that Star Films came to San Antonio. The company promised "a correct representation of the Alamo insurrection, famous in history, taken on the very ground where it took place. Many of the old houses which played an important part in the 'defense of the Alamo' are the scenes of this picture."[3]

A year later they were still talking about it. Director William Haddock said, "Already the scenario is being prepared and has necessitated delving into the old archives to obtain the correct historical setting and the infinite number of details required to be known. Of course, it would be impossible to give the siege in its entirety, but the incidents of most historic interest will be faithfully portrayed. The Alamo as it now stands does not resemble its appearance at the time of the famous battle, so we are building an exact reproduction of the structure as it then looked. Several hundred men will be required to act for the picture."[4]

A newspaper article offered a tantalizing rumor that, while an Alamo set would be built on the ranch, "in some scenes . . . the original mission will be used."[5] An ad for *The Immortal Alamo* in the *Film Index* proclaimed, "This was what the Méliès Company went to San Antonio to get, and after opposition on all sides, the Mayor finally gave his consent to the photographing of the historic Alamo, which stands in the public plaza."[6]

According to surviving stills, the genuine Alamo probably was not used in the film; the "accurate reproduction" of which Haddock spoke consisted of a small set at Hot Wells, a painted backdrop of the Alamo's facade, and some of the weathered and broken walls of nearby Mission San Jose, then in ruins. However, without seeing the actual film, we can never be entirely sure, especially because of intriguing statements such as this one from the *Film Index*: "It is by far the most ambitious work that the Méliès Company in Texas has undertaken. In the face of bad weather, the streets of San Antonio around the Alamo being crowded for the Cattlemen's Convention, the mobilization of the troops in San Antonio, and other causes, it was difficult to take pictures of the celebrated building and keep the crowds back for the grouping of the characters. But it was finally done to the satisfaction of the director, Mr. Gaston Méliès, who was actively in charge of the work."[7]

The plot of *The Immortal Alamo* centered on the historical figures Almeron and Susannah (called Lucy here) Dickenson. Susannah and her infant daughter, Angelina, were survivors of the Alamo massacre on March 6, 1836; Almeron was killed in the Alamo—but not in *The Immortal Alamo*.

It is astonishing that Méliès and Haddock could pack so much plot into so little time. *The Immortal Alamo,* a scant ten minutes or so in length, had to deal not only with the fall of the Alamo, but with Sam Houston's revenge upon Santa Anna at San Jacinto. No doubt this made for an action-packed reel, but it must have left some viewers as confused as the reviewer who scratched his head in print about the scene "showing Santa Ana's [*sic*] surrender 'as a common soldier.' One wonders why he did it."[8]

The Méliès company crowed about their extensive research, obtaining data "from direct descendants of the illustrious warriors who sacrificed their lives in fighting for their country during this siege."[9]

Reported *The New York Dramatic Mirror*: "In closely consulting Texas history in framing the story woven around the war of Texans for independence from Mexico, fiction is resorted to in a limited way. There is a consistent love story and one of the historical characters named Rose, the only man who deserted the valiant band of defenders, but was never heard of again, is made to appear as the treacherous individual of the play. This is said to be the only substantial deviation from facts."[10]

The "treacherous individual" is, of course, the fictional Navarre. And his presence is far from "the only substantial deviation of facts."[11]

A *New York Dramatic Mirror* reader, Paul H. McGregor of Temple, Texas, wrote to that publication that *The Immortal Alamo* was "weak and distasteful. They butchered history to give it a cheap appearance and have the hero kill the villain and save the heroine." After pointing out that Dickenson died in the Alamo, Mr. McGregor wrote, "Would not this true history have made a stronger play than to butcher sacred history in order to have the hero stab the villain and catch the heroine in his arms? Mockery!"[12]

The villainous Navarre was played by Francis Ford, the older brother of director John Ford who would himself enter films two years later. Interestingly, nearly fifty years later John Ford would be involved in the biggest movie about the Alamo of them all: *The Alamo* (1960), directed by John Wayne. John Ford visited the set near Brackettville, Texas, and directed several scenes in the film.

For years it has been reported that Francis Ford played the role of Davy Crockett. This inaccuracy was taken for granted for so long and by so many that I never questioned it and even perpetuated it in my book *Alamo Movies*. But I was wrong. An examination of the surviving photographs from *The Immortal Alamo* confirms that Ford played Navarre. The actor playing Sam Houston [see illustration] also looks suspiciously like Francis Ford, but I can't confirm it.

So who played Davy Crockett? Who knows?

Gaston Méliès himself appeared in *The Immortal Alamo* as the padre who presides over the bogus wedding between Lucy and Navarre. A contemporary article explains:

"The scene was among the last ones made and showed a marriage in the camp of Santa Anna at San Jacinto, where Houston defeated him. The marriage was to be interrupted by a battle and every available man was in costume for that purpose. In the emergency, William Haddock, the director, pressed Mr. Méliès into service and right nobly did he perform his part."[13]

When *The Immortal Alamo* was released on May 25, *Moving Picture World* reported that the film "will immediately rank with the important educational films. It is a very thrilling and altogether satisfactory reproduction of an important historical episode. The company deserves the highest commendation for the picture and the way it is produced."[14]

Motography agreed: "It would be a stolid audience indeed that failed to respond to the thrilling scene inside the Alamo."[15]

Over a year earlier, director William Haddock had promised that *The Immortal Alamo* would be the studio's crowning achievement: "We want something historically correct, and there will be ample romance in it. It will be, on the whole, one of the greatest films of the year, and one we believe will appeal to the masses."[16]

Barring a small miracle, "the masses" will never get another chance to respond one way or the other. No prints of *The Immortal Alamo* are known to survive.

At least three more motion pictures about the battle of the Alamo have disappeared: *The Siege and Fall of the Alamo* (1914), *The Fall of the*

Alamo (1914), and *The Fall of the Alamo* (1938). The first is the most intriguing. At five reels, it would be the first feature-length treatment of this subject. Like *The Immortal Alamo,* this film, too, was filmed in and around San Antonio. *The Siege and Fall of the Alamo* opened at the Royal Theater in San Antonio on June 1, 1914. A *San Antonio Light* critic called June 1 "the greatest day's business in the history of the Royal Theater . . . it being the first day of *The Siege and Fall of the Alamo,* the made-in-San Antonio picture play of the great historical event. The picture is a splendid piece of photography, clear in every detail, and the acting is perfect. The play seems to please the patrons and is pronounced by historians as a great production."[17]

A lengthy synopsis for *The Siege and Fall of the Alamo* was submitted to the Library of Congress for copyright, but beyond that, nothing is known about this film—who acted in it, directed it, or wrote it.

The Fall of the Alamo (1914) is an even more shadowy production. It may have starred Ray Myers and may also have been produced in Texas. Nothing more is known.

The Fall of the Alamo (1938) was a two-reel short filmed in San Antonio with a local cast. The director, Stuart Paton, is best known today for having directed the original film version of Jules Verne's *20,000 Leagues Under the Sea* (1916). By 1938 he was reduced to working with amateurs, directing this short and editing it himself in his room at the St. Anthony Hotel (where the *Wings* and *Rough Riders* companies had stayed a decade earlier).[18]

Of course, many motion pictures have subsequently been made about the siege and fall of the old mission in 1836, most notably *Martyrs of the Alamo* (1915), *The Last Command* (1955), *Davy Crockett, King of the Wild Frontier* (1955), and John Wayne's *The Alamo* (1960). The story of sacrifice, patriotism, and bloodshed seems to need a reinterpretation for each new generation of moviegoers. Gaston Méliès's *The Immortal Alamo* was certainly not the most historically authentic of the bunch, but its loss is keenly felt. Made on the same ground where the original conflict took place and filmed within living memory of the Texas Revolution, *The Immortal Alamo* was history on at least two levels at once. With the film's disappearance we have lost not only a retelling of the story of the Alamo, but a brief window into the beauties of that wild Eden: Texas in 1911.

2

SAVED FROM THE TITANIC

Eclair Moving Picture Company, Fort Lee, New Jersey. Released May 14, 1912. One reel; 1,000 feet.

C R E D I T S

In Charge of Production: Mr. Harry Raver. *Director:* Etienne Arnaud.

C A S T

Dorothy Gibson (*Miss Dorothy*); Alex Francis (*The Father*); Miss Stuart (*The Mother*); Jack Adolfi (*Ensign Jack*); William Dunn, Guy Oliver (*His Pals*).

SYNOPSIS

Miss Dorothy, who on her return home is to be betrothed to Ensign Jack, U.S.N., has written to her parents that she'll embark on the *Titanic* from Cherbourg. They and Dorothy's girlfriends are impatiently awaiting her return. She had promised in the letter to send a wireless Sunday night so that they could know the time of her arrival.

Jack, naturally, is impatient to have news of his loved one. His friend Ensign Williams, who has a friend, Bill Jenkins, in charge of a wireless post, proposes to take him there so he can communicate with the ship directly or learn if any news comes from her.

While they are telling Jenkins the object of their visit, he receives the C.Q.D. from the *Titanic*, telling of the disaster. No pen can depict the anguish of the young man and the scene the ensuing day when he calls upon Dorothy's father and mother. But the Americans on board the ill-fated ship did their duty, lived up to their "motto," always women and children saved first.

No doubt they were put into lifeboats. Some lives must have been saved, why not Dorothy's?

True, Dorothy was among the saved. Later on we find the oblivious sweethearts at the table with Dorothy's mother and father. She is requested to tell the story of the shipwreck to Jack; she does so—so vividly that one can almost imagine the catastrophe is being enacted there—more especially as a vivid vision of the fatal collision is portrayed by the camera. But the strain of recalling the stressful event is too much for Dorothy, and she faints as she finishes the story.

The next day, so impressed was her mother at seeing this, she calls on Jack and explains that if he wishes to become her son-in-law, he must resign from the Navy as his calling on the sea is too full of perils and she fears that Dorothy, whose emotions have been stirred by her terrible experiences, could not stand the strain of her constant anxiety on his account. Jack hesitates—she gives him all night to think it over. He tells his captain and friend of his dilemma, his conflict between love and duty. The bluff old commander argues in favor of the service, clinching the argument by telling him that the first consideration of a naval officer is due to his country's flag, at the same time pointing to "Old Glory" floating in the breeze. Jack understands, deciding in favor of the service.

When Dorothy's father calls for Jack's answer, he replies, "A sailor's first duty is to his flag and country." The father (impressed and happy to find such lofty and patriotic sentiment in the young man) declares that he could expect no other answer from an officer in the U.S.N. The father shows his own true loyalty as a citizen and calls Dorothy in, saying, "My daughter, there's your husband." He gives her hand over to Jack, who is overcome with surprise.

—*Moving Picture World*, May 11, 1912

THE PRODUCTION

Whenever an important, preferably sensational, news story takes hold of the nation's imagination, it is only a matter of time until it is turned into a (usually made-for-television) movie "event." Motion pictures have always, to some extent, turned to the headlines for certain kinds of hard-hitting stories. But we tend to think of this kind of instant transformation from news to drama as a relatively recent event.

It isn't. When the luxury liner *Titanic* struck an iceberg and sank in the early morning hours of April 15, 1912, with the loss of over fifteen hundred lives, the tragedy gripped the entire world. Movie exhibitors scrambled for any footage at all to present to a public hungry for information. Although there were a few genuine shots of the *Titanic,* most distributors didn't feel the need to limit themselves to these.

An angry reader wrote to *The Moving Picture News* on April 26, 1912, "As soon as the news of the *Titanic* disaster was flashed to Los Angeles, these unscrupulous exhibitors immediately went to the film exchanges and rented several old reels which show the *Mauritania* and the *Olympic* [*Titanic*'s nearly identical sister ship] steamers in action. After securing these old rainstorms [weathered, scratchy prints] they papered their lobby with fake posters and lithographs which advertised the only genuine negatives of the disaster."

Some of this footage exists today, showing ships and tugboats with their names crudely erased from each frame of film. This footage is still often represented as scenes of the *Titanic* at sea.

Similarly, Herbert Corey in the *New York Dramatic Mirror* told of a theatre owner on 34th Street in Manhattan who put up a sign in bold lettering: FIRST PICTURES OF THE TITANIC (and in small type: sunk in) OCEAN DISASTER!" Corey wrote, "The pictures themselves were the most uninteresting views of the *Titanic*'s launching. About one man in three who had been stung demanded his money back. Each would be assured if he stepped outside the gentlemanly attendant would hand it to him. Outside each was given the raucous boot."[1]

More honest theater owners were able to do sensational business with programs built around the *Titanic*. At New York's Weber Theatre "immense crowds" saw footage of the *Titanic*'s keel in Belfast, Ireland, where the ship was built; the ship's launching; the rescue ship *Carpathia*; the "hero skipper [*Carpathia* Captain Rostron] shown in realistic poses;" and "a series of views showing icebergs taken three days before the *Titanic* struck" taken by newsreel cameramen.[2]

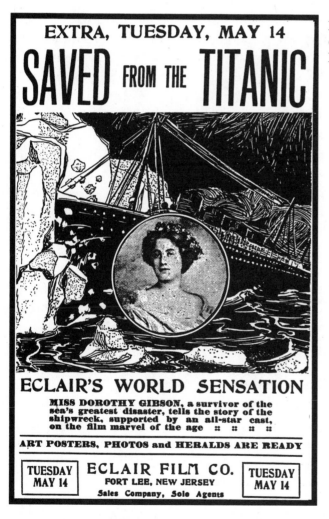

Poster advertising the film (courtesy Academy of Motion Picture Arts and Sciences)

Even news footage in 1912 could be improved upon by a little dramatic flair. After the iceberg scenes, the screen was darkened and "C.Q.D." flashed on in "vivid reality." Actually, the wireless operators of the *Titanic* were the first to eschew C.Q.D. with the newer distress signal, S.O.S., but it being only a week after the wreck, the public did not know this.

Finally, "many views of the survivors" were shown, as well as glimpses of lifeboats, life belts, and a brief visit with Signore Guglielmo Marconi, inventor of the wireless that summoned aid to the *Titanic*.[3]

These documentary views of people and events surrounding the disaster thrilled the public but didn't altogether satisfy it. For the tragedy to really connect with movie audiences, it would have to be placed in a more human, dramatic setting. By coincidence, the *Titanic* carried a passenger who not only had the wherewithall to provide that setting but the clearheaded ambition to do so in record time.

Dorothy Gibson was an actress with the Eclair Moving Picture Company, a French company with an American branch in Fort Lee, New Jersey. She was traveling in first class with her mother, returning on the *Titanic* from a holiday in Europe. The Gibsons had been playing bridge with two friends, William T. Sloper and Fred Seward, late on Sunday evening, April 14. When the steward informed them he would have to turn out the lights, they begged him to allow them to finish the rubber. "These ceremonies over," Gibson later said, "I walked down to my room just at 11:40. No sooner had I stepped into my apartment than there suddenly came this long-drawn, sickening scrunch."[4]

Although few passengers of the *Titanic* took the situation seriously at first, when the order was given to lower away lifeboats, Miss Gibson and her three bridge buddies were the first to go. They left the *Titanic* in boat 7, four of only twenty-eight passengers—less than half the boat's capacity. Once at sea, the twenty-eight discovered that the boat's plug did not fit properly (someone had to sit on it all night) and that there was no food, water, lanterns, or matches on board. Gibson complained later about a man, "supposed to be a French baron, [who] gathered all the blankets to himself. This same man, when aboard the *Carpathia,* appropriated no less than forty-five blankets to make himself a soft bed."[5]

They floated in the darkness for hours, listening to the "frightful sounds" of "ghastly cries, shrieks, yells, and moans" that "gradually died away to nothing."[6]

Miss Gibson was not the only *Titanic* passenger with a connection to the relatively new art of the motion picture. Daniel W. Marvin and his bride, Mary, were returning from a European honeymoon. The groom was the son of Henry N. Marvin, president of the Biograph Company. The couple had made headlines a few weeks earlier when they indulged in the novelty of having a moving picture camera record their wedding ceremony. Although young Mr. Marvin intended to follow his father into the movie business, he never got the chance; he died on the *Titanic*.

Also on board was Noel Malachard, a cameraman for Pathé's Weekly, a newsreel company. Malachard had been assigned by his company to take films of the *Titanic*'s maiden voyage. If he did so, the footage went to the bottom of the Atlantic with Malachard.

The rescue ship *Carpathia* arrived at the scene at about 4 A.M., and the survivors sailed into New York Harbor on the evening of April 18. History does not tells us where the idea to film *Saved From the Titanic* came from, but for it to have been completed less than three weeks after the disaster and released one month to the day after the *Titanic* sank, Dorothy Gibson must have leaped off the *Carpathia*, into a cab, and rushed over to Fort Lee without delay. In 1912, there was generally a period of about two months for a one-reel film to be produced, processed, and distributed to theaters. *Saved From the Titanic* cut that schedule to less than half.

Although well over half of this ten-minute-long film is taken up with its romantic complication, it would be particularly fascinating to see today because of its almost incidental documentary features. First, to have an actual survivor of the *Titanic* playing herself in a film about the disaster would be interesting enough. That, for the filming, she costumed herself with the very clothes—a white evening dress, long sweater, gloves, and a pair of black pumps—in which she abandoned ship, is more intriguing still. And that all this was committed to film within days of the disaster is enough to make any *Titanic* enthusiast sigh with frustra-

tion. No matter what melodramatic hokum found its way into the film—
and the synopsis suggests that there was plenty—*Saved From the Titanic*
is an irreplaceable piece of *Titanic* lore.

According to the synopsis, the wreck itself appears only in flashback
as told by Miss Gibson to her fiancé and parents at dinner. Nevertheless,
the *Moving Picture News* lauded the film's "wonderful mechanical and
lighting effects, realistic scenes, perfect reproduction of the true history
of the fateful trip, magnificently acted."[7] An earlier edition of the same
periodical, however, assured readers that the "harassing details which
might offend good taste are carefully omitted, but the story of the wreck,
the love interest, and the effects of the bitter calamity are all depicted."[8]

Saved From the Titanic was also praised for its "mechanical and vision
pictures. Miss Gibson had hardly recovered from her terrible strain in
the wreck when she was called upon to take part in this new piece, which
she constructed as well. It was a nerve-racking task, but like actresses
before the footlights, this beautiful young cinematic star valiantly con-
quered her own feelings and went through the work. A surprising and
artistically perfect reel has resulted."[9]

3

THE BATTLE OF GETTYSBURG

Produced by New York Motion Picture Company. Released through Mutual
Film Corporation. Released June 1, 1913. Five reels. Some stock footage
used in *Cohen Saves the Flag* (1913).

C R E D I T S

Director: Thomas H. Ince. *Lab Work Supervisor:* Alfred Brandt. The *American Film Institute
Catalog: Feature Films 1911–1920* suggests that Charles Giblyn may have been the film's
codirector. The scenarist may have been C. Gardner Sullivan or the team of Charles Brown,
Thomas Ince, and Richard Spencer.

C A S T

The *American Film Institute Catalog: Feature Films 1911–1920* suggests that the following
actors may have appeared in this film: Burton King, Joe King, Gertrude Claire, Shorty
Hamilton, Mr. Hadley, and Mr. Edlar. Another source names the following cast members:
Charles K. French, Enid Bennett, Herschel Mayall, Walter Edwards, Frank Borzage, J. Bar-
ney Sherry, Anna Little, George Fisher, J. Frank Burke, and Enid Markey. Still another source
claims that Abraham Lincoln was played by Willard Mack.

SYNOPSIS

This is a reproduction of the most decisive battle of the great Civil War,
following the battle day by day, and is practically historically accurate
in every detail. A pretty love story is interwoven. Other highlights are
the introduction of Abraham Lincoln, standing by the fireplace alone in
the White House, his tortured face as it reveals the anguish he suffers;
again in his office in the White House with a couple of his valued military

The president learns the fearful cost of the battle

advisors; then the climax as he stands, tall and determined, surrounded by his Army Chief of Staff and his most capable and valued members of his cabinet. He delivers the never to be forgotten "Gettysburg Address" before a privileged crowd who remained the envy of the century. Another great scene is General Lee in his last conference with all of his trusted Generals who advised General Lee to surrender.

This great venture by Thomas H. Ince to produce this great and historical epic shows again this great courage to do a deed for his country that shall be remembered with other great pictures yet to be produced by this gifted man. Mr. Ince even is considering spending as much as 2,000 feet (2 reels) on this never to be forgotten epic. The love story will tear at your heartstrings as no other motion picture has ever done. Now, the story . . .

There was a brisk breeze in the air. Lamar, editor of the *Gazette,* is the first to publish an article against secession. He and his son Jack are at dinner at the Burks' old Southern mansion when a messenger reports that a mob, headed by Major Pollard, a suitor for the hand of Virginia Burk, is destroying the Gazette office and is after Lamar to do harm to him. Even before the dinner is over the mob attacks the Burk mansion, and Lamar is taken from the dinner table on to the whipping post and beaten until he is almost exhausted. During a desperate moment, he is rescued by his son Jack and together they depart for the North. Jack, crestfallen and embittered against the South, raises a company of Union volunteers, while Jim Burk, Virginia's brother, and Major Pollard join the South. Major Pollard sends Virginia's brother on a dangerous mission through the Union lines. Lying at death's door in the home of a Southern sympathizer [he] sends for his father. Virginia and her father go to his aid. Virginia disguises herself in her brother's clothes, carries the papers to Lee that Jim has. Captain Jack Lamar, who has been following the spy, suspects that the Southern sympathizer's house conceals him, surrounds the house, and is surprised to find Jim. By a clever ruse on the part of Major Pollard, Jack is himself made a prisoner. The Major, believing that Dr. Burk, who has promised to safeguard the prisoner until called for, will allow Jack to escape for old friendship's sake, sets a trap for Jack. Pollard throws a note into Jack's room, purporting to be from a friend who will assist him to escape that night. Virginia sees through the trap and forbids Jack to go. She gets Jack a suit of Confederate uniform, gives him her favorite horse, and under cover of darkness he escapes, sending the horse back to Virginia after he reaches a place of safety.

Jim has recovered and joins his regiment. Then follows the great battle day by day. During one of the heaviest skirmishes toward the end of the war, Jim is badly wounded and made a prisoner. He sends for Jack, giving him a dying message and asking him to see that Virginia and his father are told of his death. Jack sends Jim's uniform to Virginia with a beautiful message of love and sympathy.

The story closes with a pretty picture. Two years after the war, Jack returns to Virginia's old battered Southern mansion to claim her as his bride. He finds Virginia with "Snowball," her old and trusted white horse, near their old trysting spot. Snowball seems to realize that he is a factor in this part of the story and starts to nuzzle them to see that they get together.

As they kiss — END.

—New York Motion Picture Company files

••

THE PRODUCTION

"The most stupendous effort ever put forth in motion pictures, consuming four months in its production, and presenting dramatic situations of heart-gripping intensity and spectacular scenes of awe-inspiring sensationalism. Father and son, brother and brother, opposed each other in a maelstrom of death, the tide of battle alternating through brilliant charges and acts of daring."

—*Moving Picture World* ad, May 3, 1913

••

On July 1, 2, and 3, 1913, hundreds of Civil War veterans descended on the picturesque town of Gettysburg, Pennsylvania, to mark the fiftieth anniversary of the battle that had been the turning point of the war. They wore their old uniforms, slept in tents, reenacted Pickett's Charge and spent hours chatting about the good old days a half century earlier, when they had all been trying to kill each other.

Some veterans who couldn't make the trip to Pennsylvania had an opportunity to revisit the bloody scenes of their youth in quite a different way: at the local movie theater. Thomas Ince's epic production of *The Battle of Gettysburg* was playing around the country during that same anniversary week.

Although the scrub-covered hills near Malibu, California, didn't at all resemble the lush greenery of the Pennsylvania countryside of either

The battle

1863 or 1913, the gigantic scale of the production and the vivid immediacy of the battle scenes must have struck many an aged Johnny Reb
and Billy Yank to the heart.

Ince's advertising claimed that *The Battle of Gettysburg* presented war
scenes on a larger scale than ever before attempted on the screen, and
most reviewers believed this was true: "No amount of printed description
could bring home, as does this picture, the magnitude of the Battle of
Gettysburg, and the terrifying slaughter it brought. If a cameraman had
been on the sideline during the actual battle, his film could scarcely have
given a more effective impression of the horrors of war."[1]

Motography agreed, citing, "Thousands of men battling to the death,
hand to hand, countless scenes of the most awe-inspiring sensationalism
and heroism. And then the cold, dark aftermath when the grim cloak of
death and tragedy overhung the field of battle and shut out the dreadful
scene of carnage."[2]

The synopsis from the New York Motion Picture Company files

printed above suggests that Ince at first intended *The Battle of Gettysburg* to be only two reels in length. Instead, the finished work was five reels long. The possibility exists that the film started life as a conventional Civil War drama, but the battle scenes were so powerfully effective that Ince made the decision to lengthen the motion picture. If this is the case, it appears the original two-reeler was left pretty much intact, and the massive scenes of battle were simply added on without much regard for the previously established characters. The *New York Dramatic Mirror* complained, "As to the story that occupies most of the first two reels of the picture and then is almost forgotten, not much need be said. It is the conventional situation for Civil War stories in which a girl has a lover in the Northern Army and a brother for the Confederates. The story is well handled and sufficient to form a structure on which to hang incidents of a personal nature, but the worth of the film goes far deeper: It

Delivering the immortal address

is found in a wonderful visualization of the greatest battle in American history."[3]

No reliable cast or crew list survives for the film, although Willard Mack may have played Abraham Lincoln[4] and Ann Little can be recognized in one of the surviving stills. Nor is there much reliable information about the production of the film. It was filmed at Inceville, Thomas Ince's 20,000-acre studio located near the Pacific coast just north of Santa Monica. Studio publicity claimed that 2,500 soldiers and National Guardsmen took part in the battle scenes and that $3,000 worth of "old-fashioned black powder was exploded to make the smoke of battle."[5] Ince utilized up to eight cameras during the battle scenes, making sure that the action was covered from every angle (and, one suspects, storing up Civil War stock footage for future productions).

Another film was being shot on the same location at the same time, and it is because of Mack Sennett's Keystone Company that any part of *The Battle of Gettysburg* exists today.

The first Keystone release was a comedy starring Ford Sterling, Fred Mace, and Mabel Normand called *Cohen Collects a Debt* (September 23, 1912). Released on a split reel with another Mabel Normand comedy, *The Water Nymph*, *Cohen* found its humor—what humor there was—in very broad Jewish stereotypes that undoubtedly seem far more offensive today than they did to audiences at the time.

Sennett liked the characters enough to revive them a few times over the next year or so, and when he learned that fellow New York Motion Picture Company producer Thomas Ince was filming an epic *Battle of Gettysburg* over in Malibu, he immediately took his Keystone Company unit over to the spot to ride on Ince's coattails. Sennett called his film *Cohen Saves the Flag*. Set in Civil War times, Cohen (Ford Sterling) finds himself rivals for the love of Mabel Normand with Union officer Fred Mace. Cohen is a complete boob and gets into one unfunny scrape after another, then accidentally saves the Union flag from capture. When his rival finds a way to have Cohen shot by a firing squad, he is saved in the nick of time by Mabel, riding at the head of a Union company. Cohen is regarded as a hero for saving the flag, and he has his revenge on his rival by swatting him with a sword.

As comedy, *Cohen Saves the Flag* is almost entirely dreadful. But because of the massive scenes of battle taken from the Ince production, it has a great deal of value. Sennett didn't only use some stock footage from *The Battle of Gettysburg,* he actually staged his own scenes off to the side — and out of Ince's camera range — so that his actors go through their goofy paces in the midst of quite realistic battle scenes.

The Battle of Gettysburg was first shown publicly on Sunday, June 1, 1913, at New York's Grand Opera House. The capacity crowd, noted *Motography,* "actually went wild as the stirring scenes and exciting incidents of the memorable battle were once more enacted before their very eyes. A spectacle such as this has never been witnessed by any audience in the world . . . little wonder that at the close of the film the silent and enthralled audience broke into cheering and tumultuous applause, making one of the greatest demonstrations ever heard in a theater, and incidentally paying unconscious tribute to the genius of Mr. Ince and his company."[6]

4

DAMAGED GOODS

American Film Manufacturing Company. Distributed on a states' rights basis under the Flying A banner in September 1914 and by Mutual Film Corporation, September 15, 1915. Seven reels.

C R E D I T S

Director: Thomas Ricketts; *Camera:* Thomas B. Middleton; *Adaptation:* Harry Pollard; Based on the play *Les Avaries* (1902) by Eugene Brieux.

C A S T

Richard Bennett (George Dupont); Adrienne Morrison (*A Girl of the Streets*); Maud Milton (*Mrs. Dupont*); Olive Templeton (*Henriette Locke*); Josephine Ditt (*Mrs. James Forsythe*); Jacqueline Moore (*A Seamstress*); Florence Short (*A Nurse*); Louis Bennison (*Dr. Clifford*); John Steppling (*Senator Locke*); William Bertram (*A Quack*); George Ferguson (*His Assistant*); Mrs. Lester, Charlotte Burton.

SYNOPSIS

The story opens at a college where George Dupont is studying law. He is ambitious and studious, and his nights are spent over his books while his classmates dine in cafés with girls of the underworld. One night they determine that he shall join them and, despite his protests, lure him into a café by a trick. When he sees that their object was to make him one of their number, he leaves them and returns to his room, but is strongly tempted to join them in their gay life. A struggle takes place within him, but he finally wins out, when he gazes upon the portrait of his mother.

He returns to his books and works while the others, scorning his industry, enjoy life in their own way.

Time passes and graduation day arrives. George's hours of study prove well spent, for he receives the honor of graduating at the head of his class. His friends, the young men who were "jolly good fellows," fail utterly and leave college unprepared for the battle of life which lies before them.

Among those who are with George on his graduation day are his mother and aunt, Senator Locke and his daughter Henriette, and Mrs. James Forsythe, an old friend of the family. The party returns to the Dupont home, and there a party is given in honor of the young man. Mrs. Forsythe, who has not seen George for a number of years, is attracted by his manly appearance and asks him to call at her home during the evening. George is not greatly impressed with this invitation but thinks little more about it.

He retires late in the evening without giving Mrs. Forsythe another thought — but not so with the woman. Her husband leaves on a trip, and she sends her maid to the theater. Then she telephones George and, after rousing him from bed, pleads with him to come to her at once as she needs his legal advice. The young man goes and is no sooner in the house than she uses all her wiles on him. He struggles against the temptation, but his willpower succumbs to his primal instinct, and he takes the first step on the road to destruction.

The next morning, as he reads the paper, the truth of the statement he has often heard — that interference with genuine affection can bring nothing but disaster — is brought home to him with the news that Mr. Forsythe was killed the evening before in a train wreck. The young man is heartbroken to think of the offense he has committed and his sorrow is increased when Mrs. Forsythe tells him she can now transfer all her love to him. A feeling of disgust seizes him, and he tells her he never wishes to see her again. But the seed has been sown.

Time passes and George is successful in law practice. Senator Locke and the young man's aunt plan the marriage of George and Henriette. The senator is pleased with the prospect of the money to be left the young

Richard Bennett as the tragic
hero, with Adrienne Morrison
(his wife).

people and does all he can to rush matters. George in the meantime has
become entangled with a seamstress and both believe they love each
other. Their dream is shattered one day, however, when Mrs. Dupont
sees her son with the girl. George is then told that he must become
engaged to Henriette and, to please his mother and aunt, he consents.

Henriette meets and loves him, and he appears to return her affection as he is strangely attracted to her. Mrs. Dupont sends a check to
the seamstress and tells her that she must never again see George. The
young man's aunt makes him heir to all she possesses, and Senator Locke
takes him into his law firm as a partner.

The date of the wedding is announced, and George's friends decide
to give him a farewell bachelor dinner. All plans for the affair are laid,
and George looks to it with pleasure. As he leaves home to attend it, his
mother tells him not to stay long as she will wait for him to return.
George promises her he will be home early and then goes to the dinner,

filled with anticipation of the pleasure of this last night with his old friends.

While his mother sits by the fireplace and, in a vision, sees her son among gentlemen, George and his companions are drinking and carousing wildly in one of the cafés, all being more or less under the influence of liquor. Mrs. Dupont goes to sleep as she waits for her son.

About midnight the men start to leave, and one of George's special friends telephones Mrs. Dupont that George will spend the night with him. The two men then go to the home of the mistress of George's friend, where the young lawyer meets the product and the cause of the great social disease — a girl of the streets. The couples spend the night together, and in the morning George returns home, sober and very sorry for his action.

Four weeks pass and bring many changes. The girl of the streets meets Doctor Clifford, a specialist and philanthropist, and he sees in her a spark of goodness. He cares for her, and she becomes a nurse in his employ. George's wedding is approaching, and he is very happy until he suddenly discovers that he is suffering from disease. A coward's first thought is suicide, and as he fears exposure, he buys poison and goes to a park to end his life. But the girl of the street sees him and knocks the bottle from his hands.

When the young man recognizes her, he flies into a rage and is about to kill her, but he controls himself. She tells him to listen to her side of the story. Then she says that a girl of her class is only summing up her score against society by her acts and that he was only one of the many whom she forced to suffer. She tells him how she came to the city and was ruined by a man who remained respected while she became an outcast and then how the hospitals refused to treat her. "And that is true of ninety-seven percent of the hospitals in America," she adds. Then she relates her awful vengeance on all mankind and ends by telling him how the great doctor helped her and says that he will surely help him.

George goes to Doctor Clifford, and the physician, after an examination, tells him he cannot marry for two years; if he does, he will be a criminal. To impress the fact on George, the doctor takes him to one of the hospitals where the many cases of this disease are being treated. There he sees with his own eyes the horrible results of marriages which take place in ignorance of the consequences: the little creatures, old from birth, ninety-two percent of whom die but many of whom grow up to be imbeciles and idiots. He also sees the terrible disease which has been transferred to the women by their husbands and learns that ninety-five percent of the women marrying syphilitic men are contaminated.

George returns home, determined to follow the doctor's advice, but fear of exposure leads him to another doctor, whose advertisement appears in the paper as being able to cure all ailments of men. The "quack" gives him some pills and tells him that he will be cured within three months and that to delay his marriage, he can pretend to be threatened with consumption.

George takes the pills and succeeds in delaying his marriage by the excuse, and at the end of three months is assured that he is in perfect health. The ceremony takes place, and George and Henriette are very happy. Had the marriage certificate called for a physical examination, they would have been spared a life of misery.

All appears well at first, and George is inclined to scoff at the statement Doctor Clifford made to him — but there can be no lasting happiness founded on false hope. One day George does not feel well and goes to call on the "quack." To his discomfort he learns that the fake has been driven from town. He then seeks Doctor Clifford, only to learn that he has gone to Europe. On returning home, Henriette meets him and tells him her happy secret.

After months of doubt and fear, George awaits the coming of the little stranger who is to make his household a place of even greater joy. As he paces the hall, the words of the worthy doctor — "If you marry within two years you will be a murderer" — come to him. When he is admitted to Henriette's room, however, the baby appears healthy, and he is again at rest.

A few months of happiness pass, and then one day the truth is brought to George's door with crushing force, when a doctor, called in for what George's mother believes is a slight ailment, refuses the case and sends the child to Doctor Clifford, who has returned from his trip. The great doctor tells Mrs. Dupont she must dismiss the wet nurse, as the woman is liable to become infected, and as the nurse denounces George, Henriette learns of the awful fate of her baby. She takes the infant and hurries to her father's home, and Senator Locke is about to take George's life when Doctor Clifford stops him and tells him that if he had inquired into his son-in-law's health rather than into his financial condition, all this would have been avoided.

George, recalling the horrors he saw in the hospital, cannot face the ordeal before him, and leaving all his estate to his wife, he goes to the sea. Again the coward's first thought is suicide — and this time there is no one to interfere with his purpose.

—*Motography*, September 26, 1914

••

THE PRODUCTION

Eugene Brieux's play *Les Avaries*, a powerful sermon on the tragic effect of syphilis, was first produced onstage in France in 1902. Actor Richard Bennett brought the play, retitled *Damaged Goods*, to America in 1913, where it enjoyed considerable success and endured considerable controversy, both. "In English-speaking countries," wrote one critic, "an open discussion (in whatever form) of sexual questions has always been frowned upon. The French, and indeed all the Latin races, cannot understand our viewpoint. They think we are prudish, perhaps Pharisaical."[1]

Bennett (1873–1944) was a renowned stage actor and director who is today better known for fathering three actress daughters — Barbara, Joan, and Constance — and for his moving portrayal as the dying Major Amberson in Orson Welles's *The Magnificent Ambersons* (1942). According to his daughter Joan, Bennett didn't care for motion pictures: " 'Whenever there are movie scouts out front, let me know' he used to say, 'and I'll stay home sick.' "[2] But he understood that the powerful lessons of *Damaged Goods* could reach many more people, and be far more effective, on film than on the stage. After *Damaged Goods* had played in New York for nearly a year, Bennett made arrangements with the American Film Manufacturing Company to adapt it to the moving picture screen.

"As a play," wrote a *New York Dramatic Mirror* critic, "*Damaged Goods* drove its lessons home with words rather than action. It was frankly dissertational and seemingly a most unlikely work if shorn of speech."[3] Bennett, who, although uncredited, probably cowrote the screenplay adaptation with Harry Pollard (Bennett probably had a significant hand in directing the film, too), completely reconceived the play in visual terms. With the freedom offered him by the cinema, Bennett was able to dramatize situations that had only been discussed onstage. More crucially to the visceral impact of the film, Bennett was able to show in detail the horrible results of venereal disease by visiting a Los Angeles hospital ward. *Variety*'s critic wrote, "The camera even invaded the sacred interior of an institution where it pictured patients suffering from the so-called tertiary stage and brought forth the paralyzed and twisted form for 'close-up' inspection."[4] While reviewer W. Stephen Bush commended the filmmakers for not lingering "over the horrid and morbid to titillate perverted tastes under the pretence of preaching a great moral lesson," he admitted that *Damaged Goods* would be vastly improved once "the scenes in the clinic are reduced to a flash."[5]

The printed titles of moving pictures also appealed to Bennett for their educational and informational potential. By retaining the three-act structure of a stage play (Acts I and II, two reels each, Act III, three reels), Bennett was able to place important facts and statistics on the title cards that introduced and closed each act.

Produced by the American Film Manufacturing Company, *Damaged Goods* was released under the Flying A brand on a states' rights basis in September 1914. A year later it was purchased by the Mutual Film Corporation and rereleased with a great deal of fanfare. Samuel S. Hutchinson of American Film called *Damaged Goods* "probably the greatest thing we have ever done in motion pictures. [It] is also a testimonial to the ability of the motion picture to carry over such a remarkable plot and its involved sex lesson in a clean way. None of the things that had

Bennett in *The End of the Road*, a sort of sequel to *Damaged Goods*, with Claire Adams and Joyce Fair

to be said in the speaking stage production, with the inevitable mincing of words, come in to affect the film."[6]

Although the rereleased version of *Damaged Goods* was still seven reels, as it had been the year before, reviews hint that the film had been reedited — and that some scenes had even been reshot. *Motography*, at any rate, found that "it has been strengthened by the re-editing."[7] The precise nature of these changes can only be speculated about, although it is most probable that some of the more gruesome moments from the clinic sequences were trimmed.

The premiere showing of the rerelease took place at the Broadway Theater in New York City on Monday morning, September 27, 1915. Mutual played up the considerable educational appeal of *Damaged Lives* by inviting "2,500 of those most prominent in legal, medical, official, and sociological circles."[8]

Mutual also took out large trade ads featuring testimonials from editorial writers, ministers, rabbis, congressmen, and health officials, stressing the "wholesome" aspects of the film and the fact that "no vulgarity and no unnecessary facts are permitted to appear."[9]

Although *Damaged Goods* was considered valuable mainly for its message, most reviewers made favorable statements about the film's cinematic and artistic quality. "From a standpoint of production this film can be highly recommended for its excellence," wrote *Motography*. "Artistic settings, effective lighting, and fine photography — in fact, all the essentials of a high-class presentation — play their important part."[10]

In 1917, Richard Bennett toured American Army training camps with a print of the film. That same year, from March through October, a young actor named Ronald Colman played the lead in a British theatrical version. "It would have gone on for much longer," said Edith Lester Jones, an actress in the production, "but for the zeppelin raids which stopped the audiences from coming."[11]

In 1919, a British film version was directed by Alexander Butler. Although the American *Damaged Goods* has been lost, this British version survives. Historian Kevin Brownlow points out that British censorship at that time was harsher than that in America. Consequently, the British *Damaged Goods* "came dangerously close to being a series of subtitles, interrupted merely by shots of appropriate characters."[12]

Every lost movie is a tragedy, but the loss of one like *Damaged Goods* is particularly regrettable; the film represents a glimpse at the attitudes of its era — a glimpse of a kind not readily available from other surviving period films. Audiences and critics alike found the film to be powerful and important in many ways. Today we can only imagine what kind of impact *Damaged Goods* had.

5

PURITY

American Film Company. Distributed by Mutual Film Corporation. Released
July 17, 1916. Seven reels.

C R E D I T S

Director: Rea Berger; *Story:* Clifford Howard; *Camera:* Robert V. Phelan; *Art Director:* Edward Langley; *Dance Director:* Geneva Driscoll.

C A S T

Audrey Munson (*Purity/Virtue*); Nigel de Brullier (*Thornton Darcy*); Alfred Hollingsworth (*Claude Lamarque*); William A. Carroll (*Evil/Luston Black, a Voluptuary*); Eugenie Forde (*Judith Lure*); Clarence Burton (*Publisher*); Nela Drinkwitz (*Model*); Molly Shafer (*Landlady*); Marie Van Tassell (*Truth*); Ellen Howard (*Love*); Mary Dunham (*Music*); Alice Anaroni (*Drama*); Hazel West (*Art*); Nell Franzen (*Maiden*); Wallace MacDonald (*Youth*); Ashton Dearholt (*Shepherd*).

SYNOPSIS

Thornton Darcy, an idealistic poet, is at work upon an allegorical poem, which he calls "Virtue." He devotes the first part of it to picturing the idyllic state of the earth prior to the advent of evil in which Virtue is the world's guiding spirit. Virtue is represented by a nude female figure, artlessly adorned with flimsy drapery. In the second part he introduces the Greek myth of Pandora, who releases Evil on the world.

Finishing his work for the day, Darcy falls into a light doze and upon awakening discovers that his dream girl, Virtue, has come to life in the person of a young woman clad in a simple homemade dress, kneeling on the bank of the stream gathering flowers. They become acquainted, and he learns that her name is Purity Worth and that she lives near the woods in a humble, secluded home. She makes an instant appeal to Darcy as he does to her, and they repeat the meeting in the woods, with the result that they fall in love and are engaged, in spite of the fact that there is no immediate prospect of marriage owing to Darcy's reduced circumstances. Darcy is unable to sell his poems, and the publisher will not print them for less than five hundred dollars.

Claude Lamarque, a painter, strolling in the woods, sees Purity bathing in a stream. He later succeeds in meeting Purity and makes her an offer to pose for him. She refuses but accepts his card. Purity receives

The artist in his studio (Audrey Munson and Alfred Hollingsworth)

word from Darcy that he is ill in bed and begging her to come with him. His final effort to publish his book of poems has met with refusal.

Unselfishly seeking to aid him, she goes to Lamarque, secures five hundred dollars in advance with a promise to repay him by posing for him and earning money from other artists, and at once turns the money over to the publisher to bring out Darcy's book. She binds the publisher to secrecy. Darcy is confined to his bed with a siege of illness and is only saved from death by the happy turn. Purity guards from him the secret of her share in it.

In the meantime, she poses regularly for Lamarque. Through his

Audrey Munson in a nude pose, long before the Production Code

interest in her he secures an engagement for her to pose in imitation of marble statuary at a fete given by a fashionable young widow, Judith Lure. No sooner is Darcy's book published than it excites instant attention and praise, and he becomes the lion of the hour.

In the meantime, Luston Black, an acquaintance of Lamarque, having caught a glimpse of Purity posing for the artist, has become infatuated with her. He assumes that because of her position as a model he will have an easy conquest. But Purity, despite her innocence, senses his base motives and spurns him.

Darcy, accepting an invitation to visit Lamarque, comes into the studio while Black is pressing his attentions upon Purity. He thrashes Black, who taunts the poet with the fact that his fiancée is posing in the nude. Darcy will not believe it. Purity acknowledges the truth. Darcy will not listen to Purity's explanations and casts her off. A short time later the poet sees Lamarque's finished picture of "Virtue." Darcy is quick to read the great truth that the picture is intended to convey and upon learning that Purity was the instrument through which his poems were published, hastens to her. They are happily reunited.

—Moving Picture World, August 5, 1916

THE PRODUCTION

Sexuality has been the common coin of motion pictures since they first began to flicker on a screen. From the earliest days of the cinema, there were performers who radiated erotic energy: Theda Bara, Rudolph Valentino, Asta Nielsen, Louise Brooks, and many others. During the silent period, though, eroticism was usually expressed through a code of glance or gesture; it was relatively rare to see sexual situations portrayed openly. Filmmakers considered it a sort of game to see how sexy and suggestive their pictures could be and still avoid the wrath of the local censors. Explicit sexual activity or nudity were—usually—out of the question.

(Of course, pornographic films have always been a thriving industry, but that's altogether another subject. Here we are concerned only with films that were exhibited to the general public.)

But while nudity was rare on movie screens during the teens and twenties, it was by no means unknown. Nudity—more so then than now—guaranteed a film a certain notoriety, but the filmmaker who wanted to add this element to his work found the game a little more difficult than usual. There is, after all, no way to pretend to be naked— one either is or isn't. The trick is, how to get a nude body on the screen— thereby ensuring ticket sales—without inviting censor trouble.

The solution was generally found in Antiquity, Morality, Art, or a combination of the three. Interestingly, the 1915–16 period seems particularly rich in examples of each; among them:

Antiquity: In one scene in D. W. Griffith's *Intolerance* (1916), bare-breasted maidens in ancient Babylon cavort in their bath.

Morality: Lois Weber's allegorical *Hypocrites* (1915) features a character called The Naked Truth, whose name describes her with precision.

Rea Berger and Clifford Howard, the director and writer of *Purity,* chose the Art route. Their star, Audrey Munson, was widely considered "the perfection of womanly form."[1] It was their task simply to devise a plot wherein she could pose nude till the cows came home. After all, they reasoned, if you recreate a great work of art, which happens to feature a nude woman, how can the result be anything but artistic and uplifting and educational?

To be on the safe side, Berger and Howard also added generous helpings of both Allegory and Morality to their story, making *Purity*'s nudity virtually critic-proof.

A famous artist's model, Audrey Munson had posed for the statuary and commemorative coins for the Panama Pacific International Exposition in 1915. The same year, she appeared in her first film, *Inspiration,* as, well, an artist's model. In the course of the story, Munson was obliged to pose in the nude on several occasions. The local censor boards decided that the context justified Munson's nudity, and *Inspiration* was a great success.

Purity would similarly attempt to toe the thin line between edification and salaciousness by again casting Audrey Munson as an artist's model. This time, however, instead of merely posing in the nude, she would also be featured in fantasy sequences in which she appears in famous works of art including: *Spring* by Albert Toft, *Fate* by Gilbert Ledward, *Aphrodite of Cnidus* by Praxiteles, *Musidora* by Gainsborough, and many others. Munson also recreated two sculptures for which she had originally posed: *Abundance* by Karl Bitter and A. A. Wernman's *Descending Night,* the crowning figure of the Court of Honor at the Panama Pacific International Exposition.[2]

The plan worked. Nearly every reviewer bent over backward to assure readers that *Purity* "has an artistic merit. It is cleverly produced, so cleverly in fact that none can point a finger at it and declaim it as immoral, suggestive, or salacious."[3]

Wid's Daily, a trade magazine, was not quite so taken in by *Purity's* cloak of virtue, seeing beneath it a keen and clever marketing plan. "While all this has been done in rather an artistic manner working logically into the story, the fact still remains that the picture will have its chief appeal because of the display of the nude. Certainly [the filmmakers] figured out every possible way for Miss Munson to show what she has. From that viewpoint the production is quite complete."[4]

If she read the reviews, Audrey Munson must have received very mixed messages about her appeal. While the critics constantly praise her "perfect figure," they are also quick to add that they personally don't find her body at all appealing.

"Her poses are marvels of beauty without the faintest sign of suggestiveness. Her entire conduct in dress and out is that of a refined woman, and the role she is given enforces her native purity of mind."[5]

"The sensuous is not included in Miss Munson's own character. Those scenes mentioned are never revolting and indeed one becomes acclimated to them after a while and feels surprised when Miss Munson dons clothes of the times."[6]

Rea Berger and Clifford Howard wanted to make sure that everyone came to *Purity* only for the wholesome and educational reasons for which they made it. They planted a title both at the beginning and the end of the film stating "To the pure all things are pure," which, aside from its questionable accuracy, had the effect of deflecting criticism of Munson's frequent nudity.

(*Variety* was helpful enough to point out just how frequently one could witness Munson's artistic body, stating that "a flash of Miss Munson's physical charms" came along "about every 300 feet, and this, when figured out, gives the audience about eighteen good peeks at the girl, in just about the same state of undress as she would be on entering her morning tub."[7])

Purity was filmed primarily on what several critics point out must have been a large California estate. Robert V. Phelan's cinematography was praised, although the interior design was criticized. Munson's character lives in near poverty in a small house in the woods, complained one critic, yet she "possesses a boudoir that would do justice to a Fifth Avenue mansion."[8]

Other critics slammed the slender and unbelievable plot line, ridiculing Purity's boyfriend as "a bad and extraordinarily funereal looking poet."[9] The poet is shocked to learn that Purity has been posing nude to raise the funds needed to publish his volume of poetry. "From the sample of his verse flashed on the screen," wrote one critic, "you fear the end did not justify the means."[10]

Purity was sold on a states'-rights basis by the Mutual Film Corporation. Although it seems to have been approved by the censor boards in most of the cities in which it played, the film was cut, at the behest of the license commissioner, before it could be shown in New York City, where it played at the Liberty Theater. Reviews written after that engagement began indicate that nudity was still plentiful in *Purity,* so it is difficult to determine how badly the film was cut. Nor can we know with any certainty in what form *Purity* was seen in other cities.

"Whatever may be said of the outcome as a production of art," wrote its author, Clifford Howard, "it fulfilled the company's expectations. It was the most costly film [Mutual] had ever turned out, yet by the end of the year they were half a million dollars to the good. Some towns forbade it, and others frankly welcomed it. Critics unmercifully roasted it, and critics enthusiastically praised it. Sermons were preached about

A bevy of beauties (left to right): Ellen Howard, Hazel West, Marie Van Tassell, Nela Drinkwitz, Alice Anaroni, Mary Dunham

it—pro and con. It was the first time I had ever had a hand in the creating of a sensation, and I have never contributed to another."[11]

The debate about *Purity*'s aesthetic and educational value may now seem a bit precious, particularly to our cynical age, which always wants to believe in the worst motives for everything. But it seems that at least some of the film's defenders were sincerely interested in helping to expand the horizons of a growing art form. *Purity*, whatever it may have lacked as drama or cinema, now looks like an important step toward the maturity of the cinema, one move closer to the day when motion pictures could tackle any subject, take on any point of view, without cloaking themselves in someone else's version of respectability.

6

A DAUGHTER OF THE GODS

Fox Film Corporation. Released October 17, 1916. Ten reels.

CREDITS

Presented by William Fox. *Supervised by* J. Gordon Edwards. *Director and Screenplay:* Herbert Brenon; *Camera:* J. Roy Hunt, Andre Barlatier, Marcel Le Picard, A. Culp, William C. Marshall, C. Richards, and E. Warren; *Title Editor:* Hettie Grey Baker; *Art Director:* John D. Braddon; *Technical Director:* George Fitch; *Modeller:* Herbert Messmore; *Designer of Costumes:* Irene Lee; *Master of Properties:* Joseph Allan Turner; *Chief Electrician:* F. Sullivan; *Musical Accompaniment:* Robert Hood Bowers; *General Manager:* Winfield R. Sheehan; *General Publicity Agent:* W. C. Thompson; *Manager of National Publicity:* Randolph Lewis.

CAST

Annette Kellerman* (*Anitia, a Daughter of the Gods*); William E. Shay (*Prince Omar*); Hal De Forest (*The Sultan*); Mademoiselle Marcelle Hontabat (*Cleone, Prince Omar's Hand-maiden*); Edward Boring (*The Arab Sheik*); Violet Horner (*Zarrah, His Daughter, the Sultan's Favorite*); Jane Lee (*Little Prince Omar, the Sultan's Son*); Katharine Lee (*Nydia*); Stuart Holmes (*Moorish Merchant*); Ricca Allen (*The Witch of Badness*); Henrietta Gilbert (*The Fairy of Goodness*); Walter James (*The Chief Eunuch of the Sultan's Palace*); Milly Liston (*Zarrah's Mother*); Walter McCullough (*Chief Guard*); Mark Price (*Slave Dealer*); Louise Rial (*His Wife*); Barbara Castleton.

*The star's name is spelled, interchangeably, as Kellerman and Kellermann. The former seems to be slightly more commonly used and that is the way I have elected to spell it here.

SYNOPSIS

In witnessing Mr. Fox's screen fantasy, *A Daughter of the Gods,* spectators are asked to forget, for the time being, that they are busy, practical men and women, and to become, if only for one night, children again.

For childhood is a blessing that comes but once in life, and is never appreciated until it is too late to fully realize its joys. Let us return to our mother's knee tonight, with the fairies and witches and gnomes and elves, and be as little children to enter a heaven of rich enjoyment.

Thus for three enchanting hours do we leave this world and all its cares behind.

P A R T   O N E

The Prologue

"The plaything of a little child escapes its earthly prison. And thereby hangs a tale of many years ago."

In a mythical land of Sunshine and Happiness dwell little Nydia and her parents. The choicest smiles of a Nature rarely beautiful and the carols of Song Birds make a fitting complement to their Happiness. Little Nydia finds her greatest happiness away from her parents, in communing with the creatures of brilliant plumage and the harmless animals which have retired to this haven away from possibility of harm and the Evils of mankind.

One day, the father brings to little Nydia a bird more beautiful than any she has seen. She calls it the Queen of the Song Birds and builds for it a cage that she may have it ever with her. Unwittingly she inflicts sorrow, for its mate mourns for it in the leafy home which they have built in the boughs of a spreading tree.

For many days, little Nydia enjoys the music of the Queen of the Song Birds, and then there comes a time when it leaves its cage, which

Annette Kellerman

she has left open accidentally, and goes forth to rejoin its mate. But at last Evil, which seemingly cannot be denied, enters in the form of a Cat, in reality one of the many shapes taken by the Wicked Witch, and kills the Queen of the Song Birds. Little Nydia arrives too late to prevent this while the mate of the bird looks on from its leafy bough in sorrow. Brokenhearted, little Nydia prepares a basket and in this she places the body of the song bird and consigns it to the waves. Its mate, also brokenhearted and sorrowful, speedily follows it to a watery grave. Little

Nydia returns to her parents and tells them of the occurrence and they endeavor to console her, but to no avail. Daily and hourly and the child droops and will not be consoled.

Act One:

"The land of a Mighty Sultan; and a record of many strange happenings there."

In Another Land of Equal Beauty lives a powerful and happy Sultan, secure in the love of his favorite wife and devoted to their son, little Prince Omar. Between the souls of little Omar and Nydia a distinct parallel may be traced. Here again apparently no evil can enter, yet the Old Witch one day of evil potent rises from the sea and works a mischief upon the little Prince. He has stolen away from his nurse, and his will is directed towards a boat which rests quietly by the shore of the sea upon which his father's kingdom is situated. Unable to resist the Witch's baneful influence, he enters it, and as it drifts out to sea, the Good Fairy routs the Wicked Witch but too late to save the child, for the boat is overturned, and he sinks beneath the waves.

The Sultan—his father—learns of this and summons the men of his kingdom, his guards and retainers, and directs them as they swim boldly out to find the Prince. But he cannot be found and only his little hat which floats upon the surface reveals his fate. The Sultan is inconsolable. He kneels by the sea in frenzy, and in that moment his nature undergoes a change.

Almost at the moment when Omar dies, the soul of little Nydia goes forth from its earthly casing, and the souls of the two children fly towards that place wherein all children find happiness and which is shown later as the story progresses.

"A Fairy Prince and Princess Meet."

Twenty years have lapsed, and their passage has left the Sultan a lustful, greedy, soured old man. His own harem stands in awe of his moods, his favorite no longer feels the security which his kindness formerly threw about her. No one knows what may happen next, for the soul of the Sultan is sore grieved at the death of the one dearest in all this world to him, Prince Omar. His thoughts have turned to women. He is apparently satisfied with none.

Nearby is the temporary encampment of the Arab Sheik whose daughter Zarrah is the Star of the Desert. Long has the Sheik looked upon the power and dominance of the Sultan, and summoning his daughter, as wicked and ambitious as himself, they plan against the Sultan. Her beauty shall be the power which shall attract him and hers shall be the hand which will depose him and make her father the Sheik all-powerful.

The Sheik escorts his daughter Zarrah through the streets and bazaars of the Oriental city and when at last, through many passages of Oriental magnificence, they come to the Sultan, his rapture knows no bounds when he sees the beautiful Star of the Desert. He immediately deposes his former favorite and takes Zarrah unto himself and his throne. She virtually becomes his mistress and the mistress of the powerful, warlike people whom he rules.

In the Land of Happiness where the Fairy of Good Kindness rules, we see little Nydia and Omar leading a childlike life among the blue waves which envelop them. Then it is that we see the Soul of the Song Bird in the form of the Beautiful Anitia, a free, untrammelled girl of the ocean, while the soul of the Song Bird's mate is now seen in the guise of a beautiful youth. Both souls are destined to become united, and their destinies cross in strange ways.

Zarrah, the star of the Desert, now reigns supreme in the Halls of the Wicked Sultan. Yet vague fears encompass her when the Wicked Witch visits the Sultan and tells him a Maiden called Anitia is being led by the Fates towards his Court and that she is destined to destroy him. The Sultan's alarm is great as he realizes this Evil coming upon his kingdom, and the witch at this opportune moment tells him that should he give orders for the destruction of Anitia that she—the Witch—will give him back his son, the Prince Omar. The Sultan agrees, and the witch tells him that even now a youth of noble bearing is approaching his shores who is none other than his son, the Prince.

Joyously, the Sultan hurries forth and there landing upon his shores he sees the Noble Youth and welcomes him. With equal joy, the Sultan bears him through the streets and proclaims from the balcony of his palace that this youth is his son and heir, long lost but now recovered and destined to rule for many years after he has gone. The people joyously acclaim the Prince, and as they do so, Anitia dances a strange dance upon the shadowy rocks with her sea maidens, and then the waves bear her onward to her destiny.

Anitia enters the encampment of the Arab Sheik and is welcomed and made much of. At a distance, however, the Desert Thieves see her, and becoming aware of her rare beauty, they decide that she shall bring them large sums of gold upon the Slave Mart of the Sultan's city. That night, as the shadows gather, they enter the sleeping quarters of the Sheik and inform Anitia that he is about to take her on the morrow and dispose of her in the market of the city. Anitia, believing their deceitful tales, leaves with them, and the Sheik, awakened, offers pursuit.

In the Slave Mart of the Sultan's City we behold the Evil of Man in full sway. A mother has been captured and prays that the brutal auctioneers of human flesh will not take from her the baby which she has borne and loves. Her prayer is denied, and the distracted mother, rather than witness the removal of her child and everything she holds dear, rushes upon the parapet close by and precipitates herself into the sea.

Cleone, a girl of noble family, has also been captured and her charms are exhibited publicly for those who would see and buy. As she also pleads, the Prince Omar, the Youth of Gentle Deeds and Kindness who has endeared himself to the people, visits that part of the city and overhears and sees Cleone's frantic pleas. He interferes and, buying her from the auctioneer, he removes her towards the harem of the Palace, where she is destined to become a handmaiden of the women of the Court. As they depart, Anitia is brought into the Mart by the Wicked Desert Thieves and put up for sale.

Rudely the men clamor for her and offer large sums of gold, but the beauty of Anitia is seen by the Harem Eunuch of the Sultan, a keen judge of values, and he claims prior right to buy the girl. Amid scowls concealed by obsequious bows, he removes her to the Palace of the Sultan. The Desert Sheik who has been in Pursuit arrives but also bows before the imperial authority of the Harem Eunuch.

When Anitia comes before the Wicked Sultan, the beauty of the other women pales into insignificance, and Zarrah, the reigning favorite, sees the coming death of her ambitious hopes.

All the harem women make preparations by bathing themselves for the gorgeous Oriental Festival of the Springtime. Zarrah watches the beauty of Anitia with jealous eyes and tells her to keep in the background as her work is all powerful and a suggestion from her will result in a horrible death for Anitia.

(Intermission Five Minutes)

PART TWO

Act Two

"Wherein We All Become Children Again and Fight for a Beautiful Princess."

We now revert to Mermaid Land, where happiness reigns and where little Omar and Nydia are seen in the midst of the mermaids, who carry the children from rock to rock and disport themselves in the waves.

Then comes the Festival of the Springtime. Many women dance before the Sultan and the assembled people, but none satisfy his jaded senses. When Anitia advances down the royal staircase, it is then that the Sultan, although he realizes the menace of Anitia to his own kingdom, cannot restrain the evil desires which possess him at [the] sight of her beauty. The people also are enraptured. Afterwards, the Sultan offers to make her his favorite and presses the highest rewards of his luxurious kingdom and favors upon Anitia. Disgusted by his proximity, her whole maidenly soul offended by the undercurrent of sensuality so strongly revealed in the man's manner, she refuses and thus reassures Zarrah, who has been waiting breathlessly with her own fate hanging in the balance. The Prince Omar has looked upon the beauty of Anitia with pleasure and favor, much to the sorrow of Cleone, who mourns in secret for a jot of the love which he has suddenly conceived for the beautiful maiden, Anitia.

A beguiling group of mermaids

Anitia's refusal to accept the Sultan's favors results in her being locked in the Tower, this evil suggestion coming from Zarrah, who tells the Sultan that once [she is] secure in the tower, he can wreak his pleasure upon Anitia without possible interference. Anitia is accordingly imprisoned in the Tower and there, shortly afterwards, Zarrah, the favorite, follows her and taunts her with her impending fate.

As Anitia lies prostrate under these taunts, Zarrah leaves, and the Wicked Witch appears to gloat upon Anitia's form and the success of her plans. But the Good Fairy who guards her also appears and once again puts to rout the Wicked Witch.

When the Sultan approaches, Anitia renders desperate tries to make her escape, but the guard struggles with her. She does escape, however, and leaps upon the battlements of the Tower in which she is confined and into the ocean hundreds of feet below. The Sultan notes her escape and urges after her his guards. Anitia swims desperately.

Zarrah, returning, tells the Prince Omar, and his anger and surprise are great. Zarrah secretly nourishes a love for Omar, and the Sultan, entering, finds her arms about his neck. Zarrah endeavors to explain, but the rage of the Sultan is very great.

Meanwhile, Anitia has been swimming desperately and is captured. Zarrah visits the Temple where the Wicked Witches worship and begs their assistance in destroying Anitia. They agree to aid in this destruction, but Zarrah must sell them her soul. Without hesitation she agrees to do so and departs. After she has gone, the Wicked Witches, as their first

A dramatic highlight with Miss Kellerman

operation, cause the eruption of a volcanic mountain, and the lava pours down upon the city.

Meanwhile, Anitia, who has been brought again before the Sultan, is pursued by him around the harem and strives desperately to make her escape. None seems possible, when the eruption of the volcanic mountain makes itself felt in the city and causes a temporary diversion of interest.

The Sultan now remembers the Witches' warning and denounces Anitia as a sorceress. The people below, furious at the possibility of Anitia causing the eruption, call upon the Sultan to allow them to burn her alive. To this he agrees, and the populace bring her forth to where a large post has been erected and soon it is in a blaze.

As the Sultan watches in great glee, Prince Omar also sees Anitia and goes to her assistance. This infuriates the Sultan, who arrests them both and, at Zarrah's suggestion, commands that Anitia be thrown to the crocodiles. As they take her to her fate, the Prince Omar has a heated scene with the Sultan who—doubly infuriated at this resistance—commands that Prince Omar be tied to a rock near the sea and there be drowned. Prince Omar is likewise led to his fate to the sorrow of Cleone, who has been watching.

Anitia is bound, and below in the pool coming through the sluice gate, we see the cavernous jaws of the monsters which are to devour her. At that moment when there seems no hope, the Good Fairy again becomes her savior, and the murderous, devouring crocodiles are turned into innocent swans which swim about upon the surface of the pool. Anitia, thus rescued, goes through the sluice gate and is swept, bound, into the whirlpools beyond.

Onward Anitia is swept through the cascades, unable to help herself. The rapidity of her flight, the desperation of her efforts, prevent her from sinking. As she is thrown from one rapid to another and swept further out, she is seen by the mermaid children—little Nydia and Omar—and attention is called to Anitia's plight.

The mermaids swim to her as she is about to be dashed to pieces on a rockbound coast and rescue her, bringing her in safety to the shore. There she is made welcome, but, alas, she cannot linger here as no mortal may stay among the mermaids and live. Anitia is told that she must journey to the land of the Gnomes, a strange little people—very hard working—who will treat her kindly.

Accordingly, Anitia journeys onward and bids her kind rescuers and protectors goodbye. Upon her arrival, the Wicked Witch appears and tells them that she is a spirit of evil who means the destruction of the people. The Gnomes receive Anitia with sticks and stones. They chase and finally capture her, but at the moment when they are about to execute summary sentence upon Anitia, the Good Fairy again appears and stills their fears and anger. Anitia is then made much to-do over and assigned the little cabin of state in the Land of the Gnomes.

Back in the Kingdom of the Sultan, Prince Omar is led out to his doom. He is tied by the sea-washed rock and there left to perish by the Wicked Sultan. Zarrah now thinks the time ripe for the consummation of her wicked designs. She visits her father—the Arab Sheik—and gets from him the mysterious potion which will first deaden the Sultan's mental powers and then cause the death of his body.

While pretending to lavish a wealth of affection upon the Sultan, she secretly gives the potion to the Sultan and then waits for the effects.

In Gnome Land, Anitia entertains the people by her spectacular feats of diving and swimming and becomes the popular idol.

In the Sultan's City, the people, realizing the fate to which the Prince has been condemned, grow mutinous and demand that he be released. The Sultan, furiously angry, makes plans to give them a taste of his power and to rebuke them for their desire to liberate the Prince. Sending forth his guards, a battle royal ensues between the guards and the people, and the Sultan watches with great glee the triumph of his men.

Meanwhile, in Gnome Land, the Good Fairy appears to Anitia and tells her of the troublous times going on in the realm of the Sultan. Anitia then realized the danger about to befall her lover the Prince, and marshalling the Gnomes, they set out to surround and capture the Sultan's city. As they gallop along furiously, the queer little bearded figures are changed—by the Agency of the Good Fairy—into Men of Valor, and they continue their swift rush to the city which they intend conquering.

One of the spectacular scenes in this early $1 million film

Their approach is noted by the captain of the Guards, who warns the Sultan. The people demand that the Prince shall lead them against the invader. The Sultan grows furious and tells them that he himself shall lead them, but before he can complete his intention he begins to experience the effect of the mysterious potion given to him by Zarrah.

As the news is communicated to the Sultan of his people's refusal to fight under any leadership but that of the Prince, the Sultan dies amid the rejoicing of his harem and Zarrah, whom they hail as their queen.

Then commences the terrible conflict, the Sultan's people under the leadership of the Prince, the Gnomes under the leadership of Anitia. The battle and siege wage back and forth. Large instruments are employed to cast stones. The victory rests with Anitia and the Gnomes until she and the Prince—with visors down—meet in a single combat upon the walls of the castle. This encounter results in the death of Anitia, who is thus slain by the hand of her own lover and against whom she did not realize she was fighting.

The fighting over, the sorrow and agony of the Prince is supreme. On a flowered bier by the sea rests the body of Anitia and the Prince stands with visor up and in the presence of the people is hailed as the Sultan. Pointing to the burning city, he tells them that he is Sultan of a sorry kingdom indeed and, turning, looks upon the face of she whom he has slain.

As the people retire, Zarrah comes upon the Prince and presses upon him her love. He spurns it. His heart is with the dead Anitia. Then Zarrah draws a dagger and stabs the Prince to the heart, determined at any cost to have her revenge and realize her ambition. Before she can consummate her foul intent of escape and making good her ambition, she is captured, and the vengeance of the people is wreaked upon her for the death of their beloved leader.

Then are the bodies of Anitia and the Prince consigned to the mercy of the sea upon a flowered bier. But the Good Fairy has been watching, and her intention is to reunite their souls in Death. Nearby, the happy Mermaids and the children swim, awaiting the outcome of the pleasure of the Good Fairy.

She appears upon the bier and brings back to life the Prince. But he is disconsolate at the sight of the body of Anitia which lies beside him. Saddened, the Good Fairy touches the inanimate body of Anitia with her wand, and she also comes back to life. For a single moment of bliss they are united. Then Anitia—who has been destined forever to immortal happiness—is forced to look upon the return of her lover to Death.

> "It seemeth such a little way to me,
> Across to that country,
>   The Beyond:
> For it has grown to be
> The home of those of whom I am
>   So fond.

And so for me there is no sting to Death,
It is but crossing, with abated breath,
    A little strip of sea,
To find one's loved ones waiting on the shore.
More beautiful, more precious, than before!"

She is transported to the midst of the Mermaids and becomes their Queen. But even in her immortal happiness, her soul still longs for that of Prince Omar. When last seen, she is swimming disconsolately among her followers. And all their tender ministration can do nought to ease her troubled heart.

END

—Library of Congress, with some additional
material from the original program

....

THE PRODUCTION

"The screen marvel that will never know a yester-year!"[1]

Even in a year of spectacular cinematic experiences such as D. W. Griffith's mammoth *Intolerance,* Herbert Brenon's *A Daughter of the Gods* must have left audiences breathless with amazement. "Epic" hardly describes the production; surviving photographs show huge walled cities; massive, ornate interiors; and thousands upon thousands of extras.

"For sheer material size of spectacle," wrote one critic, "*A Daughter of the Gods* outdoes anything yet seen. The mighty plain across which white and black armies charge makes one wonder at finding so much dry Atlantic island outside Cuba. The crowds of citizens and soldiers—countless, almost—which surcharge the great squares beneath Brenon's long shots make one involuntarily applaud the discipline and military technique which made this picture possible. There are wall-battles, with all the impedimenta of ancient verduning, outdoing anything in the epic film *Cabiria.*"[2]

A Daughter of the Gods had a plot every bit as complex and outsized as the production. While presenting itself as a simple fairy story, it was actually a richly textured saga worthy of Wagner's "Ring" cycle (critic W. Stephen Bush, in praising the film's musical accompaniment, wrote that "here and there I recognized a Wagnerian motif handled with uncommon skill"[3]). *Photoplay*'s Julian Johnson called the story: "As grand a tale of nereids and Necromancy, villains and voluptuaries, coryphees and combats as was ever wrought outside the Burton edition of *The Thousand and One Nights*."[4]

Director Herbert Brenon and star Annette Kellerman had filmed an elaborate fantasy, *Neptune's Daughter*, in Bermuda two years earlier and looked for a similarly exotic location for *A Daughter of the Gods*. Brenon chose a scenic spot near Kingston, Jamaica, took his company there in January 1916, and remained there for eight months, an unusually long production period, then or now.

An article in *Photoplay* magazine entitled "The King of Jamaica" gathered together some impressive statistics behind the making of the film; it is worth quoting at length here:

> [Brenon] employed 20,000 men, women, and children; spent about $1,000,000; exposed 220,000 feet (forty-four miles) of film; will use in the finished production only 10,000 feet (less than two miles); expended great sums to make sanitary a mosquito-cursed section of Jamaica so the work could go on healthfully; kept a native band playing through the days of the months so the spirit of thousands of native actors would not flag as The Story progressed; built a refrigerating plant to protect the celluloid films from tropical heat; schooled his mermaid girls to swim with their lower limbs encased in metallic mermaid tails; used up 2,000,000 feet of lumber; 2,500 barrels of plaster, 500 barrels of cement; ten tons of paper (for *papier-mâché* properties); used ten alligators, fourteen swans, ten camels, 2,500 horses, 2,000 cattle, 800 sheep, 1,000 donkeys, a flock of sparrows from New York, 500 miscellaneous animals, 2,000 lizards, 2,500 toads. And 'shot' with six cameras in unison.
>
> He put the Jamaican *siesta* out of business so far as the making of The Story was concerned; dressed up 500 island [children] in peaked caps and long beards and taught them to play as gnomes under artificial toadstools, after opening a school for them in fairy lore; let members of

his company put baby sharks in his bathtub and kept his temper in the tropic heat; gave a concert and sold $3,500 worth of seats for the British Red Cross; drove his people relentlessly from dawn to dark—and kept their loyal friendship, from Annette Kellerman, the star, down to the least considerable roustabout.[5]

Annette Kellerman was born in Australia in 1887. She gained fame for her achievements in long-distance swimming, and like Esther Williams a few decades later, she found time to swim and dive in each of her motion pictures. "The submersible star," wrote one reviewer, "is unrivaled in diving and swimming, and [in] this photoplay, taken amid settings as fantastic and Arabic as are to be found anywhere in the Caribbean, must leap from a hundred-foot tower, plunge into a pool full of crocodiles, be dashed against forbidding rocks, and fall down a waterfall."[6]

If Kellerman used a double for any of this daring work, it escaped the sharp eyes of the critics, nearly all of whom were impressed with her skill and stamina: "Miss Kellerman's dive from the tower is beautiful and the race in the ocean in which Anitia is pursued by a group of blacks who have great speed in swimming is thrilling, but no more so than the flashes of Anitia struggling to loose the bonds which hold her hand and foot while being swept along with the current and later dashed against a coral reef by vicious waves."[7]

Annette Kellerman also quickly made a name for herself by a willingness to appear nude on the screen. While not entirely unheard of during this period (see *Purity* in the preceding chapter), cinematic nudity was still by no means common. One trade paper predicted that at least part of the popularity of *A Daughter of the Gods* would be due to the "many scenes in which Miss Kellerman and many other girls appear in the nude. Yet no one can have the least grounds to complain regarding this, because this part of the offering has been delightfully handled, and there is no more reason to have a suggestive thought in viewing this offering than there would be in viewing sculpture to be found in any of our great art collections."[8]

"Audrey Munson, as exhibited in the short-lived *Purity*," wrote an-

other critic, "has nothing on Miss Kellerman, and as it has been elsewhere observed, neither has Miss Kellerman."[9]

While the long production period and exorbitant budget had made
A Daughter of the Gods into an almost universally admired motion picture
experience, it enraged William Fox, the head of the studio. He had Herbert Brenon's name excised from the print (Brenon sued and won) and
left orders that Brenon not be allowed to attend the opening at New
York's Lyric Theater on October 16, 1916.

"It was soon whispered about, however," wrote a *New York Times*
reporter, "that [Brenon] had entered in the kindly disguise that whiskers
always provide and was seated in the second row."[10]

A Daughter of the Gods was received enthusiastically by audience and
critics, and William Fox was soon proudly acknowledging his "Million
Dollar Picture Beautiful." By December, he had assembled one of the
industry's largest publicity staffs to manage the nationwide release of the
film. *A Daughter of the Gods* was released as a road show, playing "first-
class theaters at 'two dollar' prices."[11]

Fox rereleased the film in 1920 with the ad line: The screen marvel
that will never know a yester-year![12] The blurb was intended to reassure
moviegoers that they would still enjoy a movie from the dark ages of
four years earlier. Today, however, the line has an added poignancy;
"yester-year" is all this film will *ever* know. There is no future—indeed,
no present—for *A Daughter of the Gods*.

Its loss is tragic. Not only was *A Daughter of the Gods* an eye-filling
spectacle and a wildly imaginative fantasy, it might also have been one
of the masterpieces of the silent cinema.

"A distinct advance would appear to have been made in motion
picture production," wrote a critic from the *New York Dramatic Mirror*.
"The actual mechanical perfection of the film has probably never been
equaled. Camera effects, dissolves, unique photographic feats, abound.

"If the true function of the screen (as some maintain) be the portrayal of *pictures in motion*, then have Messrs. Fox, Brenon, and others
responsible for *A Daughter of the Gods* succeeded in creating a splendid
example."[13]

7

THE CONQUEROR

· ·

Fox Film Corporation. A Standard Picture. Released September 16, 1917.
Eight reels.

C R E D I T S

Director: Raoul A. Walsh; *Scenario:* Chester Blinn Clapp; *Story:* Henry Christeen Warnack;
Camera: Del Clawson; *Setting Design:* George G. Grenier.

C A S T

William Farnum (*Sam Houston*); Jewel Carmen (*Eliza Allen*); Charles Clary (*Sidney Stokes*);
James A. Marcus (*Jumbo*); Carrie Clarke Ward (*Mammy*); William Chisolm (*Dr. Spencer*);
Robert Dunbar (*Judge Allen*); Owen Jones (*James Houston*); William Eagle Shirt, Chief
Birdhead, Little Bear (*Indian Chiefs*).

· ·

SYNOPSIS

Because Sam Houston (William Farnum) has been raised in the mountains, he has little or no education. When his father (Owen Jones) dies, Sam feels as if he has lost the last friend he had in the world. He still has the Cherokee Indians, among whom he has lived since the earliest dawn of consciousness. Sam returns to civilization after the death of his father and settles in Nashville. The city was not far from where Sam lived. He made frequent trips to it, and that was how he came to meet Eliza Allen (Jewel Carmen).

When Eliza, daughter of the of the most aristocratic family in the town, discovers that Sam can neither read nor write, it means for her the end of their acquaintanceship. She laughs at Sam's ignorance and clumsiness. One day soon after Eliza has learned this awful truth, Sam goes to see her. She cannot bear the thought of receiving such a person, so she tells her Negro mammy to tell Sam that she cannot see him because she is "constrainedly unable." The Negro mammy doesn't tell Sam this. She tells him that her mistress has said she could not see him until he "strained to be constable." And so the man starts in to make good; he begins his education.

Sam decides to become constable. He asks a friend how to attain this valued position, and the friend replies, "Drinks and votes." Whiskey is dear in the Tennessee of 1825. When Sam bags a silver fox and sells its skin for a handful of silver, he finds that he has money enough for only a few votes. But his despair is short-lived. Teddy, his dog, seems to sense that his master needs money, so he quietly slips the fox skin from the shop of the dealer who had bought it and brings it back to Sam. Sam sells it again. He buys more whiskey and more votes.

When the skin is returned once more in the faithful teeth of Teddy, Sam buys more whiskey and more votes. So he keeps it up until finally he has sold that one fox skin often enough to elect him constable. Then he goes to see Eliza. The mammy answers the door again.

"Tell your mistress I am a constable now," says Sam, "and I am ready to wait upon her."

But Eliza only laughs at Mammy, sends down a message that she will not receive Mr. Houston until he is sheriff, and returns to her knitting. When Sam becomes sheriff, he finally gains admittance into the sacred quarters. When he asks Eliza to marry him, she replies, "I will when you become governor."

Sam becomes governor.

She marries him. But at the reception following the ceremony, Sam realizes that Eliza married him only to become the wife of the first gentleman of the state. He leaves in a rage. After he has gone, Sidney Stokes (Charles Clary) attempts to force his attentions on Eliza. Stokes had for many years been an aspirant to the hand of Eliza. There is something about his eyes which the girl does not like, and though she has been kind to him, she has steadfastly refused him. When his insistence becomes nothing short of insulting, Eliza's father (Robert Dunbar) interferes and is shot and killed. Sidney flees into the night, outlawed. He takes with him an undying hatred against Sam Houston, his successful rival.

[Although this plot point is not clear, it appears that Sidney is shown to be irredeemably villainous when he kills Sam's dog, Teddy. "The little dog that makes an appearance at the first is featured in a number of touching scenes with the title character, and his pathetic death, brought about by the villainy of Stokes, is as touching, if not more so, than the death of Houston's father."[1]]

In shame, Eliza goes in search of Sam, who has settled in Texas. She is captured by the Cherokees, who recognize her as a friend of the "white brother" by a picture Sam carried. She is given escort to a nearby convent.

Sidney is busy inciting the Mexicans against Texas. Soon after Sam comes to Texas, the invaders cross the boundary. Houston leads the Americans in their resistance to the Mexicans. A great battle takes place. Desperadoes, headed by Stokes, attack the settlement where Sam has made his home. He leads them against the invaders. The Cherokees come to the rescue. The marauders make to the convent, and there Stokes again attacks Eliza. Sam Houston rushes to the rescue. The Mexicans and Indians battle hand to hand.

In Eliza's room, Sam meets Sidney. The fight that ensues is terrific. It is not a battle of soldier against soldier, but of man against man, for the possession of a girl. Sam wins, and takes Eliza back to his home.

—*Motion Picture News*, September 29, 1917 and
Moving Picture World,
October 13, 1917

THE PRODUCTION

The story of Sam Houston, the Governor of Tennessee who, in 1836, wrested the vast Texas territory away from Mexico and turned it into a republic, has been brought to the screen several times. Richard Dix lent a stalwart earnestness to the role in Republic's epic *Man of Conquest*

(1939); Joel McCrea made a stern, tight-lipped Houston in *The First Texan* (1956); and Sam Elliott snarled his way through the part in a television production, *Houston: The Legend of Texas* (a.k.a. *Gone To Texas*, 1986).

The fascinating Houston shows up, at least momentarily, in most movies about the battle of the Alamo, wreaking a terrible vengeance on Mexican General Santa Anna at the Battle of San Jacinto, leading his troops into battle with the cry, "Remember the Alamo!" These cameo Houstons include Tom Wilson (*The Martyrs of the Alamo*, 1915), Edward Piel (*Heroes of the Alamo*, 1937), Richard Boone (*The Alamo*, 1960), Lorne Greene (*The Alamo: 13 Days to Glory*, 1987) and Stacey Keach (*Texas*, 1995).

While most Houston movies center on his adventures in Texas, some, like *Man of Conquest*, touch on his mysterious first marriage to Eliza Allen, which ended quickly and without public explanation. *The Conqueror*, however, allows this story to take center stage. But while the breakup of their marriage is explained in the film, Sam and Eliza don't part ways forever; in the best Hollywood tradition, history is thrown out the window in the interest of a happy kiss at the fadeout and a contrite "Can a former governor find in me a worthy wife?" from Eliza.

Farnum's leading lady, Jewel Carmen, was still a relative newcomer to films. Quite attractive, she was received relatively well in the role of the haughty, selfish Eliza. Unfortunately, it is difficult today to find enough of her films extant to adequately assess her talent. She married director Roland West in 1918 and thereafter worked only with him before leaving motion pictures in the early twenties.

Director Raoul Walsh writes in his autobiography that when he read the original script of *The Conqueror* he "didn't work up much enthusiasm" but liked the idea of working with William Farnum.[2] William Farnum and his brother Dustin were both usually cast in historical or Western roles. In fact, the year before William played Sam Houston in *The Conqueror*, Dustin had portrayed another important character in the story of Texas's independence: *Davy Crockett* (Paramount, 1916).

"William Farnum presents a splendid characterization in the part of General Houston," wrote one critic. "Both his pathetic moments when

William Farnum

he is alone and friendless—with the exception of his old hound dog—and the scenes in which he is shown as a strong and forceful leader of men, were fine examples of Mr. Farnum's art."[3]

Despite Walsh's initial lack of enthusiasm, *The Conqueror* became a major production, highly regarded for its attention to historical detail and for its rousing scenes of battle. The eight-reel production cost an impressive $300,000 (so studio publicity claimed, anyway) and utilized 8,000 extras and 1,000 horses, filming on locations in California, Texas, and Mexico. A large street set was constructed at the Fox studio to represent Nashville, Tennessee, of the 1820s, and the climactic battle takes place in the ruins of a real Spanish mission.

Walsh, who writes that he was "getting tired of redskins with blue eyes"[4] had thirty Sioux imported from the Pine Ridge Agency in South Dakota. "We were short of Indians, so I used the real ones in the close-ups and feathered and painted some cowboys for the longer shots."[5] The Sioux played Cherokees in the film.

Virtually every critic was impressed with the period detail of *The Conqueror*: "The costuming throughout is perfection itself in every detail. The women in hoop skirts, the men in ruffled shirts and stovepipe hats, make a very attractive sight and lend an abundance of atmosphere to the story."[6] But the film's explosive battle scenes were singled out for even greater praise. "In the story's big climax occur the battle scenes, which director R. A. Walsh has 'put on' in the true masterly fashion which has characterized his former accomplishments. Not only are these scenes vivid and tensely realistic, but they have a beauty which would warrant their being spoken of as masterpieces of art. The photography, naturally, has a lot to do with this. The belching cannon, the bursting shells, the white clouds of smoke, illumined by the fire below and standing out clearly in a somber sky—the whole thing has been finely executed and photographed."[7]

Wid's critic, however, thought the film too long. And, although he found that the battles scenes contained "some very effective spectacular bits . . . even the average school-child will be rather shocked to see the excessive use of high explosives throughout these clashes. In the days which were being pictured they used cannon which fired cannon balls, and didn't employ high explosives as pictured."[8] The critic also complained of the presence of an anachronistic upright piano.

However, as unified as the critics were on *The Conqueror*'s scenes of excitement and mayhem, most of them deplored the excessive use of comedy, most of which featured a buffoonish black character named Jumbo, portrayed by James A. Marcus. "Some of the comedy relief might well be spared, so far as the judicious are concerned," wrote Edward Weitzel, "but it will bring joy to the rest of the spectators."[9]

"While it gathered a few laughs," agreed the *Wid's* critic, "it seemed to run too long without a break, since there was absolutely no connection between this hokum and the story itself."[10]

One problem seemed to be that the excessive comedy in the first half of the film did not balance with the tense drama and violence of the second half. But since the most impressive moments in the film came near the end, *The Conqueror* left an overwhelmingly positive image in the critics' minds and makes it doubly regrettable that we cannot see for ourselves what *Variety* called, "a story replete with dramatic action . . . given a production that can, without exaggeration, be classed among the masterpieces of the screen."[11]

8

CLEOPATRA

Fox Film Corporation. Fox Standard Release, October 14, 1917. Eleven
reels (2 hours, 5 minutes).

C R E D I T S

Director: J. Gordon Edwards; *Scenario:* Adrian Johnson, based on the plays *Antony and
Cleopatra* and *Julius Caesar* by William Shakespeare and *Cleopatre* (1890) by Victorien
Sardou and Emile Moreau; *Camera:* Rial Schellinger, John W. Boyle, George Schneider-
man; *Film Editor:* Edward McDermott; Music adapted by Nicola Donatelli and George
Rubenstein (New York and Los Angeles engagements), performed in Los Angeles by Clune's
Auditorium Symphony Orchestra.

C A S T

Theda Bara (*Cleopatra*); Fritz Leiber (*Caesar*); Thurston Hall (*Antony*); Albert Roscoe
(*Pharon*); Herschel Mayall (*Ventidius*); Dorothy Drake (*Charmian*); Dell Duncan (*Iras*); Henri
de Vries (*Octavius Caesar*); Art Acord (*Kephren*); Hector V. Sarno (*Messenger*); Genevieve
Blinn (*Octavia*).

SYNOPSIS

Cleopatra, Queen of Egypt, craves world dominion. Expelled from Alexandria by the victorious forces of Julius Caesar, she pitches her tents
in the shadow of the pyramids, while the Roman conqueror sits in the
council chamber of the Ptolomys.

The irate Queen vows vengeance. She determines to make Caesar
a slave to her charms. She orders a chariot, and is on her way to face
the conqueror.

Caesar, enraged by the escape of Cleopatra, plans her capture. In the midst of his tirade a soldier announces a messenger bearing gifts from the King of Thrace. A huge rug is brought in, and when it is unfolded the wondrous Queen of Egypt is disclosed.

The Roman succumbs. During the amorous weeks that follow, Caesar is Cleopatra's abject slave. She instills in his mind the thought of an empire under their combined scepters. Fired with this idea, Caesar leaves for Rome to proclaim himself Emperor.

In the distant city of Abouthis, the Royal Priest of Osiris prepares his son, Pharon, to release the Egyptian people from bondage. Pharon is hereditary king to the Egyptian throne, now occupied by Cleopatra. He sets out for Alexandria to rid the land of the Siren and to assume control.

Meanwhile, Caesar in Rome makes known his ambitious [objective]. His able lieutenant, Antony, tries to dissuade him, but a vision of Cleopatra urges Caesar on to destruction. When he mounts the Senate rostrum to proclaim himself Emperor, the daggers of conspirators pierce his heart.

Pharon, posing as an astrologer, arrives in Alexandria determined to kill the Queen. While waiting for her to pass, he thrashes a slave for handling a woman and child roughly. Cleopatra witnesses the incident and is attracted to the handsome stranger. She invites him to her palace, and when he interprets a dream to her satisfaction, she makes him court astrologer.

As the days pass, Pharon gradually falls in love with Cleopatra. His vows of vengeance are dissipated like clouds, and he becomes her abject slave. He betrays his supporters and steals the treasure from his ancestors' tomb to provide for her armies.

After the battle of Philippi, the great triumvirate — Antony, Lepidus, and Octavius — divide the Roman empire among themselves. Antony commands that Cleopatra be brought before him at Tarsus to answer for the crime of aiding the conspiracy.

When Cleopatra is apprised of the command, she urges Pharon to get her the buried treasure of the Egyptian Kings. Relying upon her promise to marry him, Pharon reveals the secret. But once in possession of the treasure, she casts him aside and goes to meet Antony.

At Tarsus, she prevails upon Antony to accompany her to Alexandria. He, too, falls under her spell. Basking in the passionate love of Egypt's queen, he refuses call after call from his countrymen to return soon to quell various uprisings. Finally he leaves, promising to return as soon as possible. While in Rome he wavers and marries Octavia (Genevieve Blinn), sister of Octavius (Henri de Vries), in order to cement the strength of the triumvirate. But despite marriage, his infatuation for Cleopatra triumphs again. He returns to her and discovers that her love for him is true. Arriving at the Egyptian capital, Cleopatra spreads a great banquet in Antony's honor. In the midst of it a messenger brings the tidings that Octavius has declared Antony a public enemy; Antony unites forces with Cleopatra.

Cleopatra's forces join Antony's to fight Octavius at Actium. A day and a night the battle rages on land and sea. At the height of the engagement a false message is brought to the Queen that Antony has been slain. She leaves the fleet and returns to Alexandria.

Her desertion puts Antony's forces to flight. Raging at her action, Antony starts for Alexandria where he hears of Cleopatra's death. Unable to bear his grief, he stabs himself. As he is dying he hears that Cleopatra still is alive. He is carried to her just as the victorious Octavius rushes into the palace.

The victor gloats over the vanquished Queen as she pleads for the life of Antony. As she pleads, Antony enters and falls dead.

Pharon, still devoted to his beloved Queen, enters the chambers where she is held captive. He hands her an asp hidden in a basket of fruit. She places the poisonous reptile to her breast, and when Octavius enters again, he finds Cleopatra breathing her last—victorious to the end.

—Fox Press Book and *Motion Picture News*, November 3, 1917

· ·

THE PRODUCTION

Cleopatra is one of the American Film Institute's Ten Most Wanted lost movies. Of all the films on that sad list (named in the Introduction), the loss of *Cleopatra* is perhaps the most poignant. As much as we would love to see *The Rogue Song* or *The Divine Woman*, at least we can enjoy nearly

Director J. Gordon Edwards and his star, Theda Bara, outside her dressing room

all the other films of Laurel and Hardy and of Greta Garbo. But *Cleopatra* represents more than simply a lost film; it represents at least two lost careers.

Theda Bara starred in thirty-eight motion pictures between 1915 and 1926. No discussion of the silent cinema is complete without considering Bara's enormous, if relatively short-lived, impact on the art and on the greater culture. Yet only her motion picture debut, *A Fool There Was* (1915), and her last silent film, *The Unchastened Woman* (1925), exist today.

J. Gordon Edwards, who directed many of Bara's films, has been served no better by film preservation. Nothing of his prolific career survives, except *Drag Harlan* (1920). He died at age 58 in 1926, the year

A location scene, replete with extras, technicians, and many camels

Theda Bara retired from the screen. At the time of his death, Edwards had not made a picture in over two years, since *It Is the Law* (1924). Most of his obituaries mentioned his "plans" to return to "production work,"[1] but *Photoplay* got closer to the point: "Edwards had been a big director. Yet the last time he visited Hollywood hunting for work he couldn't get a chance. He was about to start out again on Christmas Day. He was 58 and jobless. A broken heart. They called it pneumonia."[2]

Bara's decline was neither so sudden nor so ignominious. Incredibly popular throughout the teens for her film portrayals as an amoral "vampire" who callously used men up and threw them away, the changing morals of the Roaring Twenties gradually turned her into a figure of fun. Her smoldering looks and deadly passions that once caused thrills in audiences began to inspire laughter instead.

At least Bara, whose real name was Theodosia Goodman, seems to have been in on the joke. "Theda Bara was a very amusing woman," said Colleen Moore. "She used to kid about 'Theda Bara' all the time and do lovely imitations of 'Theda Bara.' "[3] She spoofed her Vamp image onscreen in her last film, *Madame Mystery* (1926), but evidence of her

Theda in front of a pyramid made of papier-mâché and plaster

sense of humor did nothing to revive her career. Married to director
Charles Brabin, Bara lived quietly until 1955, far from the industry on
which she had had such a profound impact.

Of all lost movies—certainly of all the films discussed in this book—
Cleopatra maintains the most prominent and continual cultural profile.
The most famous portrait of Bara as the Queen of the Nile—dark eyes
blazing with angry sensuality, hands to her temples in psychic concen-
tration, breasts encircled by prophetic metal serpents—has been reprinted in countless histories of film, epitomizing the exotic allure of
Bara's image.

But although *Cleopatra* exists in the public's mind today almost entirely as a single icon, the record shows that the film itself, produced on

Trade ad

the lavish scale de rigueur in 1916–1917 (*Intolerance, A Daughter of the Gods*), must have been extravagantly entertaining.

Filmed in the summer of 1917, *Cleopatra* utilized several locations. The interiors were filmed on the Fox lot at Western and Sunset. Fox publicity claimed that one lavish tent interior featured $50,000 worth of decorations "to give it the barbaric splendor accredited to the time of the great Siren of the Nile. There were used alone, in this wonderful set, two rugs valued at $30,000."[4]

The pyramids and the Sphinx were recreated at a desert location near Ventura County, and the massive sea battle of Actium, featuring eighty ships constructed just for the scene, took place in what is now Newport Bay.

Though Fox publicity claimed that ten thousand people and three thousand horses were hired "to add color and life to the photodrama,"[5] the number is almost certainly hyperbolic. Even so, surviving photographs show that the sets and the crowds of actors and extras were truly impressive. The studio claimed that two thousand people were active behind the scenes and that the production cost a whopping $500,000.

Peter Milne wrote, "J. Gordon Edwards has furnished the picture

Preparing for a dramatic crisis: Theda Bara with Thurston Hall and director Edwards

In full regalia

with a production that belies detailed description. In settings, including entire cities, costumes, and the handling of the tremendous mobs, not still mobs, but fighting, raging mobs—he has demonstrated his ability as manager of the spectacular as never before. His work also includes some effective desert scenes with the pyramids rising in the background."[6]

Despite the splendors of the Nile that filled the screen, Theda Bara apparently had no trouble keeping the attention of the audience at all times, with upwards of fifty costume changes, many of which were risque even in the year of Audrey Munson and Annette Kellerman. "Those who like to see Theda Bara should not fail to take advantage of the opportunity afforded in *Cleopatra,*" wrote the *Dramatic Mirror*'s critic, "for certainly they will never see *more* of her. Miss Bara . . . moves throughout the two long acts with all the grace of a hula-hula dancer."[7]

"To match each costume," the Fox publicity department crowed, "the Siren of the Nile wears a complete set of jewels—fifty dazzling and different sets of baubles."[8]

Edward Weitzel, writing for the *Moving Picture World,* said that "Theda Bara as Cleopatra is always satisfactory to the eye, save that a certain grade of spectators will criticize unfavorably the very frank display of her physical charms and some of the seductive wiles she uses to ensnare her lovers."[9]

Many reviewers praised *Cleopatra*'s historical veracity and were pleased to note that some of the title cards quoted Shakespeare directly. Most of the male reviewers were quite taken with Bara's minimal wardrobe, and wondered what the various local censors would do to the film.

The local censors, however, didn't seem to mind a bit. William Fox proudly proclaimed that the film was passed by every censor board in the United States and received the commendation of the National Board of Review, which issued a statement saying, "This story, true to the main facts of history, shows the ambitious and beautiful Queen Cleopatra using her sex to juggle with the political history of Rome and Egypt. The cast is excellent and intimate details are handled with reserve. The picture abounds in magnificent settings of desert, palace, and sea."[10]

Mrs. Maude Murray Miller of the Ohio Board of Censors passed *Cleopatra* without cuts, explaining, "After a careful review of the film *Cleopatra,* produced by the Fox Film Corporation, I decided to release it for exhibition in Ohio without any eliminations. The producers have followed history in a remarkable way, and Miss Theda Bara's interpretation of the character is so skillfully and convincingly done, that I feel justified in passing the picture as it was brought to the censor offices."[11]

Cleopatra opened at New York's Lyric Theater on October 14, 1917, and over the course of the engagement, according to a Fox advertisement, thousands of patrons were turned away. Fox released the film sparingly as a road show with ticket prices up to two dollars in some venues. The following January, forty road companies were dispatched across the nation. Bara herself later said that *Cleopatra* grossed a million dollars.[12]

Prints of *Cleopatra* were known to survive in the Fox vaults well into the thirties and at the Museum of Modern Art in New York even later. However, fires at both locations reduced Theda Bara's smoldering gaze to smoking ash. No other prints have been found anywhere.

That's too bad, because *Cleopatra* must have been a great deal of fun. Maybe it wasn't a screen spectacle on the level of a masterpiece by D. W. Griffith—but then, maybe it was. The *Wid's* critic captured the way I feel about *Cleopatra* pretty well:

"I don't suppose that anybody cares whether this is good drama or not. It shows Miss Bara quite bare, in a wonderful background, and despite the fact that the action slumps very decidedly at times, the production is big enough to make anyone feel that they have surely seen an unusual and decidedly distinctive production."[13]

9

ROPED

Universal Film Manufacturing Company Special Attraction. Released January 27, 1919. Six reels.

C R E D I T S

Director: Jack Ford; *Scenario and Story:* Eugene B. Lewis; *Camera:* John Brown; *Music Supervised by:* James C. Bradford.

C A S T

Harry Carey (*Cheyenne Harry*); Neva Gerber (*Aileen*); Molly McConnell (*Mrs. Judson-Brown*); Arthur Shirley (*Ferdie Van Duzen*); J. Farrell McDonald (*Butler*).

SYNOPSIS

Cheyenne Harry is a millionaire ranch owner, but he is sadly in need of a housekeeper and voices that need to his group of cowboys, who decide that what Harry really needs is a wife, and so they write in his name to a matrimonial agency, which results in his name and requests being placed in the matrimonial journal. A copy of this falls into the hands of a group of New York society folk while they are dining at a fashionable hotel, and one of the girls, Aileen Judson-Brown, decides to answer it as a joke, saying that she is a beautiful but poor New York girl who understands housekeeping and who is longing to marry Cheyenne.

Little realizing that he is being made the butt of a joke, Harry takes the first train to New York, and there starts the comedy element strong with the uneducated cowboy in the stamping ground of fashion. Aileen's

Harry Carey in one of his easygoing but not-to-be-trifled-with roles as a stalwart of the West.

mother has but one desire in life and that is to marry her daughter to a rich man, and at first she refuses to receive the uncouth Westerner. But when she learns that a New York bank will honor his check for three millions, and when she is also faced with alternative of paying a huge amount that she owes the hotel or getting out into the cold without a cent to her name, she consents to "sell" her daughter to the Westerner, who is actually in love with the girl and fails to understand that she is marrying him solely on account of her mother's desire for wealth.

Instead of returning to his ranch, he sets up a mansion for his wife and her mother in New York, and then developments come thick and fast. The Judson–Browns continue their society pace, and Harry is relegated to the background, though there are many amusing scenes at the expense of Cheyenne. Ferdie Van Duzen, a poor but high-society bounder, continues to pay attention to Aileen, and with her mother's consent.

But the months go by, and a little Harry comes. Here the deception of the mother-in-law becomes the greater. She lies to the girl when she asks for her husband when the baby is born, and then lies to Harry, telling him that his wife is delirious and cannot see him, and bars him from the baby. But here another element enters in the [form of the] apparently dignified English butler, one of the cleverest characters that you ever saw on the screen, who shows Cheyenne how to see his own baby, and there follow several touching scenes that will bring a suggestion of a tear to everyone in your audiences.

About this time we have a switch back to the cattle ranch with the rival owner plotting to blow up the source of Cheyenne's water supply and get possession of his 50,000 head of cattle. The "boys" from the ranch discover the plot, but they decide that instead of sending a wire, they had better go in person, and since they have heard of the arrival of a "son and heir," they decided to go in person not only with the notification, but these "wise men of the West" come bearing presents for the young Harry. They come in full dress, but with their sombreros, one of them very drunk, and there are plenty of laughs to be featured here. Of course, the high-browed mother-in-law is terribly shocked, especially when they break up a perfectly good society party, but the little wife here first shows her first affection by welcoming her husband's friends.

But at the same time there comes a realization to Cheyenne that he and his wife belong on different paths that will never meet, and with the danger that threatens his interests on the ranch he goes back with the boys, without a farewell. He is in time to frustrate the efforts of the villain—but this is one point to remember: that the thrills in this picture are secondary to the heart interest and humor. Then we have some scenes back in the East with the girl wife being told by her mother that her baby has died and has been buried while she was away at a house party, and we have the first direct evidence of her love. The mother tells her that she wired Harry of the child's death but that he showed no interest, and a divorce is being arranged when the butler, a loyal and human friend of the ranchman, wires him that strange things are happening.

Cheyenne takes the "eight-thirty train." His first moment in the house is to look for the baby. He finds the covered baby bed and the other things draped in white. The mother-in-law tells him that the baby is dead and that the mother is away. But the butler comes with the information that he does not believe that the child is dead and with the warning to find the nurse. And just at that moment Harry overhears the mother-in-law and the lawyer plotting the divorce. His spirit has risen against her on other occasions, but now he drives her from the house and the skulking lawyer with her. He sends a wire to the boys "back home" and with the butler goes to look for the nurse.

Several weeks elapse, but they find her and she confesses the plot and restores the child. It happens, very conveniently, that Aileen, her mother, Van Duzen, and others are to be members of a slumming party in the section where the child has been found, that night, and here is staged one of the final scenes, and a very dramatic one. When Van Duzen sees them enter, he bribes the resort keepers to put Harry and the butler "out" if they start anything. He appears and wins his wife back, for she really loves him, and when a sneer comes from Van Duzen, he knocks him out and then the gangsters start. There is a clever touch with the butler telephoning the cowboys and their leaving their beds in their shirt-tails and joining in the fight. And there is no doubt about how it ends.

Aileen is now reconciled to her husband fully, but she does not know that the child is alive until almost the very end—and after that on the ranch comes the real honeymoon.

—Motion Picture News January 25, 1919

THE PRODUCTION

When John Ford remade *Three Godfathers* in 1948, starring John Wayne, Pedro Armendariz, and Harry Carey Jr., he dedicated the film to the memory of Harry Carey Sr.—Bright Star of the Early Western Sky."

The dedication is a poignant one; Ford and Carey were quite important to each other in the early stages of their careers. Each of their lives would have been significantly different without the other. If Ford's directorial style seems already remarkably set by 1917 and his first feature, *Straight Shooting,* it is at least partly due to the laconic, understated presence of Harry Carey. Carey was as crucial to the Western vision of the early John Ford as John Wayne and Henry Fonda would be two decades later.

(Wayne often acknowledged the influence of Carey on his own screen persona. He paid tribute to Cheyenne Harry in the famous final scene of Ford's *The Searchers* when his character, Ethan Edwards, grasps his right elbow with his left hand in the lonely gesture so characteristic of Carey.)

Ford described the films he made with Carey not as "shoot-em-ups" but as "character stories. Carey was a great actor, and we didn't dress him up like the cowboys you see on TV—all dolled up. [Carey was] sort of a bum, a saddle tramp, instead of a great bold gun-fighting hero. All this was fifty percent Carey and fifty percent me."[1]

Ford and Carey didn't exactly start out together, but they found each other early on and developed sympathetic styles. Harry Carey made his screen debut in 1909, appearing in many of D. W. Griffith's important Biograph releases, like *An Unseen Enemy* and *The Musketeers of Pig Alley* (both 1912). John Ford came along a few years later, in 1913, assisting his brother, the director-actor-writer Francis Ford, in numerous capacities: stuntman, set builder, property master, assistant director, and sometimes actor.

Ford—at that time known as Jack—began directing two- and three-reel shorts at Universal in 1917. He starred in a couple himself, but when he cast Harry Carey as Cheyenne Harry in *The Soul Herder,* released in August 1917, Ford had found the perfect alter ego. Ford and Carey were eventually to make twenty-six films together, most of which also featured Molly Malone and Hoot Gibson. With rare exceptions (1919's *The Outcast of Poker Flats,* for instance), Carey plays Cheyenne Harry, a gunfighter whose realistic sense of morality can place him on either side of the law—at least until his better nature kicks in.

The few surviving Cheyenne Harry adventures are honest, unpretentious Westerns showing both Ford's enormous debt to D. W. Griffith and the unmistakable signs of his own developing identity.

Roped, released in January 1919, was treated by critics and exhibitors as a bit of a novelty, both because of its more overt comedic elements (although there were traces of melodrama as well) and because it was a Western set mostly in New York City. Also, Cheyenne Harry is a millionaire rancher in *Roped*, whereas he is usually just a saddle tramp in his other pictures.

"In direction," wrote one critic, "one of the most difficult roles to handle is the transplantation of a character—usually the hero or the heroine—from a common environment to an aristocratic."[2] But Ford seems to have been successful in placing his fish out of water, creating fun out of Harry's appearance in a fashionable hotel "attired in primitive dress"[3] and then finding the inherent drama in his rejection by his wife's society mother and her snobbish friends.

It would take a director of unusual skill and sensitivity to at one moment immerse himself in the melodrama of a man being denied even one visit with his newborn son ("The scene is pathetic and touching to the extreme"[4]) and the next to find broad fun in the visit to New York by all of Harry's cowboy pals laden with gifts for the newborn ("It is not possible to describe the comedy they cause"[5]). Whether Ford was able to pull off this rather complex emotional seesaw is impossible to know; however, from his surviving work of the silent period, it appears he already possessed the necessary talent to do almost anything.

At least one critic, though, thought Ford and writer Eugene Lewis had not played fair with Cheyenne Harry. "The character seems 'sloppy' for a man who, having made his millions, should allow himself to be so fooled and made a nonentity by those around him, especially as he is supplying all the funds."[6]

Wid's Daily admired the "speed and action" of *Roped*. "It never slows up. [It] tends greatly towards exaggeration, both as to characterization development and the treatment of situations. They pull some bits of business here that any child could recognize as being much too much, but anyway, this is a movie pure and simple, so why worry."[7]

Motion Picture News offered exhibitors a five page "special service section" on *Roped*, filled with tips on how to sell the film. Mixed in with suggestions of ways to decorate a theater—for instance: a huge reproduction of a marriage license, surrounded by a lasso—and compelling ad copy are a few references to the world of 1919 that provide a fascinating context for *Roped*:

"When you start in to exploit this picture, forget that the war ever existed except that it gives you an opportunity to clean up. Don't let an element of it get into anything that you write or say. Do not even be tempted into saying that the spirit that Harry Carey and his cowboys show exemplified the spirit that enabled America to turn the tide of the Hun horror. Forget the battle stuff."[8]

As catastrophic as World War I had been, the worldwide influenza epidemic that raged from March to November 1918 was, to many, an even more personal tragedy. An estimated 21,640,000 people died of the flu in those horrifying months.

The marketing experts from *Motion Picture News* knew these dual horrors would still be foremost in most peoples' minds. The magazine urged exhibitors to accentuate the comedic aspects of *Roped*. "Make a straight appeal to the emotions, but make the straightest appeal to the enjoyment angle. There are a lot of your patrons who have some pangs in the heart from the war. The 'flu' hasn't left any too pleasant impressions around. We, and the rest of us, don't care to be reminded of it, but we like to get the bright side of the world before us again."[9]

Whether *Roped* helped viewers "get the bright side of the world" again is unknown. It seems to have been moderately successful, and even the critics who didn't care for it as a whole admitted that Ford had made a film that was fast and funny. It also added a new member to the Ford Stock Company: J. Farrell McDonald appeared in *Roped* as the sympathetic butler. Eventually he would act in over twenty more of John Ford's films.

Ford and Carey continued to work together until 1921 and *Desperate Trails*. After directing two more Universal features starring Hoot Gibson, Ford moved to Fox and never worked with Carey again. The two apparently had some kind of falling out and didn't speak to each other for years. But his dedication on *Three Godfathers* indicates both Ford's debt to Carey and his affection for him. *Roped* may or may not have been among their most significant collaborations, but its loss denies us the pleasure that was inevitable whenever these two bright stars of the Western sky got together.

10

THE KNICKERBOCKER BUCKAROO

···

Douglas Fairbanks Picture Corporation. Artcraft/Famous Players–Lasky.
Released May 18, 1919. Six reels; 5,003 feet.

C R E D I T S

Written and Produced by: Douglas Fairbanks; *Director:* Albert Parker; *Story:* Elton Banks [Fairbanks], Joseph Henabery, Frank Condon, Ted Reed; *Camera:* Hugh C. McClung, Glen MacWilliams; *Editor:* William Shea; Scenario *Editor/Production Manager:* Theodore Reed; *Assistant Director:* Arthur Rosson; *Art Director:* Max Parker; *Assistant Camera:* Paul MacWilliams; *Publicity:* Bennie F. Zeidman.

C A S T

Douglas Fairbanks (*Teddy Drake*); Marjorie Daw (*Mercedes*); William Wellman (*Henry*); Frank Campeau (*Crooked Sheriff*); Edythe Chapman (*Teddy's Mother*); Albert MacQuarrie (*Manuel Lopez*); Theodore "Ted" Reed (*A New York Clubman*); James Mason (*Villain*); Ernest Butterworth.

···

SYNOPSIS

(Synopsis is augmented by some of the film's original subtitles.)

THE KNICKERBOCKER
STARTS WEST

Teddy Drake, the part played by Douglas Fairbanks, belongs to the class of fortunate young chaps who waste their time and money in the clubs and on the night life of New York. His playful habit of leaping over the

tables and other articles of furniture in the aristocratic club that is honored by having his name on its roll and being general upsetter for the
organization, ends by his being expelled.

> TEDDY: "Judge! What is the matter with me?"
> FATHER: "You are inconsiderate of others."
> TITLE CARD: "And that starts Teddy Drake thinking and wanting to
> do something for somebody."

The matter is serious enough to make even Teddy take it seriously,
and he arrives at the conclusion that his thoughtlessness comes from
thinking only of himself; so he resolves to give the other fellow a thought
and try to make him happy.

> TEDDY: "I've got a hunch, Mother, that if I hurl myself out into the
> seething world, swim with the current, pick myself up where I land,
> and go to it—all will be Jake."
> TITLE CARD: "Mother doesn't know who Jake is, but anything Teddy
> says is right."

No sooner is his great idea born than he starts to put it into practice.
Selecting a spot on the map by shutting his eyes and putting his finger
down blindly, he learns he is booked for the Southwest.

> TEDDY: "West, Mother! It's a hunch! I'll pull a Horace Greeley in the
> morning."

His trip in the Pullman (Teddy: "Measure off eighty-eight dollars
and sixteen cents worth of railroad ticket going West") enables him to
test his benevolent intentions on several of his fellow passengers with
amusing consequences, but he finds he has carried his helpful creed too
far when he helps an old lady off the train and boards the wrong train
himself in his hurry to get back to his coach.

> TEDDY: "Isn't this the limited?"
> PORTER: "No, sah, it's de limit. Dis train hesitates at every li'l place
> between heah and de Mexican bawdah."

Teddy's gallantry was undertaken before he had finished dressing,
and he is minus a shirt and collar. His attempts to beg, borrow, or steal

a shirt from the passengers meet with no success until he runs into a Mexican bandit who is on his way to see his sick mother but knows the train will be searched for him by the sheriff when Sonora is reached. Teddy offers to change clothes with the Mexican. The thing is scarcely done when the train stops at the town, and young Drake meets with a red-hot reception.

The sheriff is crooked and heads a band of outlaws that is trying to get a young girl and her brother to tell where they have hidden the money they received for the sale of their ranch. At the time Teddy drops off the train, the sheriff has the girl in jail, and her brother is a prisoner in an old shack some distance from the town. The dishonest official and his pals want to get hold of the Mexican because he is one of the gang and has defied the leader.

THE   RACE   IS   ON

Dressed in Manuel's clothes, Teddy does not pause to thank the citizens of Sonora for the way they receive him, but does a flying leap for the roof of the nearest building. Then ensues a chase that outstrips everything seen before it on the screen. Up and down the town, all over the town, and all around the town goes Teddy, leaping from roof to roof like a two-legged Rocky Mountain sheep. While seated comfortably on a window ledge of the jail, he meets his future wife. She is on the inside of the bars and is the girl the sheriff is trying to rob. Her name is Mercedes.

> TEDDY: "I've been looking for a girl like you for years, but I never thought of looking in jails."

She tells Teddy about the plot against her and her brother, and where the money is secreted, in an old mission. About this time, the bandits catch sight of Teddy, and the whole town is off on the second lap of the lively free-for-all, and there is no slacking of the pace until Teddy is captured and himself put behind the bars. Another short breathing spell, then a prison escape and the third heat of the race is on. But he is caught again and about to be lynched when he is saved by the Mexican whom he befriended on the train.

Melodramatic complications come thick and fast here, and there is any amount of the hardest kind of riding, in which Doug proves himself a real buckaroo.

Everybody wants the money hidden in the old mission, but Doug gets it, only to find the mission surrounded by the crooked sheriff and his gang. Doug uses his head and manages to hold off the pack until the arrival of a U.S. Marshall, who takes care of the sheriff and his gang. Teddy's spirits drop when he believes the girl's brother is her sweetheart, but brighten emphatically when he learns that such is not the case.

> TEDDY: "I've been trying my doggondest to be unselfish and see what it's brought me."
> MERCEDES: "What?"
> TEDDY: "You, you wonderful girl!"
>
> —*The Moving Picture World*, June 7, 1919

THE PRODUCTION

"The first scene of *The Knickerbocker Buckaroo* shows Fairbanks dressed in white as a baker mixing the ingredients of a cake from six food bins labeled Mystery, Adventure, Romance, Comedy, Pep, and Ginger. He puts the sum total in the oven, and it comes out as a cake with the frosting spelling The Knickerbocker Buckaroo. Then follows the caption:

> "This is the baker who bakes the cakes;
> While you read this, the darn thing bakes."[1]

This opening scene was Douglas Fairbanks's statement of principle. He was determined to give the audience every laugh and thrill possible. Although we may never be able to prove it by actually seeing this lost film, contemporary reaction to *The Knickerbocker Buckaroo* suggests that the agile comic succeeded in his determination.

Fairbanks is best remembered today as a swashbuckler, leaping, laughing, jousting, and stunting his way through such elaborate costume epics as *Robin Hood* (1922), *The Thief of Bagdad* (1924), and *The Black Pirate* (1926).

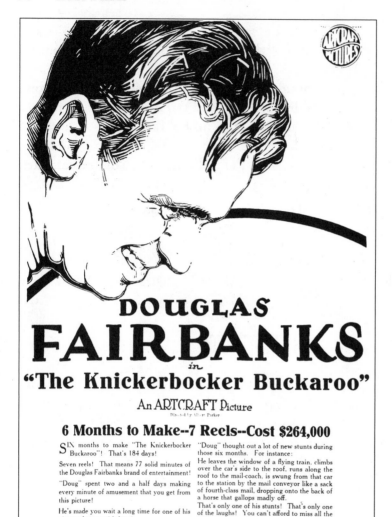

Advertising poster

But audiences a few years earlier knew him best as a comedian, albeit an athletic one. Soon after his film debut in *The Lamb* (1915), Fairbanks's enormous popularity gave him great creative control over his films; like Harold Lloyd (a performer very similar to Fairbanks in

Douglas Fairbanks in a
characteristic pose. This persona
was developed after his "go-getter"
role in *Knickerbocker Buckaroo*.

many ways), Fairbanks never officially directed any of his films, yet he
left an undeniably personal stamp on each of his action-packed comedies.

By 1919, the year of *The Knickerbocker Buckaroo* and *His Majesty, The
American*, Fairbanks worked hard to top himself each time out of the
gate. Edward Weitzel, writing for the *Moving Picture World*, said that
Fairbanks "long ago set himself a pace which should take his stories
along with record-breaking speed and leave the spectator marvelling at

their combination of machine-gun-fire fun, physical fireworks, adaptability of plot, and completeness of production. In other words, a moving picture comedy which should reflect the spirit of here and now, when airplanes are whizzing human beings through space at one hundred miles an hour and it is the fashion to run our lives on the eight-cylinder plan."[2]

On February 5, 1919, Fairbanks had formed a new releasing company, The United Artists Corporation, with Mary Pickford (whom he would marry a year later), Charles Chaplin, D. W. Griffith, and, briefly, William S. Hart. The unprecedented power and popularity of these cinema giants made incorporation a logical move, although it prompted Richard Rowland, the president of Metro Pictures to say ruefully, "So, the lunatics have taken charge of the asylum!" Before making his first picture for his new company, however, Fairbanks had to fulfill a contractual obligation with Artcraft Pictures, which released through Famous Players–Lasky.

Many stars would have walked through a quickie production just to get the Artcraft contract out of the way, but Fairbanks put everything but the kitchen sink in *The Knickerbocker Buckaroo*. He claimed in prominent trade ads that production had taken six months and that the negative cost had reached $264,000, a budget substantially higher than that of the average film of 1919. The interiors were filmed at the Lasky Studios at Sunset and Vine. Sonora, the Mexican border town in which most of the film takes place, was built in Chatsworth. It must have been quite convincing; Edward Weitzel wrote, "It is difficult to believe that the place was built by moving picture workmen."[3]

The *New York Times* agreed that the time and money had been well spent. "The Photoplay bears out the reports of the cost of its production. It was elaborately staged, where elaborateness would count, and Albert Parker, the director, must have used his good eye for scenic effects."[4]

Fairbanks's leading lady was Marjorie Daw, who appeared opposite the star in several films. Daw "scores heavily as the girl," wrote critic R. W. Baremore, "is good to look at, and displays a thorough knowledge of dramatic values."[5]

Baremore went on to say about the other actors in the film, "William

Wellman is excellent as her brother, and Frank Campeau plays the role of the crooked sheriff to perfection. Albert MacQuarrie does well in the bandit role, and Edythe Chapman is seen to advantage as Teddy's mother."[6]

William Wellman was making his film debut in *The Knickerbocker Buckaroo*. In World War I, Wellman had flown with the Lafayette Flying Corps, an offshoot of the famous Lafayette Escadrille. Decorated for his valor in combat, Wellman came home in 1918 with wounds received when his plane crashed. When the War ended, he was brought out to Rockwell Field in San Diego to instruct new flyers.

Years earlier, Wellman had met Fairbanks when the actor was in Boston appearing on stage at the Colonial Theater in *Hawthorne of the U.S.A.* One afternoon, Fairbanks watched a high school hockey match, in which Wellman was competing. Impressed by the teenager's ruthless skill, Fairbanks struck up a conversation. He ended it with some variation of, "If you're ever in California, look me up."

Wellman did just that. Legend has it that he landed his plane on a polo field at Pickfair. Since Pickfair wouldn't be built for another year, this legend doesn't hold much water, but it is true that Wellman contacted Fairbanks, reintroduced himself, and asked for a job in the movies. Fairbanks responded by giving Wellman one of the leading roles in the star's biggest production to date.

Wellman did not take to acting very well. "I saw myself on the screen," he said, "and it was really pretty frightful. My long face looked like the face you see when you look in a funny mirror at an amusement part. So I quit acting. I went to Doug and told him how I felt and he asked me, 'Well, what do you want to be?' I pointed to the director, Al Parker, and asked how much he made. When Doug told me, I said, 'That's what I want to be.' It was all pretty financial from the beginning."[7]

Wellman went on to direct such screen classics as *Wings* (1927), *The Public Enemy* (1931), *A Star Is Born* (1937), *Nothing Sacred* (1937), *Beau Geste* (1939), and *The High and The Mighty* (1954), among about seventy more. Of the sixteen silent films he directed, only five exist today.

The Knickerbocker Buckaroo was a solid hit with audiences and with most critics. "It's a regular rip-snorter," wrote R. W. Baremore. "Packed to overflowing with the Fairbanks brand of good humor, stunts, and rapid-fire action, this is a thoroughly worthwhile picture in every way, clean, snappy fun and thrills."[8]

"Neat comedy bits and slick bits of laughable business are stuck all through the picture," wrote Edward Weitzel, "and it is supplied with a line of subtitles that run neck-and-neck with the best smile getters in the release. *The Knickerbocker Buckaroo* is Douglas Fairbanks's top-notcher."[9]

The *Wid's Daily* reviewer agreed that "No Fairbanks picture ever has had more amusing or more clever titles than this one" but felt that "it is by no means the best thing that Doug has ever done."[10]

Peter Milne, however, thought it not "the fine picture that the time and money spent on it would lead one to expect. It will be liked for the same reason that a smoker likes his favorite cigarette, even after the manufacturer has started putting inferior tobacco into it."[11]

Of course, when a critic is getting a new Fairbanks "rip-snorter" every few months, he can afford to be blasé about one. Fairbanks's existing action comedies during the last years of that fascinating decade look better and better all the time. The odds seem excellent that *The Knickerbocker Buckaroo* and other lost Fairbanks films like *Bound in Morocco* (1918) would be just as funny and exciting and memorable as Doug meant them to be—if we could only get one more look at them.

11

THE MIRACLE MAN

Mayflower Photoplay Corporation. Famous Players–Lasky Corporation. Paramount–Artcraft Pictures. Released September 14, 1919. Eight reels.

CREDITS

Producer, Scenario, and Director: George Loane Tucker; Based on the novel (New York, 1914) by Frank L. Packard and the play (New York, September 21, 1914) by George M. Cohan; *Titles:* Wid Gunning; *Assistant Director:* Chester L. Roberts; *Camera:* Philip E. Rosen and Ernest G. Palmer; *Art Titles:* Ferdinand Pinney Earle.

CAST

Thomas Meighan (*Tom Burke*); Betty Compson (*Rose*); Lon Chaney (*The Frog*); J. M. Dumont (*The Dope*); W. Lawson Butt (*Richard King*); Elinor Fair (*Claire King*); F. A. Turner (*Mr. Higgins*); Lucille Hutton (*Ruth Higgins*); Joseph J. Dowling (*The Patriarch, also known as "the Miracle Man"*); Frankie Lee.

SYNOPSIS

The Miracle Man is the story of four crooks who live in Chinatown, New York, and prey upon the public by the meanest kind of trickery. Tom Burke is the leader. The Frog, one of Nature's horrible mistakes, who is able to throw his limbs out of joint and impersonate a cripple, is the most repulsive member of the gang. Rose, the girl who runs the place, acts as intermediary for the three schemers, who are always on the lookout to trick money from their associates. Rose is a pretty girl who gets money from sightseers in Chinatown that she may quit her sinful life. The Dope, a real drug fiend, pretends to be the brutal taskmaster that

Rose is forced to support by the sale of her soul and body. The scene where the four meet in their comfortable quarters to divide the day's ill-gotten gains is both novel and interesting. Here Tom Burke confides to his companions a great scheme he has hit upon to make them all rich.

Quite by accident one day Burke sees a newspaper clipping about an aged man, known as the Patriarch, in the vicinity of Boston. The man is deaf and dumb and almost blind, but has a miraculous power of healing. Burke plans a campaign of fraud. The Frog is to be taken there, in his distorted condition, gaining the sympathy and attention of everyone possible on the trip. Then they are to have the Patriarch use his power of healing on the distorted creature. He is to unwind his body quite naturally, straightening up to the erect man he is. Burke is then to advertise the cure and help the patients of the old man to open their pocketbooks and hand out their banknotes, which the gang will keep for themselves.

Rose is to pass herself off as the healer's niece whom he has never seen. Rose comes to the home of the sweet, gentle old Patriarch. She has to act a part, and she thinks constantly of her innocent, sweet self, the part she must necessarily portray to the public who visit the old man.

There is a little crippled boy living in the small town, whose father has long scorned faith in anything and will not let him go near the healer. He is feared by the frauds who think he may be the rift in the lute. Surely, they figure, this Patriarch fake, failing to cure the boy after curing The Frog, will shake the confidence of the onlookers.

The day the Patriarch performs the miracle on the Frog, Richard King, a millionaire, and his crippled sister Claire are among the town gathering. The little crippled boy, much to the disgust of Tom Burke, leads the distorted Frog to the home of the Patriarch. As the Frog's body untwists itself under the Patriarch's healing hands, the little boy becomes imbued with a terrible sense of suggestion! He watches the Frog's movements, then attempts to put his own foot on the ground. He straightens the crippled muscles, his eyes glowing with a wondrous light, and suddenly finds he can walk. He rushes up to the Patriarch and flings himself at the latter's feet in thanks.

Simultaneously, the same wonderful psychological power takes possession of the millionaire's sister. And she rises—and walks. The girl is restored to health, and her overjoyed brother gives Burke a check for $50,000 as his contribution to the healer. Young King does something else. He sees in Rose an innocent young girl of great beauty, falls is love with her, but goes away without declaring his feelings.

Awe-stricken by what he has seen, but still determined to carry out his plan for commercializing the old man's mysterious power, Burke goes ahead with his advertising of the miracles, and patients begin to pour into the town and repay the healer in gifts of money, checks, and jewels.

The peaceful, harmonious atmosphere of the little cottage where the gang live in disguise under the power of the old Patriarch's personality gradually has its effect. Rosie finds her point of view of life changing. The millionaire falls in love with her—for what he thinks she is—and in a subtle way helps her back to ideals. She becomes a product of wholesome womanhood.

The Frog, who finds life on a farm the best environment he has ever known, decides to stay. He scorns the offer of money. And the dope fiend, whose viewpoint has been made over and strengthened also by this environment, decides to make his future in the little town with a pretty little farm maiden.

Burke is furious when he finds out that his pals are deserting him, and that Rose is beginning to understand that his love for her is merely a base passion. When she repulses him, the crook is ready to kill her. The return of King, who has determined to ask Rose to be his wife, almost leads to Burke's killing him. But the girl finds that her heart really belongs to Tom, and her influence and that of the healer opens the gang leader's eyes to the light.

And when the Patriarch passes on, he leaves behind him four mended lives—who have changed their views and have been made over into wholesome, healthy human beings by the power of suggestion he so unconsciously exerted on them.

—Moving Picture World September 13, 1919 and
Exhibitor's Trade Review July 26, 1919

THE PRODUCTION

Some of the films discussed in this book were not particularly treasured in their own times. They received negative or mixed reviews, perhaps didn't fare well at the box office. Today, they seem important to us for reasons that may have eluded contemporary audiences or critics.

But *The Miracle Man* was almost universally acclaimed. Walter E. Greene, vice-president of Famous Players–Lasky Corporation, called it "One of the greatest pictures, not only of the year but of all time."[1] While Greene's reaction can be chalked up to mere (if understandable) studio hyperbole, the critics agreed with his assessment of the film.

"As a study in genuine human beings," wrote *Photoplay*'s Julian Johnson, "as an exhibition of the instinctive triumph of the better nature when that better nature has a chance, as a perfect fabric of life as it is lived—alternately funny as a Chaplin and pathetic as a Warfield scene— and as an adroitly constructed drama, rising from climax to climax and never missing a telling point, I do not recall that the silver sheet has ever offered anything better than this and few pieces as good."[2]

Wid's Daily was more succinct: "This isn't just a picture—it's a sensation."[3]

In an era when motion pictures were nearly always discussed in terms of stories or stars instead of directors (D. W. Griffith, Thomas Ince, Cecil B. DeMille, and a few others are exceptions), *The Miracle Man* was praised primarily for the direction of George Loane Tucker.

Tucker (1881–1921) was highly regarded by his peers as an innovative director of taste and skill; when he died at the age of forty, *Photoplay* called him "First of the Immortals."[4] Aside from his powerful white-slavery exposé, *Traffic in Souls* (1913), however, virtually nothing of Tucker's work is available for reevaluation. Historian William K. Everson writes that Tucker's "instinctive grasp of film-making [evident in *Traffic in Souls*] suggests that he may well have been one of the major talents of those early years."[5]

Film historian Kevin Brownlow agrees, writing that Tucker's death cut short "a career of exceptional promise."[6]

Famous Players–Lasky released a sketch of Tucker's life which, due to the dearth of information about him, is worth reprinting here:

George Loane Tucker was born and reared in Chicago and was allowed by his wise parents to determine along what lines he should shape his life course. So, several years later, discarding his cap and gown at the University of Chicago, he joined the staff of a Western railroad.

At twenty-one, he was chief clerk in the Maintenance of Way department of the company and soon thereafter found himself promoted to the position of Contracting Freight Agent, the youngest man in Chicago who had ever held that or a similar position. But cruel fate intervened, and with the crushing loss of his young wife, who died while giving birth to a son, all but wrecking his life, he resigned his position and faced the future almost without hope.

A friend suggested the stage. The idea struck his fancy. It would mean travel, new faces, pleasing distraction. And presently George Loane Tucker found himself interviewing some of his mother's old associates in the theatrical world.

Motion pictures were beginning to make their influence felt about then, and Tucker made a strike into the new field. He wrote a scenario, but stipulated that he act in the picture himself. He did, and with a success which, if not startling, assured him that there was where his future lay. He decided to be a producer. D. W. Griffith was in the new game at that time, and he and Tucker got their heads together and evolved a distributing plan.

Those were the old Biograph days, when the stars of today were then staff workers or supers. Any old reel picked from out the myriad hosts of old-timers will show such celebrities as Clara Kimball Young, Maurice Costello, Kate Price, and others playing in the same picture as staff casts.

"Let's try something big and worthwhile. Even if we fail we shall have gained that much experience," said Tucker to his associate.

The sound philosophy of the idea struck Griffith "between the eyes." They shook on it. And George Loane Tucker made the first million-dollar American picture, *Traffic in Souls,* the scenario of which he wrote himself. The subject was one of the chief discussions of the day. Society ate it up and discussed it over the tea table. Schools and churches were lecturing on the great vice. And New York, ready for the picture, went to see it and was astounded by the magnificence of the production. Tucker made a million dollars' profit on it, and from that moment the million-dollar picturization of the great questions of human interest has been Tucker's chosen work.[7]

England heard about *Traffic in Souls*. She sent for the great producer, and he forthwith became Director General of the London Film Company. Typically American in spirit, typically American in personality, energy, and ingenuity, not to mention his remarkable imaginative powers, Tucker allied himself with some of the big authors, including Hall Caine and Anthony Hope, and gave to the British public and the world *Rupert of Hentzau, The Christian, The Prisoner of Zenda, The Manxman,* and other screen masterpieces.

But America called him back again. He became Director General for the Goldwyn corporation. Soon thereafter he personally directed *The Cinderella Man,* one of the biggest hits of the 1917–18 season. Then followed several other productions which he supervised, but the initiative of this born producer had to assert itself again. He didn't want to supervise; he wanted to produce. He wanted to make his very own pictures. And because he wanted to—he did.

Virtuous Wives was the first special under his new plan. It was released by the First National and proved to be a tremendous success, so much so that it was heralded in some quarters as the greatest picture of 1918."[8]

Tucker married British actress Elizabeth Risdon while in England.

The Miracle Man had been produced on the stage by George M. Cohan, who had adapted the script from a novel by Frank L. Packard. Despite Cohan's considerable popularity, the play was not particularly successful. Tucker bought the motion picture rights to *The Miracle Man* after teaming with Isaac M. Wolper, a Boston merchant who aspired to be a movie producer. With a budget of $120,000, Tucker could not afford big stars for the film, so he chose such capable actors as Thomas Meighan, Betty Compson (then appearing in comedies made by Al Christie), and Lon Chaney.

The Miracle Man was filmed at the Robert Brunton Studios (today, Paramount Pictures) on Melrose Street in Hollywood over about four weeks in the Spring of 1919.

When the film was released that Summer, it earned about $3 million.

Lon Chaney and Joseph Dowling

The staggering success of the little film immediately created three stars—
and one star director. Unfortunately, George Loane Tucker would only
live to write and direct one more film, *Ladies Must Live* (1921), a melodrama featuring Betty Compson.

Though the synopsis of *The Miracle Man* suggests a conventional
story of redemption, audiences were moved—in some cases, stunned—
by the extraordinary power of the film. *Variety*'s critic describes one such
memorable scene:

> "We have a long shot here, down the path to the house, the old
> man waiting, sublimely calm, unseeing, without hearing or the power

of speech. While all look on, the Frog crawls forward, stages his fake recovery, and gets to his feet. From Tom's mouth suddenly the cigarette drops, others show great amazement, while almost every spectator at Cohan's Theatre felt that sudden contraction of the throat which precedes a sob. All this because suddenly the little boy started forward, dropped one crutch, then the other, and ran down the path into the old man's arms. The girl, rising from her invalid chair, follows him more slowly. These two cures were real."[9]

Part of this scene is all that exists of *The Miracle Man*. It was included in a Paramount short, *Screen Highlights #1*, released in 1935.

James Cagney recreated this sequence in *Man of a Thousand Faces* (1957), an entertaining, if inaccurate, film biography of Lon Chaney.

Hobart Bosworth as "The Miracle Man" in the 1932 version

(Interestingly, Cagney also portrayed George M. Cohan, who played Tom Burke on the stage, in *Yankee Doodle Dandy* (1942).) But Cagney's performance, fine though it is, can only suggest the emotional power that the original scene had on its audiences.

"This scene has a wallop such as the screen has seldom disclosed," wrote one critic, "and the wonderful part about it is that it is pure drama, thereby proving for all time that wild tactics are not necessary to deliver real thrills."[10]

Chaney had appeared in dozens of films since his screen debut in 1912 but *The Miracle Man* firmly established him both as a star and as the cinema's leading purveyor of the grotesque. Calling his performance "some of the best work of his career," *Exhibitor's Trade Review*'s Charles E. Wagner predicted that Chaney's "character study . . . will entrench him firmly in the ranks of film players."[11]

Thomas Meighan, wrote *Photoplay*'s Julian Johnson, "has played men good, bad, and indifferent [but] he has never done anything which can be even remotely compared to his virile and engrossing delineation of Tom Burke.

"And, virile and keen as Meighan is, so Betty Compson, whom you once knew only as a bathing-suit comedienne, is keen and true and ultra-feminine in her visualization of Rose. She is a beautiful, sensuous thing indeed. I have never seen a creature more gloriously physical."[12]

Only *Variety* expressed reservations about *The Miracle Man*'s structure, claiming that nothing much happened after the healing scene. "Mr. Tucker starts his story slowly, ends it badly, and lets it drag perceptibly after the big scene."[13]

But that is virtually the only dissenting voice. The overwhelming admiration by audiences and critics for *The Miracle Man* makes its loss very keenly felt. It was certainly among the most important and influential motion pictures of its era. It may even have been, as the studio that released it claimed, "a masterpiece of masterpieces."[14]

12

HOLLYWOOD

Famous Players–Lasky Corporation. Paramount Pictures. Production number 788. August 19, 1923. Eight reels; 8,217 feet.

CREDITS

Presented by: Jesse L. Lasky. *Director:* James Cruze; *Adaptation:* Tom Geraghty; *Story:* Frank Condon; *Camera:* Karl Brown; *Assistant Director:* Vernon Keays. *Original title: Hollywood and the Only Child.*

CAST

Hope Drown (*Angela Whitaker*); Luke Cosgrave (*Joel Whitaker*); George K. Arthur (*Lem Lefferts*); Ruby Lafayette (*Grandmother Whitaker*); Harris Gordon (*Dr. Luke Morrison*); Bess Flowers (*Hortense Towers*); Eleanor Lawson (*Margaret Whitaker*); King Zany (*Horace Pringle*); Roscoe Arbuckle (*Fat Man in Casting Director's Office*).

STAR CAMEOS

Gertrude Astor, Mary Astor, Agnes Ayres, Baby Peggy, T. Roy Barnes, Noah Beery, William Boyd, Clarence Burton, Robert Cain, Charlie Chaplin, Edythe Chapman, Betty Compson, Ricardo Cortez, Viola Dana, Cecil B. De Mille, William deMille, Charles De Roche, Dinky Dean, Helen Dunbar, Snitz Edwards, Douglas Fairbanks, George Fawcett, Julia Faye, James Finlayson, Alec Francis, Jack Gardner, Sid Grauman, Alfred E. Green, Alan Hale, Lloyd Hamilton, Hope Hampton, William S. Hart, Gale Henry, Walter Hiers, Mrs. Walter Hiers, Stuart Holmes, Sigrid Holmquist, Jack Holt, Leatrice Joy, Mayme Kelso, J. Warren Kerrigan, Theodore Kosloff, Kosloff Dancers, Lila Lee, Lillian Leighton, Jacqueline Logan, May McAvoy, Robert McKim, Jeanie Mcpherson, Hank Mann, Joe Martin, Thomas Meighan, Bull Montana, Owen Moore, Nita Naldi, Pola Negri, Anna Q. Nilsson, Charles Ogle, Guy Oliver, Kalla Pasha, Eileen Percy, Carmen Phillips, Jack Pickford, Mary Pickford, Chuck Reisner, Fritzi Ridgeway, Will Rogers, Sennett Girls, Ford Sterling, Anita Stewart, George

Stewart, Gloria Swanson, Estelle Taylor, Ben Turpin, Bryant Washburn, Maude Wayne, Claire West, Laurence Wheat, Lois Wilson.

· ·

SYNOPSIS

Angela Whitaker was a movie fan who attended regularly at the local picture palace and dreamed of the day when she herself could go to Hollywood and occupy a room and bath in the Celluloid Hall of Fame. Finally, she went, taking Grandpa along with her, in the hope that the widely advertised climate of California might either kill him or cure him—it didn't much matter which. Left behind in Centerville, Ohio, are Aunt Margaret, old Grandmother Whitaker, and Lem Lefferts, Angela's "steady."

On her first day in Hollywood, Angela starts out on the rounds of the studios in quest of employment, leaving Grandpa parked on the hotel veranda and complaining bitterly. Angela had been fed with stories of girls like herself who had gone to this strange place and achieved instantaneous success; consequently she believed that she need only present herself at any casting director's window and wait for the celebration to start.

She trudges about from one studio to another, walking along miles of boulevards while the sad pepper trees of Hollywood nod their sympathy; but none of the movie producers evince the slightest interest in her, and she doesn't see a single contract all day.

So, weary and worn, she returns to the hotel—to find that Grandpa has been picked up by William deMille as a valuable "type" and has been working in pictures all day. Angela is delighted, for this means a prolonged stay in Hollywood. They move to a bungalow court and settle down. A resident of the court is Horace Pringle, young author of the picture story *Beware the Avenging Hand!* Almost at once Horace recognizes that Angela was born to be the star in his play, so he haunts the path of a movie magnate with cards bearing the inscription: Beware the Avenging Hand!—which sinister inscription reduces the magnate to a state bordering on nervous prostration.

By this time Grandfather has become a rather swagger and gay old sport and is regarded as a popular peer by the boys and likewise by some of the girls.

Back in Centerville, Lem, while pressing pants, is taking care of Grandmother and Aunt Margaret. In time they hear of the change in Grandfather and decide to go to Hollywood to rescue the brand from the burning. In an uproariously funny scene, Lem has a dream of what Hollywood will be like. At length, the trio arrives in the film capital prepared for the worst.

Immediately, Aunt Margaret flounces over to the studio to snatch Grandfather from the jaws of Hell if she has to drag him out bodily. At a moment when the great, remote Cecil B. De Mille is quietly explaining the urgent need of a cyclonic woman, Aunt Margaret bursts in as if conjured by his thought, flailing with her umbrella right and left. Mr. De Mille is delighted, and before Aunt Margaret realizes what has happened, she is engaged for the part. Grandmother is also ordered to be on hand tomorrow to play a certain role.

That night, Mr. De Mille gives a dinner at his home for the aforementioned movie magnate, and Angela and Horace resolve to use the occasion to give Horace's story a final push. Angela's first move is to plant a card at the magnate's plate warning: Beware the Avenging Hand! The great man, upon glimpsing it, drops like a rag into his chair. This is Horace's cue. He comes in brandishing a gun and yelling like a maniac, "Beware the Avenging Hand!" A wild scene ensues. Then Lem, who has followed Angela, bursts through a window, extricates Angela from the melee, wrests the gun from Horace, and puts up a spectacular fight, which culminates in Horace being thrown through a window, and Lem is justly proclaimed a hero.

Mr. De Mille selects Centerville for the premiere of his picture. The town is delirious with joy when its now-famous sons and daughters return to do the occasion honor. The star of the picture is Lemuel Lefferts, idol of a million fans, while featured in support are Grandfather, Aunt Margaret, and Grandmother Whitaker. But the scene which brings forth the loudest acclaim of all is the newsreel depicting the actual Hollywood wedding of Lemuel Lefferts and Angela Whitaker.

And the twin children which resulted from this union are engaged to act in the movies even before they have been graduated from the cradle.

—Paramount Story Department and *The Best Moving Pictures of 1922–1923* by Robert Sherwood

••

THE PRODUCTION

Hollywood was billed as "A James Cruze Production with the World's Greatest Cast." Even today, that claim seems hard to dispute. Not only did almost every star on Paramount's roster make an appearance in the film, so did such major "outside" figures as Charlie Chaplin, Douglas Fairbanks, and Mary Pickford. In every case, the stars were presented as themselves, casually introduced into their scenes to give the Hollywood background unusual verisimilitude.

The huge number of movie stars in *Hollywood* caused two problems. The first was simply one of coordination. James Cruze spent eight months in preproduction, a long time for the period. "It wasn't easy to catalogue all the stars in that eventful community," wrote Robert Sherwood, "and at the same time maintain the continuity of his story. It was a weary, painful job, but he and [scriptwriter Tom] Geraghty kept at it until they were sure they had done it right."[1]

The second problem was, paradoxically, casting the film. With so many major stars in supporting roles, *Hollywood*'s fictional characters had to be portrayed by unknowns. Hope Drown brought an unfortunate name and a minimum of stage experience from a stock company in San Diego to this, her first and only film role. Cruze had discovered Luke Cosgrave on stage in Salt Lake City while Cruze was on location for *The Covered Wagon* the year before. *Hollywood* was Cosgrave's first role in a film, but it was only the beginning of a long career as a character actor.

Comedian George K. Arthur had recently immigrated from the music hall stages of England. He, too, would spring from his film debut in *Hollywood* to many more film appearances as a screen comic.

James Cruze directs a scene from an early film in which Hollywood satirizes itself. The players are William de Mille, Owen Moore, Hope Dalton, Luke Cosgrave, and Sid Grauman.

Although the dramatic success of *Hollywood* depended almost entirely on these newcomers, they did not receive screen credit on the film itself.

Hollywood was the brainchild of Frank Condon, who was perplexed at the sameness of all the movies about movies that followed in the wake of the popular novel *Merton of the Movies* by Harry Leon Wilson (which would itself be made into a film in 1924). "In writing the story," Condon said, "I aimed at no great moral reform, nor did I strive to satirize, or reveal secrets of the movie folk, who, as a general rule, have no more secrets than other people. All I planned to do was to write a yarn wherein the beautiful and innocent young heroine did not get a job."[2]

It is the film's amusing conceit that everybody *except* the heroine gets work in the movies right away. Even when she settles down with her hometown boyfriend (now a movie star) and gives birth to twins (named Doug and Mary) her *twins* become movie stars; so does Angela's parrot. But Angela Whitaker, vowed Condon, would be a heroine "who not only did not get a job in the movies, but who did not get a job anywhere. She could starve, for all I cared, but she certainly would not go to work, as long as I had anything to do with her. I even refused to find employment for her in a restaurant, or a drug store."[3]

The one time Angela comes close to getting a job, she is asked whether she has any experience. She replies with an enthusiastic, "Yes!" Too bad, she is told. They are looking for people without experience.

Although Angela is entirely unsuccessful, her comeuppance is more gently ironic than painful. She begins the film as a cocky girl, secure in the knowledge that she has what it takes to become a star. People are constantly saying to her, "You ought to be in pictures," to which her reply is an immediate, "I know it!" At the end of the film, as the chaos of a movie set breaks all around her, a stagehand says, "You're lucky. You don't have to work in pictures." Angela replies, "I know it!"

"The moral of the story," claimed *Harrison's Reports*, "is that it is not easy for a young girl to obtain a position in Hollywood as an actress, and that it is better for her to stay home, marry and have children."[4]

Condon's satire first appeared in *Photoplay Magazine*. Jesse Lasky, head of Paramount Pictures, read it and had the story purchased on September 30, 1922, for two thousand dollars. Several writers had a go at coming up with a good script, but director Cruze didn't like any of them until Tom Geraghty was given the assignment in early 1923. The idea to stock the film with familiar Hollywood stars was Condon's.

Hollywood was filmed at many locations around Hollywood, including Paramount and Universal Studios and several stops along Hollywood Boulevard, including Grauman's Egyptian Theater. The filming was completed on May 3, 1923, at a cost of $201,959.14

According to the script, now in the Paramount Files at the Academy of Motion Picture Arts and Sciences (AMPAS) Library in Beverly Hills, *Hollywood* poked knowing fun not only at the moviemaking community but at audiences, censors, and movie conventions themselves.

The opening scene is in Centerville, at the Palace Theater—formerly Murphy's Saloon but now the home of the cinema art. In the social center of this thriving mid-Western town is the Centerville Purity Club. They are looking at a poster for *The Perils of Potsdam* and are incensed because the word "dam" is in the title. When we see the poster again a few scenes later, it reads *The Perils of Pots*, with a piece of paper over the "dam."

We even get to see a few scenes from *The Perils of Pots*[*dam*], including these titles:

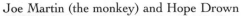

Joe Martin (the monkey) and Hope Drown

"How dare you bring me here . . . alone?"
"I brought you here because I love you!"
"Why? Why am I always misjudged? Will no one ever understand me?"
"You may carry out your murderous . . . and . . . and . . ."
"Wait a minute . . . I can't read them big words . . . and . . . and . . ."
"Don't you know this is a silent drama!"

No sooner do Angela and Grandpa step off the train in Hollywood than the place is littered with movie people: They see (and don't recognize) Bebe Daniels, William deMille, Jack Holt, Thomas Meighan (buying candy and toys for some children), Alfred Green, and others within their first moments in town. Later, Angela runs into Sid Grauman, Gloria Swanson, and Theodore Kosloff at the Egyptian Theater; they are there for a premiere. Swanson offers Angela the use of her limousine (since her driver isn't busy at the moment) to go to a studio for an audition, but of course Angela doesn't realize whose car she is in. Still later, in the Hollywood Hotel lobby, Angela complains, "I'm just a little disappointed. I thought we'd see movie people around everywhere, but we haven't seen a soul."

Mordaunt Hall, in the *New York Times*, details a few more star cameos:

> "Mary Pickford and Douglas Fairbanks emerge from their home "Pickfair," the latter with his long hair grown for *The Thief of Baghdad*. Pola Negri presides at a banquet, and Jack Holt is pictured carrying piles of letters from admirers. Ben Turpin rolls his eyeballs, J. Warren Kerrigan appears with wind-blown hair, and Nita Naldi flashes her vampish optics. Will Rogers throws a lasso around a garrulous quartet of players to hurry them to the train, and Baby Peggy and Dinky Dean are seen on friendly terms.
>
> One of the humorous situations is where a fast-walking, fast-talking plain woman approaches Charlie Chaplin in the Hollywood Hotel, informing him that she enjoyed his last picture so much. Just as Chaplin is beaming his appreciation she concludes her remarks by calling him Mr. Warren Kerrigan."[5]

Almost every scene is played for laughs, but one sequence must have been disturbing in the extreme.

Angela is visiting a casting office. Off to the side sits a lonely figure —
Roscoe "Fatty" Arbuckle, whose career was ruined in 1921 when he was
accused in the death of a starlet. Although acquitted of the charges, he
had been banned from the screen.

Several girls in bathing suits enter from a door marked DRESSING
ROOMS. They all wave gaily to Arbuckle as they hurry by. He nods to
each of them, but he does not even smile.

One girl is offered a swimming part. She won't take it. "Not for one
day's work. I've just paid three bucks for this marcel."

The casting director replies, "Well, you're out."

The girl indicates her hair, showing it to Angela. "The very idea of
spoiling *that* for a day's work!"

As the girls turn away from the window and stop, facing the camera,
Arbuckle looks up at them with a thoughtful, reflective expression but
does not intrude his gaze on them. The new girl nonchalantly dismisses
the unsuccessful application for work. "Come on, let's gip a ride to Universal City." She starts out, Angela following along like a faithful dog.
As they pass the camera out of scene, the casting director goes to the
window and closes down the wooden shutter. Arbuckle looks up, rises,
then starts to go, but stops to roll a cigarette.

There is a note in the script (written by Condon? Geraghty?) reading: "I think we can get an effective reaction on playing him very quietly — not even introducing him as the audience will recognize him immediately. The idea conveyed here is supposedly a big one — that the
lovable comedian, through unfortunate circumstances, has been forbid-
den to go to work and now sits in an empty waiting room as if awaiting
a call at the very bottom where he began."[6]

Mordaunt Hall, for one, did not find Arbuckle's appearance to be
in good taste. "[It] will not whet public desire for his reintroduction to
motion picture enthusiasts. He is at the casting director's window, which
is slammed down, leaving the obese comedian with naught else to do but
walk away with others for whom there is no work. However, none of
the interest in this photoplay hinges on this incident, and nothing would
be lost by its elimination."[7]

His cameo was viewed more kindly by critic Frank Shelton, "[Arbuckle] is the big surprise. It is probably a bit of diplomacy. If Roscoe gets a hand every time this picture is shown and the folks thus show that all is forgiven—we believe that it will not be long before the fat funmaker will be in our midst again."[8]

This, of course, did not turn out to be the case.

The mixture of the hilarious and sober must have lent the film an interesting flavor; in many ways *Hollywood* seems among the least sentimental, and most factual, of Hollywood stories.

Cruze, however, did indulge his propensity for fantasy in a dream sequence: "In one episode he visualized a dream in which the Centerville pants presser imagined himself a knight errant who had journeyed to the twentieth-century Babylon to rescue his girl from the clutches of that dread dragon, the Cinema. It was utter insanity. The various stars, garbed as sheiks, licentious club-men, aristocratic roués, bathing girls, apaches, and the like, moved about in weird confusion through a distorted nightmare. There was slow motion photography, reverse action, and double exposure; no sense was made at any given point."[9]

Today, *Hollywood* would have the added resonance of its documentary record of lost Hollywood: the studios, the streets, the nightclubs, and the theaters, all captured on film when the city was still somehow poised between small town and world capital. In February 1941, Paramount considered remaking the film and asked a reader to look over the script and screen the film itself. The reader's report said: "This was a hilariously funny picture in 1923, and since the basic situations are practically unaffected by the passing years, it possesses all the ingredients for an equally funny remake."[10]

Indeed, the humor might have translated quite well to a later era. But how could any film, in 1941 or 1991 or 2021, ever recapture what was lost when *Hollywood* disappeared: a party at Pola Negri's house, a ride in Gloria Swanson's limo, a William deMille film set, the crushing finality of a "closed" sign slamming down before Roscoe Arbuckle's tragic face. There have been other movies about movies—lots of them—but *Hollywood* caught a place, a time, and perhaps a truth, that none of those that followed ever could have.

13

PIED PIPER MALONE

· ·

Famous Players—Lasky Corporation. Paramount Pictures. Released February 4, 1924. Eight reels; 7,264 feet (77 minutes). Working titles: *Uncle Jack, Everybody's Uncle, Everybody's Uncle Jack.*

CREDITS

Presented by: Adolph Zukor and Jesse L. Lasky. *Director:* Alfred E. Green; *Scenario:* Tom Geraghty; *Titles:* Booth Tarkington and Tom Geraghty; *Story:* Booth Tarkington; *Camera:* Ernest Hallor; *Assistant Director:* Jack Boland.

CAST

Thomas Meighan (*Jack Malone*); Lois Wilson (*Patty Thomas*); Emma Dunn (*Mother Malone*); Charles Stevenson (*James P. Malone*); George Fawcett (*Captain Clarke*); Cyril Ring (*Charles Crosby, Jr.*); Claude Brook (*Charles Crosby, Sr.*); Joseph Burke (*Mr. Thomas*); Peaches Jackson (*Betty Malone*); Charles Winninger (*Louie, the Barber*); Hugh Cameron (*Photographer*); Dorothy Walters (*Housekeeper*); Pearl Sindelar, Marie Schaefer, Elizabeth Henry, Jean Armour, Blanch Standing, Mollie Ring (*The Malone Sisters*); Charles Mussett, Walter Downing, Henry Mayo, Lawrence Barnes, David Wall, Ed Williams (*The Malone Brothers*); Helen Mack, Marilyn McLain, Florence Rogan, Rita Rogan, Louise Jones, Marie Louise Bobb, Louise Sirkin, Billy Lauder, Charles Walters, Edwin Mills, Leonard Connelly, Bobby Jackson, Dorothy McCann, Billy Baker, Marshall Green, Douglas Green (*Children*).

· ·

SYNOPSIS

Jack Malone is the thirteenth child of the Malone family. He has six brothers and six sisters, all his senior. The boys have all settled down to stable business pursuits; they seem to have gobbled everything in town, so it left Jack nothing else to do except go to sea. He has been on a two years' cruise on the *S.S. Langland* and returns in time for the Golden Wedding Anniversary of his parents, but before going to sea again he wins the promise of Patty Thomas, the pretty schoolteacher and daughter of the mayor of the town, that while he is away there will be no one else in her life.

Jack is especially popular with the children of the New England town of Old Port. He is their "pied piper." Charlie Crosby, second mate of the *Langland*, always has claimed Patty as his girl, the rivalry between the men becoming rather acute. Charlie gains the disfavor of Captain Clarke for his drinking while ashore, and Jack is promoted to his position. Crosby shows his resentment by trying to brain Malone with a boat hook, but the Captain sees the [?] just in time to ward off the blow with his arm, which is broken by the impact.

A great storm is encountered at sea, and water gets into the ship's boilers. Jack, with the Captain disabled and drinking heavily to forget his pain, and with Crosby in irons, decides to release the latter; he needs every man. But all of Jack's heroic efforts cannot save the *Langland*. The Captain and Charlie get into the lifeboats, while Jack and the engineer succeed in launching the last boat and are picked up by a tramp steamer bound for Samoa.

In the meantime, Charlie returns to Old Port and spreads the report that Jack and the Captain were drunk and that he tried to save the ship and couldn't. The townspeople turn against Jack and Captain Clarke; that is, all save Mr. and Mrs. Malone and Patty, whose heart has been won by the lovable Jack. The children, too, continue to love him as before.

Upon his return, Jack endeavors to bring Clarke back into the good graces of the community and finally lands him another ship. When he goes to the Captain's room, he finds that he has gone to the town's only "blind tiger" with Charlie Crosby and has been there all night playing poker. Jack accuses Charlie of beating the Captain [while the man was] drunk. There is a fight and Malone gives Crosby a beating. While he is taking the staggering Captain to his room, many persons see him. There is a buzz of excitement. All believe that Jack and Clarke are drunk again. Even Mrs. Malone and Patty are terribly alarmed.

Mr. Thomas and several of the leading citizens hold a meeting to draw up an order that Captain Clarke must be driven out of town or go to jail. Charlie's father rushes into the gathering and tells the committee that Jack Malone has assaulted his son. This brings an order for Jack's departure also. When Jack arrives home, his father tells him that he has been drunk and that he will have nothing to do with him.

After he leaves, the children Malone had sent to Patty with a box of candy arrive and tell her that they had walked home with Jack after he had taken the drunken man to the hotel. This opens Patty's eyes; she sees her mistake. She tells her father that they have done Jack a grave wrong.

An effort is made to stop Jack. Just as the boat is leaving the dock, Patty rushes down to the water's edge and tells Malone that she knows he is guiltless and that she will be waiting for him. Jack insists time after time as the vessel leaves the dock that he loves her. The ship moves away with Patty throwing kisses to Jack who returns them, promising an early return home.

—"Scenario for Thomas Meighan, Esq., by Booth Tarkington"—
from the Paramount Story Department

THE PRODUCTION

Thomas Meighan is another of the casualties of the vagaries of film preservation. Most of his films have disappeared. Even those that exist are by no means accessible to general audiences. Once wildly popular, Meighan has been mostly forgotten by all but those with a serious interest in the silent cinema.

There was a time, however, when Meighan's name on a marquee carried almost as much weight as that of Chaplin, Valentino, or Fairbanks. Audiences responded to his robust screen presence. Even at his most heroic, Meighan remained approachable; fans felt they knew him personally. When author Booth Tarkington visited Meighan on the Sing Sing prison location of *The Man Who Paid* (1925), he was amazed to find all the prisoners treating the actor like a treasured pal. " 'Hello, *Tom!*' they called voluminously," Tarkington wrote, "and the voices were hearty and cordial, for they were greeting a man who had proved himself their friend. Meighan smiled and colored a little, pleased but shy."[1]

From the evidence, it appears Meighan was similarly popular with his coworkers. "If you knew Tommy, you had to love him," said Lois Wilson, his costar in *Pied Piper Malone* and four other motion pictures. "I don't think he had an enemy in the world. Everybody loved Tommy. He was a very easy actor to work with, but he had his favorites, and he was so popular that he could choose me for the picture. He'd say, 'I want Lois Wilson in this.' He found me easy to work with, so I always felt that was a great compliment."[2]

Meighan must have also found it "easy to work with" *Pied Piper Malone*'s director, Alfred E. Green. The two made eight features together: *Back Home and Broke* (1922), *The Bachelor Daddy* (1922), *The Man Who Saw Tomorrow* (1922), *Our Leading Citizen* (1922), *The Ne'er-Do-Well* (1923), *Woman-Proof* (1923), *Pied Piper Malone*, and *The Man Who Found Himself* (1925). Meighan and Green also both appeared in scenes in James Cruze's all-star *Hollywood* (1923). Green's name is another that has essentially disappeared from the pages of film history, despite his long, prolific, and successful career. He directed Bette Davis in her Academy Award–winning *Dangerous*, (1935) and provided solid vehicles for Mary Pickford, Colleen Moore, George Arliss, Edward G. Robinson, and John Barrymore, as well as entertainments as varied as *The Gracie Allen Murder Case* (1939) and *The Jolson Story* (1946).

While Meighan, early in his career, was playing the lead in Indiana-born humorist George Ade's stage play *The College Widow*, he and Ade became good friends. "If I was in a tight place," Ade once said, "I'd rather have Tommy Meighan by my side than any other man alive."[3] Later, when Meighan became powerful enough in motion pictures to choose his own collaborators, he urged Ade to start writing for the screen. They worked together often, producing *Back Home and Broke* (1922), *Our Leading Citizen* (1922), *Woman-Proof* (1923), *The Confidence*

George Fawcett

Lois Wilson

Man (1924) and *Old Home Week* (1925). Their friendship led to Meighan's introduction in 1922 to another well-known Hoosier: Booth Tarkington.

Many of Tarkington's novels had already been made into films, notably *Penrod* (1922) and *Alice Adams* (1923). He had written a few entries in Goldwyn's series of *Edgar* shorts in 1921 but had never turned his hand to writing features. Meighan urged him to do so, and the result was *Pied Piper Malone*, a slight tale about a sailor, beloved by all the children in town, who must prove himself innocent of bad conduct to win the heart of the girl he loves and the trust and respect of his fellow

Alfred E. Green, the director

townspeople. Tom Geraghty wrote the scenario based on Tarkington's story, and Tarkington and Geraghty collaborated on the titles.

Filming was scheduled to begin in the autumn of 1923, and Green searched for the proper location throughout the preceding summer. Although *Pied Piper Malone* is set in the (fictional) New England fishing village of Old Port, Green realized that the approaching winter would make filming difficult Way Down East. He headed south, down the East Coast, looking for a stand-in, and found it in the charming little coastal city of Georgetown, South Carolina.

At 2:40 in the afternoon, on November 6, 1923, a special train pulled into the Georgetown station. The train, consisting of four Pullmans and a baggage coach, held about seventy members, cast and crew, of the Thomas Meighan Company.

No motion picture had ever been filmed in Georgetown, and the populace turned out in force to greet the movie people. Mayor J. W. Wingate headed a delegation of merchants and civic leaders, and after a few speeches of welcome, the actors and crew members from Hollywood were dispatched to homes all over town. No member of the company — even Green and Meighan — stayed in a hotel during their Georgetown sojourn.

Although stars Lois Wilson, Emma Dunn, Charles Stevenson, George Fawcett, and other members of the cast arrived in Georgetown that day, Meighan himself was not on the train. Just days earlier, his father had become gravely ill, and Meighan was summoned to his bedside. Soon after Meighan's arrival in Pittsburgh, his father died, and while Green and the Meighan Company headed for Georgetown, Meighan stayed in Pennsylvania for his father's burial.

Filming began immediately on Wednesday, November 7 on "certain portions of the picture not necessitating the presence of the principal actor."[4] Most of the scenes shot in Georgetown concentrated on the lovely waterfront and North Island, which was accessible only by boat. Among the other Georgetown landmarks used in the film was the Revolutionary War home of General Lafayette.[5]

The plot called for Malone (Meighan) to be regularly surrounded by a flock of children, a situation that expanded on his popular *The Bachelor Daddy* (1922) — "only more so, for instead of five youngsters, about fifty are seen in support of the star."[6] Most of these children were recruited locally. Two of them, Marshall and Douglas Green, aged four and two respectively, were the sons of the director.

Meighan arrived in Georgetown on Saturday, November 10. There was bad weather the following Tuesday, but the rest of the week was "bright and crisp, perfect conditions for taking pictures for the screens."[7] Although the company planned to move down the coast to Charleston for scenes involving a steamship and a four-masted schooner, a Georgetown shipping firm, The B. A. Munnerlyn Company, came up with both.

The *Baltimore and Carolina* steamer was used in scenes shot off the coast of Georgetown, and a schooner was chartered from a local businessman.

Georgetown was delighted to be hosting the movie folk, and the chamber of commerce gave an informal reception and dance in their honor on November 16 at the Winyah Indigo Society Hall. Meighan, Wilson, and their Hollywood cronies danced to the "splendid music"[8] of the Elks Band, and cast member George Fawcett regaled the crowd with "a very witty and eloquent speech, which was much enjoyed."[9] On the evening of November 23, the Meighan Company returned the city's kindness by presenting a benefit performance at the Winyah School Auditorium. The admission price of $.50 for adults and $.25 for children went toward the Health Fund of the Civic League, a fund for caring for undernourished Georgetown children. The theatrical evening earned $700 for the fund, of which Meighan himself kicked in $100.[10]

Meighan, Green, and company left Georgetown on Monday, November 26. "Many warm friendships were formed," wrote a *Georgetown Times* reporter, "and a firm bond of mutual regard established between this company and our citizens. Incidentally, it has been estimated that between ten and fifteen thousand dollars of good, hard cash was put into circulation here as a result of this visit of the Movie Stars."[11]

The *Pied Piper Malone* company moved north to New York City's Chinatown, to shoot early scenes of the film that take place in the Orient. After the warmth and hospitality of their three weeks in South Carolina, the company was unprepared for the hostility waiting for them in the Big Apple.

Actually, the trouble to come had less to do with *Pied Piper Malone* specifically than with the general attitude of American film toward Asian characters. Furious at the repeated racial stereotypes of films depicting Asians as deceptive, opium-smoking white slavers, a small riot was brewing by the time the film company arrived. Angry residents of Chinatown ripped the Mandarin costumes from the Chinese extras.[12] "Stones, fruits, and ancient vegetables were thrown," said one report of the incident. "So were lamps and old shoes."[13] The actors and crew took cover until the police arrived and restored order.

At the same time, Green began filming an exciting storm-at-sea sequence. Late one night the special effects crew hit Meighan, Fawcett, and the other "sailors" with repeated blasts of water to simulate storm waves. Large water tanks were placed overhead, just out of camera range, which periodically dumped out water near the actors. One five-hundred-gallon tank opened accidentally as it hung just ten feet over Meighan's head. He leaped aside in time to avoid the powerful wave. "Had it hit him," *Photoplay* claimed, "he would have been swept off the deck into Long Island Sound."[14]

It is an indication of how much less time it took to finish a motion picture and get it onto movie screens in 1923 than today to note that principal photography on *Pied Piper Malone* was not completed until the middle of December 1923, and the finished film was being reviewed by mid-January. The film opened at New York's Rivoli Theater on January 27, 1924.

Variety found *Pied Piper Malone* to be "one of the best of the most recent Meighan-starring productions. It is a decidedly human story with the love interest paramount. While there is not [any] great big thrill that stands out other than the sinking of a steamer in a typhoon in the China Seas, it is a picture that will hold the interest."[15]

The *New York Times*, however, thought the story "flimsy and improbable" and found the production "wearying, especially toward the end."[16] Tarkington's story was "pretty thin stuff," said another critic, who also felt the film's many children were not particularly well used. "[Malone] attracts all the children because of his personality and because he is kind to them. But he is no magician, no Pied Piper. They follow him at a respectful distance because the title demands it—and because the idea is written into the plot. But the scene is unconvincing. The children appear uncertain in their movements—and probably were difficult to handle."[17]

Several critics complained of unconvincing plot point. The scene in which Jack leads the drunken Captain Clarke home in full view of an emerging church congregation seems to have rubbed nearly every reviewer the wrong way. "He might have waited until the services were over," sniffed Laurence Reid.[18]

"There is quite a bit of human interest in the story," wrote C. S. Sewell, "and Meighan is cast in a very sympathetic role. There is, however, very little of the intimate insight into childhood psychology that has characterized most of Booth Tarkington's works, and the picture will doubtless disappoint this author's followers. Well made from a production standpoint, and portrayed by a high-class cast, it should prove pleasing to the average audience; but will probably not be considered as up to the standard of entertainment value usually found in a Thomas Meighan picture."[19]

Harrison's Reports agreed that the story was "devoid of dramatic incident and of suspense" but admitted "that the star's performance is, as always, above criticism."[20]

Perhaps these reviewers were right, and *Pied Piper Malone* was simply a forgettable little trifle. But many a terrific movie has overcome a routine plot. When I think wistfully of *Pied Piper Malone,* which I will never see, I feel the excitement of the citizens of Georgetown, South Carolina, in the autumn of 1923, thrilled to have movie folk in their midst. I picture the beautiful and precious images of that city, which should have been preserved on film forever.

Not much of a story? How ironic that today the story is all that's left. And everything that had the potential to make the film lovely, exciting, funny, and memorable—the performances, the direction, the cinematography—are irretrievable, never to surface again to prove those critics wrong.

14

SO BIG

First National Pictures. Released December 28, 1924. Nine reels; 8,562 feet. (*So Big* was remade in 1930 in a two-reel production starring Helen Jerome Eddy and directed by Eddie Foy; in 1932 in a feature version starring Barbara Stanwyck and directed by William A. Wellman; and in 1953, starring Jane Wyman and directed by Robert Wise.)

C R E D I T S

Supervisor: Earl Hudson; *Director:* Charles Brabin; *Editorial Director:* Marion Fairfax; *Scenario:* Adelaide Heilbron; Based on the novel *So Big* (1924) by Edna Ferber; *Adaptation:* Earl Hudson; *Camera:* T. D. McCord; *Art Director:* Milton Menasco; *Film Editor:* Arthur Tevares.

C A S T

Colleen Moore (*Selina Peake*); Sam De Grasse (*Simeon Peake*); John Bowers (*Pervus De-Jong*); Ben Lyon (*Dirk DeJong*); Wallace Beery (*Klaas Poole*); Gladys Brockwell (*Maartje Poole*); Jean Hersholt (*Aug Hempel*); Charlotte Merriam (*Julie Hempel*); Dot Farley (*Widow Paalenburg*); Ford Sterling (*Jacob Hoogenduck*); Frankie Darrow (*Dirk DeJong as a Boy*); Henry Herbert (*William Storm*); Dorothy Brock (*Dirk DeJong as a Baby*); Rosemary Theby (*Paula Storm*); Phyllis Haver (*Dallas O'Meara*).

SYNOPSIS

After returning from a tour of Europe with her father and finishing a course at a fashionable finishing school in the year 1888, Selina Peake is shocked to find that her father is a gambler and has been killed by accident in a gambling den. Left penniless, she gets a job as a schoolteacher in the Dutch colony at High Prairie and finally marries Purvis DeJong, a dull-witted and poor farmer, and soon finds that her life is one of drudgery, lightened only by her love for her little son, Dirk, whom she calls So Big.

Purvis dies and Selina, in old clothes, reduced to abject poverty, peddles vegetables. The father of her former school friend advances her a little money, and by stinting and hard work, after eighteen years she has made the farm pay and educated Dirk as an architect, and he wins a competition.

Dirk is loved by an artist, Dallas, who has helped him, but he owes much of his success to Mrs. Storm, a discontented wife, who persuades him to elope with her.

Selina learns of this, and while begging the pair to give up the wild idea, Mrs. Storm's husband enters and threatens to name Dirk as correspondent in a divorce suit. Selina pleads so for Dirk that Storm consents to drop the matter. Thoroughly repentant, Dirk goes with his mother to Dallas.

—Moving Picture World, January 17, 1925

THE PRODUCTION

"The picture should prove suitable more for small communities than for big theaters in large cities."

—Harrison's Reports, January 7, 1925

"Its appeal certainly will be only to the better class audiences. In the small towns they may wonder what it is all about."

—Variety, January 7, 1925

When Edna Ferber's novel *So Big* was published early in 1924, its success was immediate and vast. It sold hundreds of thousands of copies, gaining the kind of fanatic devotion among readers that would become typical of Ferber's books. A book—then and now—couldn't be that popular without Hollywood's horning in to get a piece of the action—and First National didn't waste any time in doing just that.

The studio purchased the screen rights to *So Big* in May 1924. Adelaide Heilbron was signed to write the adaptation, which she completed the first week in June.

Charles Brabin was signed on as director in July, and production began on August 11, 1924.

The star of *So Big*—in a role that demanded a fine dramatic actress who could age from sixteen to sixty in the course of the film—was, to everyone's surprise, Colleen Moore.

Although Moore was one of the most popular stars in moving pictures, she was usually cast in sassy comedies. Appearing in films from 1917, her real breakthrough came in *Flaming Youth* (1923; also a lost film), in which she played the prototype flapper, a bobbed-haired Jazz Baby, the icon of a new generation of young people. F. Scott Fitzgerald wrote about the Jazz Age in his scandalous novel *This Side of Paradise*. He said later, "I was the spark that lit up *Flaming Youth*, Colleen Moore was the torch. What little things we are to have caused all that trouble."[1]

Flaming Youth had been incredibly popular at the box office, as had most of Moore's starring vehicles, but the executives at First National—who included her husband, John McCormick—weren't altogether pleased at the prospect of such a drastic change of pace as *So Big*. However, as Miss Moore was not the first or last movie star to discover, box-office success spells increased clout. She wanted the role of Selina Peake and she demanded it. And she got it.

Ben Lyon was hired in August, just as filming got underway. Lyon had just finished costarring with Gloria Swanson in P. C. Wren's Foreign Legion melodrama *The Wages of Virtue* (1924) when he reported for work as Colleen Moore's son in *So Big*.

So Big was Charles Brabin's first picture under his new First National contract. He and his wife, Theda Bara, came to Hollywood from

Colleen Moore and John Bowers

New York for the duration of production, staying in a lavish suite at the Beverly Hills Hotel. Brabin had been directing films since 1911. Many of his films are stylish and expertly made, but he had a reputation in Hollywood for inefficiency. His very public firing from M-G-M's massive (and catastrophic) Italian production of *Ben-Hur* nearly ruined his career once and for all. *So Big* offered Brabin the chance to redeem himself by making a good and successful film.

"Mr. Brabin was really—as far as I was concerned—he was the director who could get the most out of me," Colleen Moore said many years later. "It was just wonderful working with him, just wonderful. I enjoyed every minute of it. I liked all of my directors. They weren't difficult, and I worked well with all of them, but I had a special rapport with William K. Howard and Charles Brabin."[2]

So Big was filmed at United Studios (today Paramount Pictures) at 5451 Marathon in Hollywood. The location work, depicting High Prairie, a suburb of Chicago, was done in Downey, California, then a rural community.

Brabin and company gave a great deal of attention to accurately depicting the periods in *So Big*, carefully selecting clothes, hairstyles, and furnishings to recreate an era on the screen. Moore claimed that she stopped listening to jazz while *So Big* was in production, listening only to music of the eighties and nineties on an old-fashioned gramophone to stay in the mood of her character. (It is interesting to note that in 1925 the 1890s were considered ancient times.) All of the work seems to have paid off, since nearly every reviewer, when writing about *So Big*, mentioned "the meticulous attention to detail in providing the correct atmosphere of those sweet and simple grandmother's days. These sequences will be a treat for the oldsters."[3]

It was while shooting one of these charming period scenes that tragedy nearly struck. Character actress Cissy Fitzgerald was cast as the Widow Paalenburg. One day in early September, while shooting a scene in which she was driving "the first automobile ever used in Chicago," Fitzgerald lost control of the vehicle and ran into a truck. She was thrown over the hood, striking her face on the truck. Fifteen stitches were required to close the wound and doctors at Downey Hospital predicted that her face would be scarred for life.[4]

Although Cissy Fitzgerald's injuries did not prove critical—she continued appearing in films into the thirties—she was replaced by Dot

Farley a few days later. Brabin complained that he had to reshoot half of the month's scenes.[5]

The remainder of the production was uneventful, except for a few days in late September when Colleen Moore came down with "klieg eyes."[6] This was a relatively common affliction in the early days of movie making caused by looking directly into the powerful, open-arc flood-lights called "kliegs" after the Kliegl Brothers who invented them. (A twenties gag: "Who knocked the *L* out of Klieg?") Klieg eyes were painful but generally cleared up after a few days' rest.

So Big opened in early January at the Mark Strand Theater in New York City. In those days, a trip to the movies involved a great deal more than just a movie. Before *So Big* began, audiences at the Mark Strand were treated to an orchestral overture, excerpts from *Serenade* and *Fair Andalusia* sung by Kitty McLaughlin and a male chorus, a film short, *The Humming Bird,* and a playlet, "Days of '88," which served as a prologue to the feature film. Finally, *So Big* played, to nearly unanimous acclaim for Colleen Moore's work. Calling her performance "astonishingly fine," the *New York Times'* Mordaunt Hall also praised the "resourceful and imaginative" direction of Charles Brabin.[7]

"*Flaming Youth* proved that Miss Colleen Moore is an actress of talent," wrote another critic. "*So Big* now confirms that fact."[8]

Variety's critic "Sisk." wrote one of the more perceptive reviews, pointing out the film's successes and correctly predicting its commercial fate:

"That it is one of the most artistic pictures ever produced is beyond question. That it is the medium wherein Colleen Moore exceeds the wildest expectations by her portrayal of an old woman is also indisputable. That the famous Ferber novel has been handled intelligently and with a fine directorial sense is something else that can't start an argument, but whether it will draw money at the box office is doubtful."[9]

Colleen Moore wrote in her autobiography, "In spite of the critical acclaim, *So Big* made only a few hundred thousand dollars' profit instead of the usual million. Mr. [Richard] Rowland [executive in charge of production at First National] and John [McCormick, her husband] both said to me, "All right, you've had your fun, Now, will you go back and give the public what it wants from you?"[10]

Colleen Moore remained a star for the remainder of the twenties. Her last film, *The Scarlet Letter,* was released in 1934. She was not a casualty of sound but of image. Like Mary Pickford's, Moore's image was a youthful one; audiences didn't want to see her act like an adult. Since she *was* an adult, and the youthful roles began to bore her, there was nothing to do but call it a day.

But while *So Big* may not have set any box office records, it did allow Moore to experiment with different aspects of her talent and personality. She was to make several more dramatic pictures (notably William K. Howard's *The Power and the Glory* (1933), written by Preston Sturges and costarring Spencer Tracy) and gave intelligent and beautifully measured performances in each of them.

While *Flaming Youth* may be the quintessential Colleen Moore film—and it, too is lost—*So Big* was always her favorite. Sadly, it will never get the chance to become *our* favorite, too.

15

THE FLAMING FRONTIER

Universal Pictures. Released September 12, 1926. Nine reels; 8,828 feet. Some stock footage used in the twelve-part serial *The Indians Are Coming* (Universal, 1930).

CREDITS

Director and Story: Edward Sedgwick; *Scenario:* Edward J. Montagne, Charles Kenyon; *Adaptation:* Raymond L. Schrock; *Camera:* Virgil Miller; *Musical Director:* Dr. Hugo Riesenfeld; *Technical Advisor:* Col. George L. Byram, U.S.A., retired.

CAST

Hoot Gibson (*Bob Langdon*); Anne Cornwall (*Betty Stanwood*); Dustin Farnum (*General George Armstrong Custer*); Ward Crane (*Sam Belden*); Kathleen Key (*Lucretia*); Eddie Gribbon (*Jonesy*); Harry Todd (*California Joe*); Harold Goodwin (*Lawrence Stanwood*); George Fawcett (*Senator Stanwood*); Noble Johnson (*Sitting Bull*); Charles K. French (*Senator Hargess*); William Steele (*Penfield*); Walter Rodgers (*President Grant*); Ed Wilson (*Grant's Secretary*); Joe Bonomo (*Rain in the Face*).

SYNOPSIS

Westward Ho! 1876, and the tide of civilization was still pushing, pushing, pushing—and always toward the West. The copper-colored Indians were growing restless and jealous of the ever new encroachments upon their hunting grounds. On the plains, settlers and soldiers were blazing the way for the new civilizations, while back East, in Washington, unscrupulous politicians and profiteers were selling whiskey and arms to the Indians.

It was at this period that America first heard of Custer. He sought to bring peace between the new white settlers and the Indians, but this, of course, was against the interests of those who sought to capitalize upon those disturbances.

The story of *The Flaming Frontier* centers on Bob Langdon, who is first seen as a pony express rider. Through the influence of General Custer with Senator Stanwood, Bob secures an appointment to West Point. There he becomes friends with Stanwood's son Lawrence and falls in love with Stanwood's daughter Betty.

Stanwood is a real friend of the Indians, and to discredit him, the corrupt Indian agent Belden seeks to frame up a scandal involving Stanwood's son Lawrence, a weak-willed tough, and Belden's daughter Lucretia. There is a scandal, but Bob, to shield the Senator, takes the blame. When he is before the head of the school and refuses to offer an explanation, Betty believes the worst of him. Bob is expelled and returns West, to Custer's command.

Even there, Bob refuses to tell General Custer the true story of his expulsion from the Academy, even though his heart is breaking because of his love for Senator Stanwood's daughter.

Not satisfied at the outcome of his scheme, Belden plots with Sitting Bull to cause an uprising of the Indians and arranges [it] so that Custer and his command are lured into a trap. Custer is misinformed about the number of Indians he is up against and attacks them at the Little Big Horn. Custer commands four hundred men, while Sitting Bull's army numbers in the thousands. Bob is sent to Major Reno for reinforcements, but Reno fails to act in time.

Custer and his men are slaughtered.

Lawrence Stanwood, who is in Custer's command as an officer, makes a confession to his chief just before the fight, and his story is included in the last dispatches of the Indian fighter.

The profiteers are delighted at Custer's defeat, but their joy is short-lived. Bob leads the angry settlers and the soldiers that were left at the garrison against Belden and rescues Betty, who is in Belden's power.

In the fight that follows, Belden is killed and his entire settlement burned to the ground. Lawrence's confession vindicates Bob and secures for him the commission in the Army that he rightfully should have had. Bob is reappointed to the Army and wins Betty.

—Culled from several sources—including *Moving Picture World*, April 17, 1926; *Exhibitor's Review*, February 20, 1926, and *Variety*, April 7, 1926.

THE PRODUCTION

On June 25, 1876, as the United States geared up for its Centennial celebration, George Armstrong Custer made the biggest mistake of his life. He and about 225 troopers of the Seventh Cavalry crossed the Little Big Horn River in Montana in search of "renegade" Sioux Indians under Sitting Bull. Custer intended to attack their villages and subdue the Sioux, forcing them back to the reservations where they were supposed to be exiled.

Custer believed they might come across up to eight hundred warriors and so had already split his command into three segments to facilitate the search. In fact, Sitting Bull was followed by more than seven thousand Indians, at least two thousand of whom were warriors. On a ridge near the Little Big Horn, in a place the Indians called Greasy Grass, Custer and his command were wiped out. The victorious Indians under Sitting Bull lost only a handful of warriors.

The violent and dramatic story of George Armstrong Custer's bad day at the Little Big Horn was a natural subject for the movies. The saga had already been brought to the screen at least a dozen times before Universal released *The Flaming Frontier* in 1926. The first Custer film was Selig's *Custer's Last Stand (On the Little Big Horn)* (1909).[1]

Nineteen twenty-six marked the fiftieth anniversary of the Battle of the Little Big Horn; the year fairly overflowed with Custer films. Anthony J. Xydias's Sunset Pictures released a low-budget version, *With General Custer at Little Big Horn*, starring John Beck as Custer; Robert Frazer and Clara Bow appeared in *The Scarlet West*, an interracial love story that leads to Custer's last stand; and Custer makes a cameo ap-

Trade ad

The Entire Industry Will Vote This the Most Glorious Picture of the West Ever Made!
THE
FLAMING FRONTIER
Mightiest of Thrillers—A Glorious Epic of America's Last Frontier
An Edward Sedgwick Production
Presented by
CARL LAEMMLE
with this great assemblage of stars HOOT GIBSON—DUSTIN FARNUM—ANNE CORNWALL Eddie Gribbon, George Fawcett, Kathleen Key, Harold Goodwin —Joe Bonomo—Harry Todd—Noble Johnson—Ward Crane—C. K. French.
The Last Word in Great Westerns—the Ultimate in Great Thrillers!
A UNIVERSAL SUPER PRODUCTION

Trade ad

pearance in Metropolitan's *The Last Frontier,* which also features Western heroes like Wild Bill Hickok and Buffalo Bill Cody (Jack Hoxie).

That year was also the twentieth anniversary of Universal Pictures. Universal's head, "Uncle" Carl Laemmle, decided to celebrate both of these momentous anniversaries by making *The Flaming Frontier* the biggest Custer film of them all and one of Universal's most expensive and elaborate productions of the year.

A replica of Fort Hays, Custer's outpost, was built with apparently painstaking detail in the hills of the San Fernando Valley outside Universal City. A duplicate of Crane City was constructed near Pendleton, Oregon. Though studio publicity claimed thousands of extras were used, that's probably an exaggeration. However, surviving stills indicate there were indeed hundreds of participants in the battle scenes, including scores of "real Indians." Several published reports claimed that the budget exceeded four hundred thousand dollars.

Universal crowed on endlessly about the research poured into making *The Flaming Frontier* "the greatest of its kind."[2] Colonel George S. Byram, U.S.A., retired, an 1885 West Point graduate, was enlisted as the film's technical and historical advisor, supervising the battle scenes and military accessories. Byram had, he claimed, made the original survey of the battlefield for the U.S. War Department report. Studio researchers, claimed Universal publicity, also talked with old Indian scouts and with veterans of the Indian Wars.

Director Edward Sedgwick wrote the story himself. In typical Hollywood fashion, he wove a fictional story through the Custer saga both to provide some romance for the picture and also, one suspects, to make sure that the film had a hero who could actually survive for a happy ending. Although Sedgwick's plot seems needlessly melodramatic, reviewers found *The Flaming Frontier* to be refreshingly authentic.

"*The Flaming Frontier* makes no effort to be imposing or impressive," wrote one reviewer. "Its objective is to pictorially present a few pages from American History which followed upon the heels of the Civil War in a simple, direct manner. The foul politicians, false friends who surrounded President Grant, whose intrigue polluted the West, robbed the

Indians of that which the Government believed they were receiving and finally culminated in the tragic slaughter of American troops known as 'Custer's Last Fight,' form the essence of the plot. In an effort to unfalteringly and faithfully follow history's path, the love interest has been submerged. But after all, this is the story of the struggle of the pale face and the red man, the soldier and the brave. The battle scenes are well handled, the gathering of the tribes and the assembly of the troops will stir the blood of all—especially the adolescent viewer."[3]

Nearly all the reviewers were mightily impressed with *The Flaming Frontier*'s spectacle, particularly regarding Custer's Last Stand, which was "magnificently handled and wonderfully thrilling. Thousands of real Indians were used in the big battle scene and to see them coming from all sides in huge droves, literally dotting the landscape, to watch them at their campfires listening to the exhortations of the chiefs and medicine men and then bursting into wild, rhythmic war dances preparatory to taking the field, are sights long to be remembered."[4]

But as thrilling as the action scenes were, the *acting* scenes were not received nearly so positively.

"So far as acting goes, the picture reveals little or none," wrote a reviewer. "The characters are according to pattern. Hoot Gibson in the role of Langdon rides magnificently, like a streak of lightning, but he cannot ride forever, and in close-ups, away from his horse, he scarcely suggests either the youthful cadet or the loftiness of character we associate with a hero who allows his career to be blasted to protect somebody else. Gibson also makes use of a dark, unpleasant wig while on the plains, which gives way to his own light hair when at West Point and which reappears on his head when he returns to the West."[5]

The only prominent naysayer among the critics, regarding the film as a whole, was *Variety*'s "Fred.," who found *The Flaming Frontier* to be "an ordinary western. As a matter of fact, it really seems regrettable that a story abounding with so much red-blooded historical fact would have been so terribly butchered. The gathering of the Indian tribes, the dances before the battle, the battle itself, and all of the scenes in these sequences are so badly handled and directed that the least said about them the

Anne Cornwall and Hoot
Gibson, the romantic leads

better. Suffice it to say that Indian scenes had the same shot repeated
again and again until they became tiresome. The battle stuff was awful."[6]

Hoot Gibson, *The Flaming Frontier*'s Bob Langdon, was already a
popular Western star, appearing in dozens of Universal features and
two-reelers. Gibson had been acting in films since 1912 and had established a casual, laconic, realistic cowboy persona, at odds with more
flashy stars like Tom Mix. Even an epic like *The Flaming Frontier*—obviously a motion picture with big fish to fry—had to accommodate itself
to Gibson's personality, making sure he had some of the comic scenes at
which he was so adept and also could indulge in plenty of the fast riding
that his fans loved: "Hoot Gibson can rouse a house to enthusiasm simply
by swinging on and off a horse in full gallop."[7]

Dustin Farnum had been in semiretirement for over two years when
he returned to the screen to play General Custer in *The Flaming Frontier*.
Farnum had already played his share of historical figures, including *David
Garrick* and *Davy Crockett* (both 1916), but was best known to audiences

for his Western roles in films like De Mille's *The Squaw Man* and *The Virginian* (both 1914).

    The Flaming Frontier was Farnum's last film, and he apparently made the most of it. Even *Variety*, who hated nearly everything about the movie, admitted that Farnum, as Custer, "was all that could be asked."[8]

    Moving Picture World called Farnum's performance "excellent,"[9] and *Motion Picture News* said he gave "a splendid performance."[10].

    Universal gave *The Flaming Frontier* class-A treatment. For its premiere, a special musical score was written and conducted by Dr. Hugo Riesenfeld. One magazine article reported that Dr. Riesenfeld had made a special study of the U.S. Army and the Indians of 1876 "and has unearthed a creation called 'the frontier horn,' which reproduces the Indian war cry and was used by them in battle. One of these horns, claimed to have been used by Chief Gall in the battle of the Little Big

Dustin Farnum as General Custer, advising Chief Crazy Horse to keep off the war path.

Horn, has been lent to Universal for the period of the engagement."[11] Although the use of this "frontier horn" is almost certainly a piece of press-agentry, it does point out how close, historically, were the battle and this film version of it—closer than we are today to the beginning of World War II.

Virtually all silent films were color tinted for mood: blue for night, amber or green for day, red for battle or a passionate love scene, and so on. *The Flaming Frontier* was tinted in this way. One reviewer pointed out a particularly effective moment. In the climactic scenes—the burning of Belden's headquarters—the flames were tinted red to "heighten the melodramatic effect."[12] This scene was also noted for its "clever camera work."[13] Indeed, according to one critic, "The picture abounds in many scenes of striking beauty, with great sweeping landscapes, and has been superbly photographed."[14]

The Flaming Frontier premiered at New York's Colony Theater at midnight on Saturday, April 3, 1926. Every one of the theater's eighteen hundred seats was occupied, and in the back of the orchestra were "standees three feet deep."[15] Guests had received golden invitations and gold coins, inscribed with an Indian head and the name of the film. "Indian villages" were set up in stores adjoining the Colony in which souvenirs were on sale and "relics" were on display.

In the lobby were buglers from the 71st Regiment Armory, along with Chief Red Eagle and several Indian braves. The buglers were there for the length of the run, blasting bugle calls several times daily to announce the next performance.

Although the invited audience was composed of "prominent government and military officials, stage and screen stars, directors, producers, etc.,"[16] the guest of honor was Brig. Gen. Edward S. Godfrey, U.S.A., retired. In 1926, Godfrey was eighty-five years old. Fifty years earlier, at Little Big Horn, he had commanded Troop K, Seventh Cavalry under Custer. After fighting off Indians for two days while awaiting General Terry's relief column, Godfrey arrived at the massacre site to help supervise the identification and burial of the dead. In 1908, he wrote one of the definitive accounts of Custer's defeat. It is fascinating to imag-

Custer's Last Stand

ine this old soldier sitting among New York sophisticates, watching the most momentous period of his life being turned into a romantic fiction starring Hoot Gibson.

Among the audience in the Colony Theater that night were producer Samuel Goldwyn, actors Clara Kimball Young, Alice Joyce, Al Jolson, George Jessel, and the descendants of some of Custer's command. Also present were Groucho, Chico, Harpo and Zeppo—the Four Marx Brothers.

Ironically, Custer's widow, Elizabeth, lived in New York City at the time. We have no way of knowing whether she saw this or any other film depicting her husband's death.

The screening, which ended at 2 A.M. Sunday morning, was an

Finding General Custer's body after the massacre

unqualified success. The *Universal Weekly* proudly printed many of the glowing reviews:

The *Morning World:* "Universal has put out in *The Flaming Frontier,* a glorious Western, an adventure with the vigor of those lusty fighting days of the historical novels. A tremendous movie!"

The *Daily News:* "A great spectacle and full of thrills."

The *Herald-Tribune:* "The scenes when the Indians come from the East, from the West, from the North and South—these scenes are magnificent! The photography and the vast natural settings are impressive; Custer's Last Stand, the awesome ride of the brave Seventh, with the menacing redskins closing in on every side—these scenes were thrilling."

The *Evening World:* "The director, Edward Sedgwick, did splendidly. . . . Wonderfully staged and marvelously photographed Battle of the Little Big Horn."[17]

The Flaming Frontier was greeted with similar enthusiasm wherever it played, both by critics and by general audiences. It was one of Universal's most successful films of the period, due in part to a revolutionary new form of publicity. Universal utilized a "Radiobile" — a circus wagon, decorated with *Flaming Frontier* posters. The wagon was motor driven and equipped with a calliope and a microphone and made a cross-country tour, broadcasting to the curious crowds that gathered around it.

In addition, Universal had one hundred thousand letters sent to school principals and teachers all across the United States, stressing the patriotic and educational elements of *The Flaming Frontier*.

All of this helped make the film successful, but it did nothing to make the film permanent. Within just a few years, the film was even more lost to history than its subject. No prints now survive.

However, it is not *completely* gone. In 1930, Universal produced a serial, released in both silent and sound versions, called *The Indians Are Coming*. It starred Col. Tim McCoy, Francis Ford, and Allene Ray. The serial concerned a long wagon train journey that is continually attacked by Indians. Many of these epic attacks used stock footage from *The Flaming Frontier*.

While *The Indians Are Coming* does not invoke the name of Custer, it is worth noting that star Francis Ford—brother of director John Ford—had himself once played Custer in *Custer's Last Fight* (1912); he also directed the film.

These few surviving scraps of *The Flaming Frontier* are not, of course, enough. It seems a particularly tragic loss, especially if we believe some of those who were fortunate enough to see the film in 1926:

"It contains an abundance of the best elements of the dramas of the great open spaces, an excellent story plus the thrill of the patriotic angle and the glamour of dealing with an exciting historical event, is punctuated with comedy and shows excellent characterization. It excites, thrills and entertains and inspires."[18]

The surviving photographs bear out the epic qualities of *The Flaming Frontier* and all those critics who praised it probably weren't wrong. However, as promising as their endorsements sound, I'd still like to know what Groucho thought of it.

16

"THAT ROYLE GIRL"

Famous Players–Lasky Corporation. Paramount Pictures. Production number 301. Released December 7, 1925. Ten reels; 10,253 feet.

CREDITS

Presented by: Adolph Zukor and Jesse L. Lasky. *Director:* D. W. Griffith; *Screenplay:* Paul Schofield; *Photography:* Harry Fischbeck and Hal Sintzenich; *Art Director:* Charles M. Kirk; *Film Editor:* James Smith.

CAST

Carol Dempster (*Joan Daisy Royle*); W. C. Fields (*Her Father*); James Kirkwood (*Calvin Clarke, Deputy District Attorney*); Harrison Ford (*Fred Ketlar "the King of Jazz"*); Marie Chambers (*Adele Ketlar*); Paul Everton (*George Baretta*); George Rigas (*His Henchman*); Florence Auer (*Baretta's "Girl"*); Ida Waterman (*Mrs. Clarke*); Alice Laidley (*Clarke's Fiancée*); Dorothea Love (*Lola Neeson*); Dore Davidson (*Elman*); Frank Allworth (*Oliver*); Bobby Watson (*Hofer*).

SYNOPSIS

Chicago. Up to the age of 20, Joan Daisy Royle has known nothing of life except what she has observed from her doll-faced, cheap, drug-taking mother and a charming but nevertheless fuddling stepfather. When she learns that this man she adores and calls "Father" isn't her real father, she decides to shift for herself. She has kept pretty straight despite all the pitfalls and finds inspiration in Saint-Gaudens's statue of her ideal, Abraham Lincoln, in Lincoln Park.

The Royles make one of their many moves—to avoid rent—and in their new "home" Joan meets Fred Ketlar, an orchestra leader who has great abilities as a composer. Fred falls in love with Joan, but she treats him as a friend because she believes in his genius. Also, he is married.

One night as Joan passes Mrs. [Adele] Ketlar's flat, she sees the shadows of the woman and some man, whom she thinks is Fred, but on second look she doesn't think it is. A little later, Fred calls on her, and after she stops his advance he leaves in a huff.

Mrs. Ketlar is murdered, and Fred is arrested for the crime. The police take Joan for his mistress and browbeat her. The district attorney, Calvin Clarke, is a New Englander, transplanted to the West, and he has the old "sons of the American Revolution" idea: Anyone who arrived after 1700 is not desirable. So he has decided to get rid of the "foreign" element. Having heard the names Royle and Ketlar, he makes up his mind that here are two more victims. They are tried, convicted, and sentenced before he arrives on the scene.

But strange to relate, he falls very hard for Miss Royle, even after his background and training. Ketlar lies about how he spent the evening, and makes his case look bad. Joan's stepfather lies, too, which doesn't help any. Calvin goes right on planning his conviction of Ketlar, but he keeps getting hints and notes about "George Baretta," an underworld figure who was known to be involved with Adele Ketlar.

The case comes to trial. Joan makes a fine impression in her direct examination by Elman, Ketlar's attorney. Calvin reveals some lies about the whole thing, which disqualifies her testimony, and bewilders the jury. Fred is convicted of the murder, and Joan determines to clear his name simply because "right is right." She appeals to District Attorney Clarke, but he says he can do nothing.

Joan, disguised, enters Baretta's headquarters, the Boar's Head Inn, with the aid of a venturesome reporter. Together, they get evidence of Baretta's guilt. Joan is discovered, but suddenly a terrible cyclone crashes through the city. The inn is destroyed and all the gangsters—Baretta included—are killed.

Joan and Clarke telephone the governor in time to save Ketlar from imminent execution.

Fred tries to persuade Joan to marry him, but she refuses. She loves Calvin. Chorus girl Lola Neeson takes Fred away from Joan, and they get married. Clarke hears about it and goes to see Joan. He tells her how much she means to him and she accepts him. Clarke takes her in his arms in tender betrothal.

> —Paramount Story Department, the *American Film Institute Catalog* [1921–1930], and various reviews

THE PRODUCTION

Although D. W. Griffith is rightfully regarded as one of the masters of the American cinema, not all of his films were created equal. Griffith produced one masterwork after another in the teens—*The Birth of a Nation* (1915), *Intolerance* (1916), *Broken Blossoms* (1919), to name just the most obvious ones—yet no sooner did the twenties hit than the quality of his work began to slide rapidly and alarmingly.

The reasons for Griffith's decline are too many and complex to go into here. But I don't believe I am painting with too broad a brush when I mark as the beginning of the end the day in 1925 when Griffith signed a contract with Famous Players–Lasky/Paramount. Previously, with his own D. W. Griffith Productions (which distributed through United Artists), the director had the freedom to make films as he saw fit. At Paramount, he was just another hired hand, compelled to take on projects that he might otherwise have avoided—like *"That Royle Girl."*

Griffith must have seen from the start that things weren't going to go smoothly with Paramount. He took his first film under the new contract (*Sally of the Sawdust* (1925), starring Carol Dempster and W. C. Fields) away from Paramount and released it through United Artists. Although it isn't a particularly good film, *Sally of the Sawdust* was commercially successful. Paramount immediately put Griffith, Dempster, and Fields together again for a follow-up.

Unfortunately, *"That Royle Girl"* had already been turned down by most of Paramount's top directors, and Griffith didn't want to do it himself. In a plaintive letter to Paramount head Adolph Zukor, he com-

Carole Dempster and W. C. Fields

plained that he didn't think he could make a good film of *"That Royle Girl."* But Zukor and Jesse Lasky insisted.

Although there's no way to tell if Griffith was able to pull something interesting out of his bag of tricks, on paper *"That Royle Girl"* doesn't really sound like his cup of tea. Its Jazz Age aura could hardly be more alien to Griffith who, as an artist, was always far more comfortable in the past than in the present.

Edwin Balmer's original story had been purchased by Paramount on April 20, 1925 for thirty-five thousand dollars (the film in its entirety cost $607,000). It was quickly adapted for the screen by Paul Schofield (later to write *Beau Geste* (1926) for director Herbert Brenon) and filming began in Chicago late that summer. This location footage of 1925 Chicago would undoubtedly be among the more interesting facets of *"That Royle Girl"* today; Griffith filmed at Edgewater Beach, on Lake Shore Drive, and in Lincoln Park, where Daisy Royle talks to her hero, Abraham Lincoln — or at least to his statue by Saint-Gaudens.

Another reason to regret the loss of the film is the presence of W. C. Fields, even though *Variety* claimed he didn't "belong in the picture. He has nothing to do, and does it just like a man with nothing to do would do it."[1] In Griffith's *Sally of the Sawdust* the previous year, Fields provided virtually all of the film's bright spots; even some of his title cards unmis-

Mr. Fields as an object of tittering

takably evoke his persona and characteristic use of language. It's possible
that he similarly shone in *"That Royle Girl."* But his drunken, oblivious lout
of a father seems neither funny nor poignant on paper, while his irre-
sponsible dad in *Sally of the Sawdust* was both. His interaction in *Sally* with
Carol Dempster was touching and believable, and perhaps their chemistry
survived the uninspired story of *"That Royle Girl."*

Despite *Variety'*s negative opinion of Fields's contribution, most
other critics acknowledged his humorous impact on audiences:

"W. C. Fields, that inimitable zigzagging pillar of drollery, might
have been used to more extensive advantage," wrote Michael L. Simmons. "The audience met his every appearance with bubbling murmurs
of mirth, but his appearances were all too few."[2]

Harrison's Reports agreed. "It seems as if Mr. Fields has caught the
spirit of the average spectator, because one hears nothing but giggles
wherever he is ushered into a scene. The scene where he lights his cigar
and, instead of putting the candle back in the chandelier puts the cigar
into it and then places the candle in his mouth should draw roars of
laughter."[3]

Carol Dempster, appearing in her sixth feature with Griffith, was
an actress of charm and skill. Since it is believed Griffith cast her so
often because he was in love with her, Dempster remains rather underrated as an actress. Happily, most of the rest of her work with the director survives, so we can at least imagine the kind of performance she
delivered in *"That Royle Girl."*

Critically, Dempster's "versatile portrayal of the title role"[4] was generally well received. "She is in turn gay, grave, saucy, tearful, vivacious,
and lovable, with a competence that is entertaining and impressive."[5]

Mordaunt Hall of the *New York Times* found a refreshing physicality
in Dempster's performance. "Occasionally [she] is called upon to emu-
late Tom Mix, Douglas Fairbanks, and Richard Dix in acrobatic stunts,"
he wrote, "especially when she escapes through the flustered coterie of
scoundrels. There is no denying that she gives a splendid account of
herself in these wild passages, especially when she escapes from a building hand-over-hand along a painter's ladder conveniently placed for the
escapade."[6]

It is indicative of the great esteem in which Griffith was still held in 1926 that even those critics who didn't care for *"That Royle Girl"* went out of their way to find something good to say about it. Mordaunt Hall particularly admired a scene where Daisy Royle "pauses at a partly opened door before entering a room, and one perceives only half her face with one of her bright eyes as she hesitates wonderingly."[7]

While reviewer Michael Simmons found the story to contain only "the slightest suggestion of plot," he acknowledged Griffith's mastery in making certain that "real entertainment will result. 'Meller' [old-fashioned melodrama] reigns supreme, but it's all good meaty box office stuff."[8]

And most of the critics agreed that the climactic cyclone was masterfully filmed. "When it strikes a building, it makes it collapse like a house of cards. Roofs and sides of houses are seen crumbling, and trees uprooted and carried away as if mere toys. In short, it is as realistic a reproduction of a tornado as it could be made by human ingenuity. It thrills one to watch it."[9]

Variety thought *"That Royle Girl"* was too much of something that wouldn't be so hot at any length, advising that at least thirty minutes be trimmed before the film went into general release. One hundred and fourteen minutes was "a terribly long time to sit through any picture — no matter how good, [and this is] the poorest thing Griffith has turned out in a great many years."[10]

"That Royle Girl" opened at New York's Mark Strand Theater on January 10, 1926. During a tense moment when Daisy Royle is being pursued by "an individual with an evil eye," the film broke, and the screen was dark for several minutes. "But the hiatus instead of hurting the interest in the story rather heightened the suspense."[11]

After the screening, Griffith, Dempster, and James Kirkwood took to the stage and spoke briefly to the audience. Although the hundreds who made up the overflow crowd at the Strand that night seemed enthusiastic about *"That Royle Girl,"* it was not a harbinger of great things to come. It was respectably successful at the box office but was far from a hit. This must have been particularly galling to Griffith, since he made it clear that he had directed the film only for commercial reasons, to allow him to indulge his "art visions and . . . creative dreams and [the] vistas of the golden glow of humanity . . . as I once did in *Broken Blossoms,* the most artistic picture I ever produced."[12]

"That Royle Girl" is one of the American Film Institute's most wanted lost films, but the indications are strong that it is probably the least worthy movie on that sad roster. It would certainly be interesting to see — W. C. Fields in *anything* is worth the effort — but its loss is far less painful than that of most of the other films in this book.

Perhaps this is because — happily — the great majority of D. W. Griffith's work survives. Since we can evaluate the films he made before and after *"That Royle Girl,"* we can get a fairly good idea of the way he would have handled this project. And since we also know that his heart wasn't in the film, it seems probable that he didn't go out of his way to make it transcend its unpromising origins. And if you don't think Griffith could triumph over the most preposterous balderdash, making compelling art out of nearly nothing, then you haven't seen *Way Down East.*

For whatever magic Griffith was able to work with this scenario, for the location footage of Chicago in the twenties, for the climactic cyclone, and for the performances of Dempster and Fields — let's hope that one day *"That Royle Girl"* returns to us, to prove all of our worst suspicions wrong.

17

THE LAST MOMENT

Samuel Freedman–Edward M. Spitz. Distributed by Zakoro Film Corporation.
Released February 15, 1928. Six reels; 5,600 feet.

CREDITS

Director/Writer/Film Editor: Paul Fejos; *Photography:* Leon Shamroy.

CAST

Otto Matiesen (*The Man*); Julius Molnar, Jr. (*The Man as a Child*); Lucille La Verne (*The Innkeeper*); Anielka Elter (*A Woman*); Georgia Hale (*His Second Wife*); Isabelle Lamore (*His First Wife*); Vivian Winston (*A Woman*).

SYNOPSIS

It is a scientific fact that the human brain extracts all the experiences from life and at times crowds them all into one short moment.

View of a man drowning, his hand reaching out in a vain effort, and down he goes again; and as he thus acts, there are flashes of his life coming before him. He is stationary, a mere onlooker as it were, while all these scenes are passing over him. It is a clown that is drowning, and the first thing he remembers is the nursery and the nursery rhymes.

In a room we see children busy over reading and arithmetic.

In the schoolroom, a girl is studying at her desk, while a boy is at the blackboard, and the lady teacher is severely scolding him.

In a home, the father is rough with his little daughter as he looks at the poor report card. He wants to beat her, but the mother steps in and interferes, as the shadows on the wall show how the cruel father is about to beat the child.

Then, the Church bells are ringing. In the Church, the boy is kneeling at the communion railing and receiving at the hands of the priest his first Holy Communion. In the same Church is the statue of the Blessed Virgin, and the boy is kneeling in front of it, praying.

The years have slipped by, and in a home there is a birthday cake with candles upon a table. It is the son's birthday, and he is a young man by this time. Among other birthday gifts he has received a watch and from his mother a copy of Shakespeare, which delights him more than anything else. He cannot wait, but opens it right then and there to *Hamlet*, at the soliloquy, and he reads it to them with much feeling.

View of a stick beating a bass drum. It is a circus drum, and as the scene is widened there are seen many circus posters stuck over everywhere depicting the famous Collette, the dancer and acrobat. He stands there at the posters and looks, with artistic eye, at the female figure and admires it, and hopes to be able to get acquainted with the original.

View of a dancer's feet. The camera moves up and reveals the knees and upper legs and the flimsy dress and finally the full figure of Collette, and our young man looks on her with admiration.

After the show he leaves the place and stops outside and again looks at the poster displaying Collette.

In his home we see this young man sitting at his table, pen in hand and all flustered, evidently writing a love missive to his beloved Collette. On the table there is a candlestick with seven lit candles. He thinks and muses, and as the hours fly by, the candles burn lower and lower, and finally they go out.

At the Circus we find our lover sitting on a box near Collette's door, and soon a man requiring the box makes him get up. But there is another right opposite this one, and here he sits and waits and whistles merrily. At last she comes out of her dressing room, all made up for her act, and [with her] on his arm they both leave the scene.

Clock at home shows 10 P.M. and the son is coming home from his visit. As he enters the parental room, his father is waiting for him, loaded with invective, and [the] father starts at once to upbraid his son for his shameful behavior. For a little time the son lets his father rave on, and when the latter is done raving, the son dives into him and replies in the same manner, which the father resents. He never suspected this, and says that he is through.

In his bedroom the son is seen packing up his few things, among which is the volume of Shakespeare. His packing done, he now leaves the house.

At the front porch, as he is leaving the door, his mother accompanies him and weeps bitterly and hugs him close to her. She takes her picture out of her locket and hands it to him. He puts it into his watch case. Then, kissing his mother once more, he leaves her, and again and again looks back at her. She blesses him and wishes him godspeed, and then the door is closed as [the] mother goes back in.

View of [a] stool standing at the steps of a railroad coach. A man is stepping up and entering. In the coach our young man is seen taking his seat.

View of the track as seen in front of the moving train.

View of the wheels of the locomotive and the steam issuing.

View of the whistle blowing.

Another view of the track with a sharp curve ahead.

View of the locomotive bell ringing.

View of our friend sitting in his chair, musing and thinking. Before his eyes there passes the picture of his mother, of Collette, and of his angry father, and he thinks of his home.

View of the train dashing around a curve.

In the distance can be seen the seashore with [a] sailing vessel at anchor. He is anxious to get away from it all as far as possible and thinks if he could get on board that ship he might get away far enough. With longing eyes he looks out.

View of the ship deck; men hoisting the sails.

In a rowboat our friend is speeding towards the wharf where the sailing vessel is anchored. View of the expanse of ocean as seen from his skiff and the sailing vessel in the distance.

View of the ship deck and close-up of compass and gong.

In the hold. Our friend has found his way in unperceived. He is frightened, for he hears a sailor coming and tries to hide behind some boxes, and tries to be as quiet as possible, but the man seems to be looking for something and accidentally stumbles upon the stowaway. Roughly, he drags him out and up.

On deck we see the sailor dragging the young man roughly out of the cabin door; he sets him to work, and after some abuse, leads him into the Captain's quarters.

In the Captain's cabin, the sailor brings in the stowaway and presents him to the half-drunk Captain, who hits him. The lad tumbles backwards upon the bed.

Next we find him scrubbing the companionway with soap and water.

In his bunk we find him lying in his bed; the volume of Shakespeare is his only companion, and he amuses himself much by reciting to himself, much to the annoyance of the rest of the crew, and when it is getting too much for them, the one in the upper berth sticks down his foot into the youth's bunk. He understands the signal and quits reciting.

On deck we now see our friend in the rigging, standing like a proud king, fanned by the breeze and feeling free and happy.

View of a calendar, and one by one the leaves are torn off as the days pass.

At last they have reached land again, and in the streets of a city we find our young friend walking along, looking at the sights and wishing for some kind of an excitement.

As he walks along the sidewalk, he comes to the lower section of a seacoast town. It is night and the sidewalk is dark, when all of a sudden a door is opened, and the flood of light from the room is thrown upon the sidewalk. A man staggers out and leaves the door open. Our young friend steps up to the door and looks, and above the door sees a huge beer bottle hanging, as a sign. He looks in and finds it is a saloon where men and women are carousing. After looking and wondering whether he ought to go in, he enters.

View of the dancers and of the piano man playing.

He stands a little back by himself and looks upon the scene.

In the corner of the room there is an elderly woman, evidently one of authority about the place, the way she frowns at the girls as they come and ask her for the different bottles, and she deals them out, and scolds them when the liquor doesn't seem to go fast enough. When he sees a chance, he goes up to this woman and wants to know if it is alright for him to recite something to the company. The woman says alright, if the rest are willing to listen.

The man at the piano has gotten tired of playing by hand, so he turns a crank to make the piano play. Our friend has leaped upon the table and starts reciting his Shakespeare, but the carousing mob has no heart or ears for such things, and the drinking and dancing and gambling are going on as if he were not there at all. But he keeps on just the same, to the few who show a little interest, half intoxicated though they be.

By the piano stands a good-looking dancer who is quite interested in the recitation and more in the reciter.

View of a row of bottles, and the pendulum of the clock seen swinging back and forth through them, an ominous shadow.

He, too, has been drinking, and the stuff is telling on him. He has the girl in his arms and loves her. She, in her foolishness, pulls his watch and chain out of his pocket, holds it up for a moment, and then drops it on the floor, and the watch falls to pieces. Mother's picture is face up, lying among the wreck. She then asks him for a dance, and as they dance toward the watch, first she, then he, step upon mother's picture. Then, in his intoxicated condition, he sees the shining thing on the floor and sees it is his watch. He excuses himself to the girl and on his hands and knees he crawls among the dancers, and just as he almost has his watch and the picture, it is shuffled away from him. After several trials he picks it up, looks at the picture, sees how it has been damaged by being trampled on, and replaces it in the watch case. Then he goes out into the night.

In a stage[coach] he is seen riding, when the horses shy at something. There is a runaway and a wreck.

Typewriter is writing the daily report sheet for the doctor of a case: how the night was passed and other items.

View of an operation chair being wheeled in, and our friend on it. The nurse puts ether on him preparatory for the operation.

View of the various instruments and paraphernalia.

The operation performed, we see him lying in bed, the nurse being very kind to him and giving him the medicine. He wakes up and sees the nurse and sees her smile and is at once attracted to her. He pets and kisses her hand as she hands him the spoon.

Then in time he is fully recovered, and again we see the typewriter writing the report of recovery for the doctor.

Our patient is now well again, and this bright morning we see him standing upon the hospital steps, taking fond leave of his favorite nurse. As he goes down, she accompanies him and then with another fond look he departs, and she ascends again the steps.

Again we find ourselves in a saloon, with a close-up of a gambling table, the cards and chips much in the foreground.

Upon another table stands our poet and actor, and he is reciting his Shakespeare to the unappreciative audience while the tobacco smoke is curling and blowing up around him, almost stifling him; but he keeps on. Close-ups of the different ones around the tables as they listen and watch, most of them indifferent. When he is done, there is no little applause and hand clapping, and he stands upon the table, amidst the smoke, and bows himself out and descends.

Among the ones that have interestedly listened to him is a gentleman, hidden away at a table, all by himself. When our friend comes down from the table, the man calls to him. The young man steps up to him and takes a seat. The man tells the youth he has been much pleased and impressed with his reading and wants to know if he would consider an engagement, and hands him a card, for he is a theatrical man. The young man is happy and agrees, and the other tells him to come to his office in the morning and talk over the contract. The manager leaves, and the young man is happy.

Next day, at the appointed hour, we find our young man in the manager's office. They discuss the contract and the part he is expected to play and he is exceedingly happy, for the dream of his whole life has at last come true.

Typewriter writes contract for Casino Theater.

In his dressing room we find out young actor, making up for his part as Hamlet.

Stage as seen from the wings. He is stepping upon the stage and recites his lines.

View of the audience and their wild applause as he is done.

Outside, at the stage exit, there waits his sweetheart, the nurse. After the show he is seen coming out, and finding her there, he is agreeably surprised. They whisper something lovingly to each other and leave the scene.

In the park we see the two lovers walk on, arm in arm. They are happy as a pair of schoolchildren and romp around, catching each other. They love each other fondly.

View of two wedding rings and two love birds; then, two other birds fighting in a cage.

They are now married and in their parlor we see them sitting, one in one chair, the other in another, their backs to each other. The first squall has struck the marriage ship.

In the sink of the kitchen can be seen the pile of unwashed dishes.

In the bedroom, we find them both in bed, fighting and quarrelling with each other.

Then there appears the statue of Justice standing upon the table of the divorce judge, with the gavel lying upon divorce papers. View of him and her, with quite a space between them. The divorce is granted.

Then through the scene there appears the pendulum of time as it strikes to and fro, to and fro. Then there appears the scratched and dimmed and mutilated picture of [the] mother, the pendulum still beating back and forth.

Now, in a parlor, we find our young man with a new flame; he is making new love to Collette.

At the door there is seen a finger pushing a button.

In the parlor, the two are alarmed, especially she, when a man enters. Angered at seeing the actor with his wife, he hands him the card for challenge to a duel to avenge the husband's honor.

Again we see how the sheets are torn from the calendar, day by day, and at last we find our actor friend in a solitary, unfurnished room. He is sitting at the table when the husband enters with the swords and seconds and lets him choose.

Then a chalk line is seen being drawn upon the floor. The two men are fighting the sword duel, and the husband is killed.

In the dressing room of the theater, the calendar again is torn day by day, to show the flight of time. In the theater he again is playing Hamlet to an appreciative house.

After the performance we see a great crowd gathered at a café, where people are playing at roulette and dancing and drinking, and we see our actor friend ambling through the mob to the roulette. He steps up and puts down some money and luck is with him, for he just scrapes the money in to himself. Then to win still more, he sets down the whole winnings, and loses it all. Then he leaves the table in disgust. As he passes to the stairway to get his hat and coat, the head waiter recognizes him as the one who used to recite in the saloon. Down the stairs comes that same girl with whom he made so free in that same saloon, and she also recognizes him, but he pays no attention to either of them.

At the Casino Theater, our friend is playing the part of Pierrot and on the stage (as seen from the wings) is playing and singing, and the audience is much pleased. When he is done, he returns to the wings, where a stagehand is waiting for him who hands him a dispatch. It is a note that his mother is critically ill and that he should come home without delay. Not even waiting to change clothes, he runs from the theater in his clown costume, through the streets.

Close-up of a candle almost burnt down. It gets lower and lower, flickers and sputters, and then goes out. Mother is dead.

Through the streets, running at high speed, the son arrives at the steps of the home [from] where he has been exiled all these years. He is loath to enter. He is just about to open the door and go in when the door opens and men are carrying out a casket. Before him they stop, and in his memory he sees upon the black casket the vision of the scene in the saloon, the lovemaking with the dancer, the broken watch and mother's picture trampled underfoot. He weeps at the memory, and they carry the casket by him out of scene. For a moment he stands; then he follows them.

In the churchyard is seen a shovel throwing dirt into the grave. Then, when the little mound is heaped up, we find the clown standing there, looking sadly upon it.

Now, war is declared. To forget his sorrows, our friend has joined the forces, and we see him fighting in the trenches, while the [shells] are bursting all around him.

In the trench his pal is hurt, and to amuse him and make him forget his troubles, the actor makes a doll out of his handkerchief and starts a Punch and Judy show, at which the wounded man laughs heartily. But the life blood is slowly oozing away, and with a smile on his face, the pal expires in the arms of the actor.

Peace has been declared, and the forces are again returned to their peacetime occupations.

Close-up of a notice at a theater, announcing the date for rehearsal.

View of a stage, with director in foreground, while in the background the actor is rehearsing a room scene with an actress and others in the play. In the scene the girl is supposed to rush up to him and say, I LOVE YOU, and she does this so realistically, and she really means it, that he is dumbfounded. Their eyes meet in mutual understanding, the hands meet in a loving clasp.

We see them walking arm in arm along the garden path to a little fish pond. They sit down on a rustic bench and love and kiss each other.

View of the two pair of hands and the minister placing the wedding rings thereon.

View of the organist's hands playing upon the keys the "Wedding March."

In the church, view of the wedding couple leaving the sanctuary.

Arrived in their home, the two newlyweds are very loving to each other, kid each other, make faces at each other, then kiss.

In the bedroom, they are both in bed. She is awake but he is still asleep, and she is just itching to caress him and wants to stroke his hair, but is afraid she may wake him and she doesn't want to do that.

At the theater, our friend is again playing the part of the Clown. The orchestra is playing, and he appears upon the stage and sings and plays.

In his dressing room after the performance, the phone rings. He answers. It is the maid from his home talking excitedly that something is wrong and for him to come home at once. All worried and excited, he leaves the room in his costume and runs through the streets. He arrives at his home, enters the hall—nobody there—then hastens up the steps to his wife's bedroom.

In the bedroom he finds the doctors and nurses with their backs to the bed. He goes to the bed and finds that the only woman he ever loved has been snatched from him. His heart is torn in agony. He goes to the next room and stands by the mirror of the dressing table and looks at himself: the Clown. As he looks down he sees a motto card saying: "This world's a stage, and in our life we are all called upon to play many parts." He looks at himself. He is playing the part of the Clown just now. With a hysterical laugh he picks up a candlestick and dashes it into the mirror, and there he sees himself reflected in the thousand pieces. Sad and despondent, he leaves the room, dragging his cloak after him. Life is not worth living anymore.

Through the garden he walks, down to the brink of the lake, still dragging his cloak after him. He wades into the water, deeper and deeper, and sees the distorted image of himself as he disturbs the water. Deeper and deeper he goes and at last sinks out of sight. His hand comes up once more and he is gone.

Through the water he seems to see his last vision of his mother, his angry father and his last beloved wife.

Upon the surface of the water we see remnants of the Clown's garments floating. A few bubbles come up, and now all is still.

S Y N O P S I S   N O T E

A special note about this synopsis is in order. It comes from a collection called *Silent Synopses* at the Margaret Herrick Library of the Academy of Motion Picture Arts and Sciences. It is not known who wrote it, except that he or she was a theater musician. One theory is that this musician wrote detailed synopses of films as a way of planning the musical accompaniment. There are dozens of such synopses in this collection, and there must have been hundreds originally. Except for correcting spelling and punctuation errors, I have elected to leave this sometimes naive writing alone. All the other synopses in this book come from the studios or from trade magazines. But this is an extremely valuable record of a person literally scribbling down everything that he sees. If the syntax of this synopsis is a little skewed, its immediacy and life are invaluable. This screening of *The Last Moment*, by the way, occurred at an unknown city's Casino Theater on Sunday, November 18, 1928. Coincidentally, the Casino Theater is also the name of the theater in the film in which our hero appears as Pierrot.

....

THE PRODUCTION

When Paul Fejos died on April 23, 1963, the *New York Times* mentioned his career as a filmmaker only as a kind of afterthought. It was his position as president and research director for Wenner-Gren Foundation for Anthropological Research that made him noteworthy in the *Times*'s eyes. In fact, Fejos's career was even more diverse than that. Born Pal Fejos on January 27, 1897, in Budapest, he received a medical degree at the Royal Hungarian Medical University in that city. During World War I he served on the Italian front, indulging his interest in the theater by organizing plays for the soldiers.

After the war he designed sets for operas and in 1919 began directing films for various studios. He came to the United States in 1924. After working for a while in a piano factory, Fejos began working as a bacteriologist for the Rockefeller Institute of Medical Research in New York. His desire to make motion pictures led him to California two years later.

Fejos supported himself briefly by working in a commercial clinical laboratory at a Los Angeles hospital. The work, however, kept him too busy to pursue landing a job at a studio, so he quit and began living on the streets, sometimes sleeping in orange groves where he could at least steal some food. He also boxed professionally now and then, earning five dollars per round—"plus cauliflower ears, which were with him as long as he lived."[1]

A meeting with Edward M. Spitz, a would-be producer, led Fejos

Otto Matieson (*center*) in a still from the film *The Salvation Hunters*. No stills from *The Last Moment* are available.

to begin work on a feature film that would, in his words, "be timeless."[2] He explained to Spitz his theory "that the motion picture does not use one of its greatest assets, and that is that one can be, regardless of time and space, anywhere, and that the jump in time or in space can be made without pain for the audience. So one can designate loss of time by a candle which burns down, and so on. I told him I wanted to make a film this way. I also told him that I would like to make a story which happened during an impossibly short time. He said, 'How short?' I said, 'A second, a fraction of a second.' "[3]

In *The Last Moment*, Fejos wanted to tell the story of a man's life, as it flashes before his eyes in the split second before he drowns. This basic idea was later used in Mervyn LeRoy's *Two Seconds* (1932) starring Edward G. Robinson as a man dying in the electric chair, who reviews his life in, as the title suggests, two seconds.

Spitz told Fejos that he was "either crazy or you're a genius!"[4] and gave him five thousand dollars to get started.

Fejos got *The Last Moment* made with more chutzpah than cash. He talked Georgia Hale, recently Chaplin's costar in *The Gold Rush* (1925), into appearing in the film for free. Otto Matiesen, a struggling actor, eagerly accepted the gratis leading role just for the exposure [Matiesen continued in minor roles in films until the early thirties]. Fejos convinced the general manager of the Fine Arts Studio, at 4500 Sunset Boulevard, to rent him studio space by the minute so that Fejos could move onto a set as soon as another company was through with it, and then leave quickly when the real paying customers were ready to shoot again.

He then met with a representative from DuPont and somehow talked the company into providing on credit all the raw film stock he needed.

Because it proved to be impossible to coordinate the availability of his actors with his sporadic access to his sets, Fejos had to be creative. When Georgia Hale was available, he filmed her close-ups, but when she wasn't, he used a double whom he filmed from the back. Often he found himself filming scenes in which the two leading players figured and in which neither actor was present. Many of the scenes of the romance, marriage, and breakup of the characters played by Hale and Matiesen consisted of shots of hands, lips, church bells, calendar pages, love birds in a cage that dissolves to two black crows biting each other. "There was a shot," Fejos later remembered, "of a bedroom and a bed, with just two heads—you couldn't see who they were—and the man reached over and yanked the pillow away from the woman. So there were all sorts of symbolic shots, suggesting that the marriage had gone on the rocks. Then came a hand holding a gavel . . . [and the] interlocutory decree. I mean, this was in seconds, and it meant five years. And the whole film was made this way. The aim was to make it in kaleidoscope-like speed, as it might seem in actuality to the hero when he was dying."[5]

Fejos completed *The Last Moment* in about three months, reportedly for a budget of about thirteen thousand dollars. Now, however, he faced an even more daunting task: finding a distributor. He showed the film to two influential critics, Welford Beaton of the *Film Spectator* and Tamar Lane of *Film Mercury*. Both men were completely overwhelmed by *The Last Moment*. Headlining his review, "Introducing to You Mr. Paul Fejos, Genius," Beaton called the film "one of the most outstanding works of cinematic art that was ever brought to the screen."[6] Beaton told Charlie Chaplin about *The Last Moment;* after Chaplin saw it, he arranged for United Artists to distribute the film. Its critical success led to the offer of a Universal contract to Fejos.

Fejos's cinematographer was a young man named Leon Shamroy, who had only been shooting features for about a year. He later called *The Last Moment* "the first of my experimental films."[7] Shamroy claimed that he "promoted $4,000 and the stage space for it, arranged laboratory work, and everything. It was the first silent picture made without any explanatory titles, it was all done in subjective camera."[8]

Shamroy was later to become one of Hollywood's most honored cinematographers, winning Academy Awards for *The Black Swan* (1942), *Wilson* (1944), *Leave Her to Heaven* (1945), and *Cleopatra* (1963). But he won nothing for *The Last Moment,* he claimed—not even another job.

"Fejos was a charming guy," Shamroy said, "but a charlatan. He double-crossed me. When the picture was shown and everyone liked it, [Universal's] Carl Laemmle [Jr.] signed us up as a team, but Fejos deliberately left me out in the cold. He shunned me completely, even though I had contributed so much, and I was literally starving because of this."[9]

The Last Moment previewed in the Beverly Theater in Los Angeles in November, 1927, and opened in New York on March 12, 1928. All the critics lauded its artistic effects, while doubting whether there was much of an audience for this sort of experimentation. "It's a picture for the Greenwich Village faddists to chew over," said *Variety*, which also called the film an "interesting, freaky, and slightly morbid arty picture."[10]

The *New York Times*, on the other hand, called it "remarkable" and filmed with "a wonderful aptitude for true cinematic ideas" and "an enviable fund of imagination."[11]

"Fejos displays considerable imagination in his direction and is apparently an adherent of the Continental school which goes in heavily for unique camera angles," wrote the *Film Daily*. "Parts of the production are extremely interesting; parts are not. An intelligent experiment."[12]

Paul Fejos stayed in Hollywood only a few more years, indulging his experimental tendencies when possible (he is credited for devising, with cinematographer Hal Mohr, the camera crane, which he first used on his 1929 production *Broadway*) and directing the French and German versions of George Hill's *The Big House* (1931). The only film of Fejos's that can easily be found these days is *Lonesome* (a.k.a. *Solitude*, 1929) an early experiment in cinema verité. He returned to Hungary in 1931 and made films there, as well as in Austria and Denmark, for the next decade. When he came back to America it was to join the Wenner–Gren Foundation to continue his career as an anthropologist.

With *Lonesome* as our only clue today, Fejos seems to have been an extraordinarily gifted filmmaker. *The Last Moment* may or may not have been his best film, but it is certainly the one he made at his most unfettered. By all accounts, Fejos manipulated cinematic techniques with a freedom that must have been exhilarating, even if the film itself wasn't entirely successful. "Here we see a motion picture cut free of its established mould and striving for a purer form," as one critic put it. "*The Last Moment* is another milestone at which our hopes for the motion picture can be replenished and our enthusiasm renewed."[13]

18

THE ROUGH RIDERS

Paramount Famous Players–Lasky Corporation. Released March 15, 1927.
Premiere version: Thirteen reels; 12,071 feet. Release version: Ten reels;
9,443 feet.

CREDITS

Presented by: Adolph Zukor and Jesse L. Lasky. *In Charge of Production:* B.P. Schulberg; *Producer:* Lucien Hubbard; *Director:* Victor Fleming; *Screenplay:* Robert N. Lee and Keene Thompson; *Titles:* George Marion, Jr.; *Adaptation:* John Fish Goodrich; *Story:* Hermann Hagedorn; *Photography:* James Wong Howe and Burton Steene; *Editor in Chief:* E. Lloyd Sheldon; *Assistant Director:* Henry Hathaway; *Business Managers:* Sidney Street and Tom Fortune; *Cutter and Clerk:* Susannah Whaley and Eda Warren; *Second Cameraman:* Rex Wimpy; *Assistant Cameramen:* Otto Pearce and Bob Rhea; *Special Effects:* Roy Pomeroy; *Musical Score Composed and/or Compiled by:* Dr. Hugo Riesenfeld.

CAST

Noah Beery (*Hell's Bells*); Charles Farrell (*Stewart Van Brunt*); George Bancroft (*Happy Joe*); Charles Emmett Mack (*Bert Henley*); Mary Astor (*Dolly*); Frank Hopper (*Theodore Roosevelt*); Col. Fred Lindsay (*Leonard Wood*); Fred Kohler (*Sergeant Stanton*); Ed Jones (*Double for Frank Hopper*).

SYNOPSIS

America, 1898. Cuba struggling for liberty. Spanish oppression — America protests. The *Maine* goes to Havana Harbor. Suddenly, without warning, one night the *Maine* is blown up. Wild excitement. Much oratory. Official investigations. A single man with the courage to act —

[Teddy] Roosevelt. In one hectic afternoon his acting secretary of the Navy gives the orders which get the Navy mobilized. War comes. Volunteers are called for. With his friend Leonard Wood, Roosevelt organizes the Rough Riders.

From every corner of the U.S.A. recruits assemble at San Antonio — cowboys, prospectors, Indians, silk-stockings; East and West, North and South, rich and poor — millionaires, college athletes, gamblers, law officers, and fugitives from justice. The welding of this extraordinary aggregation of independent individualists into a regiment makes veteran officers despair. There never was a rodeo like the first "mounted drill" — but Roosevelt does the job — because he is human and hasn't forgotten how to laugh.

Among the characters who crowd the foreground are three with whom we are specially concerned — a gay young blade from New York, Van; an attractive young Texan, Bert; and Dolly. There are other characters who play a big part in the story — Leonard Wood, strong, quiet, human; a hard-boiled top-sergeant; a cowboy named Happy Joe who skips jail to enlist; and a sheriff known as Hell's Bells, who likewise enlisted in order to be near his man — these all weave in and out of the story; but the romance belongs to Van and Dolly and Bert with the regiment as a background, and Roosevelt dominating them all.

Bert has been devoted to Dolly since childhood. She has agreed — almost — to marry him. When the lighthearted, powerful New Yorker comes to thrill her in spite of herself, Bert is like a faithful collie. But Van is like a greyhound who ruthlessly pushes aside the less aggressive lover. Dolly is momentarily carried away by the sweep of her own feelings for him. She does not admit that she loves Van, but Bert instantly senses the force of the new element which has entered their placid relations. In a jealous rage he goes to Van, strikes him, and is knocked down with one brutal blow. In the dramatic scenes which follow, Van, Bert, Dolly, Top Sergeant Stanton and Roosevelt himself are closely involved.

The regiment goes to Cuba, and Dolly is left behind. Van and Bert are forced to bunk together, and although at first they hate each other, they later grow to be great friends. Meanwhile, Roosevelt has won the admiration and affection of all by his courage, his hardihood, his warm human sympathy, and his complete devotion to their interests. In Cuba, as in San Antonio, he is the friend and father and brother, inspiring, leading, laughing, eating out of the same cup, sleeping under the same blanket, nursing them in sickness, fighting for their rights, bucking authority always for the sake of the underdog. He is everywhere in the story as he is everywhere in the regiment. The last sight of him in Cuba is not as the hero of the famous charge, but as the warm human being, sacrificing himself to help one of his "boys."

The romance ends where it began — in San Antonio. But until the survivor of the two lovers gets out of a cab at Dolly's house, the audience doesn't know whether it is Bert or Van. We see them again — for the last time — six years later — at the White House. Statesmen are waiting, but the Rough Riders have the precedence. In the White House, as in Cuba, the Colonel's deepest interest, first and last, is in the common affairs of "his boys."

—Paramount Story Department

THE PRODUCTION

"There is just enough history about *The Rough Riders* to satisfy those who like history and not enough to drive away the picture fans."
—*Motion Picture News*, March 25, 1927, p. 1035

In December 1925, Paramount producer Lucien Hubbard announced that the studio would soon make a film called *The Rough Riders*, the story of Theodore Roosevelt and his famous regiment of volunteers who served so heroically during the Spanish–American War. A news item in *Motion Picture News* stated that Hubbard and Roosevelt's official biographer, Hermann Hagedorn, would soon leave for Cuba to scout locations — and to seek the cooperation of the Cuban government.

"The picture will be produced on a lavish and impressive scale," the article went on to say. "It will be filmed in Hollywood with locations in Cuba and New York. It is hoped to enlist the aid of thousands of Cubans in the war sequences of the picture. Whoever is chosen to play the role of Roosevelt will be surrounded by a cast of brilliant names."[1]

Scenario writer James Shelley Hamilton (*North of 36*, 1924; *The Air Mail*, 1925) had completed a treatment on October 27, 1925; it was this version that sold Paramount on the project, but it was almost immediately scrapped. Several other writers tried to come up with a good plot, but their treatments were also found wanting. Hubbard himself took a crack at distilling the complex historical saga into a manageable screen melodrama, turning in his first attempt on June 9, 1926. This, too, was missing something, so Hubbard assigned the troublesome project to writers Robert N. Lee and Keene Thompson, who worked from an original story by Hermann Hagedorn. John F. Goodrich then adapted it into a screenplay. The titles were turned over to George Marion, Jr., who had written witty titles for everything from *Ella Cinders* (1925) starring Colleen Moore to *Son of the Sheik* (1926), Rudolph Valentino's last film.

One of Hollywood's best directors, Victor Fleming, was assigned to the picture. Having started out directing Douglas Fairbanks's action comedies in 1919, Fleming had quickly established himself as a tough, virile director who knew how to get the job done with a minimum of fuss. More crucially, he had an almost infallible commercial sense. Throughout his long and distinguished career his films were nearly always popular with both critics and audiences.

The cast included Charles Farrell and Mary Astor as the romantic interests and Noah Beery and George Bancroft as the comedy backup. Charles Emmett Mack also had a role. It was his next-to-last film. On March 17, 1927, just as *The Rough Riders* opened, Mack was killed in an automobile accident while filming *The First Auto* with Gibson Gowland and Patsy Ruth Miller.

Teddy Roosevelt look-alike Frank Hopper, a Los Angeles book agent, was cast only after Paramount tested hundreds of applicants. The role apparently demanded very little acting, and Hopper seems to have acquitted himself well enough: "While he occasionally overemphasizes the characteristics of that indomitable American, his resemblance to Colonel Roosevelt is extraordinary."[2]

On Monday, August 9, 1926, the first scene of *The Rough Riders* was

Charles Farrell and Charles Emmett Mack enlist to do their bit in the Spanish-American war. George Bancroft is handling their luggage.

shot on the Paramount lot. The scene featured Frank Hopper in a replica of Roosevelt's office in the White House. The week was devoted to White House scenes, and on the following Saturday, August 14, the entire company left by train for San Antonio, Texas. They arrived the next Monday.

San Antonio had been the site of Roosevelt's original recruitment and training of the real Rough Riders, and Paramount decided to film these scenes at the old fairground where it actually took place. The lovely Texas city rolled out the red carpet for Fleming and the *Rough Riders* company. An official delegation met the train, and a military ball was held the evening of the first day to honor the arrival of the moviemakers.

A tender moment when Mary Astor wonders if she should permit Farrell's kiss.

The company stayed at the historic St. Anthony Hotel. What made things interesting around the place was the fact that William A. Wellman's *Wings* company was staying at the same place.

"San Antonio became the Armageddon of a magnificent sexual Donnybrook," wrote Wellman in his autobiography. "The town was lousy with movie people, and if you think that contributes to a state of tranquility, you don't know your motion picture ABCs.

"To begin with, all the young actors in *The Rough Riders* and *Wings* [which starred Clara Bow] fell in love with Clara Bow, and if you had known her, you could understand why. She took care of it—how, I will never know. They were handled like chessmen, never running into one another, never suspecting that there was any other man in the whole world that meant a thing to this gorgeous little sexpot—and all this maneuvering in a hotel where most of the flame was burning."[3]

Frank Hopper as Colonel Theodore Roosevelt gives Charles Farrell his orders. The stern sergeant is Fred Kohler.

Clara Bow was similarly popular outside the St. Anthony—but presumably for different reasons. She was "fairly mobbed by a thousand students of Texas State University when she visited the campus lately . . . and early in the same week she addressed the members of the State Senate and House on the subject of aviation."[4]

The Rough Riders company was in San Antonio for forty-eight camera days, filming from August 20 to October 14, 1926. "While there the company filmed the mobilization and training of the Roosevelt regiment and the battles of Las Guasimas, Kettle Hill, and San Juan Hill."[5]

Years later, cinematographer James Wong Howe said, "I always remember the sight of four hundred buckjumpers trying out their skill in breaking horses for our tests in San Antonio; there was so much dust you couldn't see anything except vague figures flying dismounted through the air."[6]

Fleming and his cast and crew arrived back in Los Angeles the first week of November and after a brief respite, moved up the coast to Santa Cruz, where they filmed for twenty-one days. In addition to the 150 cast and crew who arrived from Hollywood, extras recruited in Santa Cruz consisted of 600 U.S. troops, 350 Spanish and Cubans, and 250 Negroes. Among the scenes filmed in Santa Cruz were those depicting the landing of Roosevelt and his regiment on Cuban soil.[7]

One epic—and apparently effective—scene was filmed not on location, but within the confines of a Paramount stage: the sinking of the Maine was accomplished in a studio tank using miniatures.

And, finally, the closing scenes of the film incorporated newsreel footage of Teddy Roosevelt's inauguration, alternating documentary long shots with close-ups of Frank Hopper.

After a series of previews, Fleming brought his actors back into the studio to reshoot some of the scenes. The filmmakers had enormous trouble trying to decide how to end the film and seem to have reshot the climactic scenes several times, alternating between a tear-jerking finale and the happy ending that eventually won out. This final stage of production lasted from December 28, 1926, to January 8, 1927.

After all was said and done, *The Rough Riders* cost Famous Players–Lasky $1,410,000.

Farrell and Mack in the field.

The Rough Riders opened as a road show presentation at New York's George M. Cohan Theater just over two months later, on March 15, 1927. Dr. Hugo Riesenfeld had composed a musical score for the occasion that was liberally padded with hit songs of the 1898 period: "A Bicycle Built for Two," "Annie Rooney," "Good-bye, Molly Darling," "A Hot Time in the Old Town Tonight," "After the Ball," and many others.

Variety's "Fred." complained that the look of the film didn't reflect its high budget and that the entire enterprise didn't seem "special" enough for a road show. "There was considerable trouble with the film before it was finally ready to be shown, and when it finally did arrive on Broadway, it proved to be more or less of a disappointment."[8]

The less demanding *Harrison's Reports* found that the film contained "a genuinely sympathetic love story with plenty of pathos and human interest values as well as countless thrills, fast action, patriotic glow, and military atmosphere that stirs the blood. Its appeal will be strong to the middle-aged picture-goers who remember the days of 1898 . . . but the younger generation will also be thrilled by its melodramatic power and moved by its tender love romance."[9]

Most of the other major critics were similarly enthusiastic about the epic sweep and judicious use of humor and sentiment of *The Rough Riders*. The *New York Times*'s Mordaunt Hall found that the intermission marked a definite change of mood in the film and its audience: "Filled with excellent fun during the first half; the latter part is delivered over to sentiment and heroics. The romance in this film is quite plausible, but the efforts to elicit tears are too prolonged. The comedy relief that reigns in the first chapters of this photoplay is missing for quite some time in the latter episodes."[10]

Although no prints of *The Rough Riders* survive, a few reels of action outtakes exist in the Library of Congress. These consist mainly of the training sequences in the old fairground in San Antonio, although some battle footage exists as well.

Was *The Rough Riders* a great film? We can never know, but it certainly had a great deal going for it. Victor Fleming's surviving work of the period is excellent. Critics of the time compared it favorably to such epics as *The Covered Wagon* and *The Big Parade*, and it was produced at the same time that the studio was making *Wings*, the first film to win the Academy Award as Best Picture and an acknowledged classic. Add to that a solid cast of fine actors, and we can safely assume that *The Rough Riders* must have been pretty thrilling stuff.

Even if it missed the mark, though, it would be a fascinating and important discovery, should a print turn up somewhere. If that were to happen we could judge for ourselves the film that one critic called "100 percent pure unadulterated American entertainment with just enough mixture of real drama to make it stand out as a production which cannot fail with any class of audience in any class of theater."[11]

19

TIME TO LOVE

Paramount/Famous Players–Lasky Corporation. Production number 648. Released June 18, 1927. Five reels; 4,926 feet. Working titles: *Ten Minutes to Love, Dying For Love, Elvira and the Phantom.*

CREDITS

Presented by: Adolph Zukor and Jesse L. Lasky. *Associate Producer:* B. P. Schulberg; *Director:* Frank Tuttle; *Screenplay:* Pierre Collings; *Story:* Alfred Savoir; *Photography:* William Marshall; *Assistant Directors:* Russell Mathews and Sidney Brod; *Unit Manager:* Arthur Koch; *Cutter:* Verna Willis; *Clerk:* Jane Loring; *Second Cameraman:* Lionel Linden; *Assistant Cameramen:* George Hoffman and A. B. Chatfield; *Property Man:* Frank Hughes; *Assistant Prop Man:* Lou Asher; *Grip:* Kenneth DeLand; *Assistant Grip:* Wade Harlen.

CAST

Raymond Griffith (*Alfred Sava-Goiu*); William Powell (*Prince Alado*); Vera Voronina (*Countess Elvire*); Josef Swickard (*Elvire's Father*); Mario Carillo (*First Duelist*); Pierre De Ramey (*Second Duelist*); Helene Giere (*Elvire's Guardian*); Alfred Sabato (*Hindu Mystic*).

SYNOPSIS

Opening Title: "There are only two cures for love—marriage and suicide."

On a rustic bridge over a lovely river, a little man [Alfred] in a silk hat is determining on suicide. He writes a final, despairing note, pins it to his lapel, binds his eyes, and jumps off into nothingness. He lands, however, in a canoe, to the intense surprise of the boatman and his passenger, the beautiful Princess Elvire. Alfred is almost senseless from the impact. When he glimpses the face of the beautiful girl, he passes right out. In a vision, he thinks himself dead; [he] sees her garbed with a halo like the saints in paradise, while the boatman looks like a devil from the pit. Elvire, meantime, reads the note on his lapel. Alfred is dying for love.

Alfred soon comes to, finds out that his divinity is a mortal, thank God, and proceeds to make the best of his opportunity. They become so enraptured of each other that the boat nearly goes over the falls, and Alfred has to wade ashore, carrying the Princess. Luckily, they land right on her estate, where an excited duenna tells Elvire that her father demands her presence immediately. Before she leaves, Elvire gives Alfred a rendezvous for two o'clock.

In the salon of the ancestral Chateau, Elvire finds that her father is waiting to betroth her to Prince Alado, a gentleman for whom she has a lively dislike. However, the papers are already signed, and there is apparently nothing to be done.

Broken-hearted, Elvire escapes into the garden while the guests toast her and the groom. Here she is met by a newcomer, a former flame just back from a trip. He starts in to protest his devotion, but the Prince enters, overhears, and before she can explain, the Prince slaps the stranger and is challenged to a duel.

Elvire thinks that this is very funny; the stranger happens to be the best dueler in France. The Prince fails to see the joke. He is much worried. Luckily for him, at that moment Alfred hurries up. The Prince meets him and falls on his neck. They are old friends. Alfred must help him out by fighting the duel for him since he, the Prince, has just become engaged. Alfred agrees, fights the duel, wounds the adversary; in fact, always anxious to oblige a friend, Alfred immediately fights a second adversary whom the Prince insults for that purpose.

Elvire, who does not even know of Alfred's arrival, thinks that this marvelous fighter is the Prince himself. During these episodes, the father of Elvire, a gentleman given to the study of the occult, is in session with a crystal gazer. The distracted Princess thinks of a plan, takes the mystic aside, and bribes him to rap "no" in answer to an inquiry concerning her forthcoming marriage. They all agree to the test, including the Prince.

They sit. Suddenly, they are interrupted by a number of raps citing "yes." Elvire is furious, thinking that the mystic has double-crossed her, when in trips Alfred; it was his knocking at the door that they had heard. Alfred rushes to Elvire, only to learn that she is the Prince's fiancée and the girl for whom he has been fighting. In the madness of despair, he slaps the Prince; then, becoming contrite, begs his pardon. But unfortunately it is an old Spanish custom, peculiar to the Prince's family, that every insult means a duel.

Alfred agrees privately to a fake duel; thereafter, he will leave for Argentina, now that he is convinced that he has no hopes of Elvire. The duel takes place near an open grave, dug for the occasion, to give a touch of realism. At the first firing, the Prince, nervous, knocks Alfred's hat off. Alfred, thinking the Prince has double-crossed him and meant to slay him, starts in to murder his adversary. He is pacified. A second exchange of shots is ordered and Alfred falls as per schedule. Just as he falls, up dashes Elvire and casts herself upon his prostrate body, kissing and caressing him. There is more than a suspicion that Alfred kisses her back, but the Prince assures her that Alfred is dead and hurries her off. As he leaves, a clod of earth sails out of the grave and mysteriously catches the Prince on the neck.

Elvire drives off brokenhearted. Alfred runs up to the Prince and begs to be let off his promise but the Prince is obdurate. Alfred has given his word of honor; he must stay dead. Alfred sits down and thinks and thinks.

At the Chateau, preparations are [a]foot for the wedding. It is stormy outside. Elvire is feeling very low. In through a window steps Alfred. He sees Elvire in an attitude of dejection [and] determines upon a plan, the outcome of which is that Elvire is startled almost to death by the appearance of a figure dressed in a sheet, which floats across the room and addresses her in a sepulchral voice, telling her that he, Alfred, has come back to Earth to inform her that he has a twin brother, almost identical with himself, and any attentions bestowed by Elvire on said brother would be highly appreciated.

The apparition floats out of the room and almost immediately in pops somebody looking very much like Alfred. Elvire, for some reason, doesn't like the supposed brother, and while Alfred is trying to win her over, the Prince comes in. Immediately, Alfred jumps on him, calling him the assassin of his brother. The Prince, frightened, blurts out the truth about the fake duel. Elvire, hurt and chagrined, turns her back on them both. The father comes in. Alfred is seized and thrown out, and the marriage ceremony commences.

Suddenly, in the midst of a prayer, the bride disappears from their midst. Alfred has appeared on a balcony overhead, reached down, drawn Elvire up and run off with her. They are soon running off; the family give chase.

The only escape for the moment is by means of some large hampers loaded on an army truck. The hampers turn out to be the baskets of captive balloons, and before Alfred and Elvira know what is happening, they find themselves up in the air and serving as a target for army gunfire. They are almost shot to pieces [and] have to throw away all their superfluous clothing in order to keep afloat. Their anchor gets entangled with a train, and they are drawn through tunnels at inconvenient moments. Finally, they have to descend to safety via the parachute. Scantily clad, they crash, by coincidence, through the roof of the Chateau and fall into place before the minister in time to complete the interrupted ceremony. This time, however, Alfred is the groom.

—Paramount Story Department

THE PRODUCTION

"At this particular moment in the history of the Silent Drama, Raymond Griffith leads all comedians in points of ingenuity, imaginativeness, and originality."

—Robert E. Sherwood[1]

Most students of movie comedy will find those words baffling, even perverse. After all, when Robert E. Sherwood wrote them in 1926, it

Raymond Griffith and Vera Voronina

was easy to find a theater still playing Chaplin's *The Gold Rush* (1925). Buster Keaton's inventive *Battling Butler* was in release; so were Harold Lloyd's *For Heaven's Sake* and two of Harry Langdon's finest: *Tramp, Tramp, Tramp* and *The Strong Man*. All of those great comedies continue to play to appreciative audiences; they epitomize that rich period of cinema.

Only a true aficionado of silent comedy, however, has even *heard* of Raymond Griffith's trilogy of films from that year—*Hands Up, Wet Paint* and *You'd Be Surprised*—much less seen what survives of them (which seems to be only *Hands Up*).

But we don't have to see much of Griffith's work to keenly regret the fact that there isn't more of it still around. *Hands Up* is delightfully wry and ceaselessly inventive—and its plot holds no more promise, in cold type, than does that of *Time to Love*. That *Hands Up* is so funny and compelling suggests that God—and Griffith—was in the details. The joy comes not so much in what happens, but in how Griffith and his characters react to circumstances. In that sense, since the plot of *Time to Love* is the only part of the film that remains, it is even more "lost" than other lost films. What subtle gesture or raised eyebrow or sudden burst of lunacy might have ignited an audience with laughter? We don't know. We *can't* know. All we have is the blueprint—and, in comedy especially, that just isn't enough.

Raymond Griffith's screen persona was a dapper, ironic, imperturbable dandy. He loved to devise completely outrageous circumstances to which he could respond in the quietest, subtlest ways. Griffith would have been the perfect actor and filmmaker to bring the stories of P. G. Wodehouse to the screen; both of them loved combining dry wit with slapstick.

As a screen technician, Griffith was directly at odds with the "Sennett style," yet that is precisely where he began his screen career. His suave urbanity didn't blend in comfortably among Sennett's vulgar, mugging comics, but when he stepped behind the scenes to work as a writer and story editor, his genius for brilliantly timed gags began to assert itself. He might have been a great screenwriter or director; in fact, like his comedic peers, Griffith usually wore far more than one hat, uncredited, on his film sets.

Raymond Griffith has been compared, quite properly, to Max Linder on the one hand and Charley Chase on the other. Like Linder, Griffith was usually resplendent in immaculate evening dress: top hat, opera cape, cane. Like Chase, his characters were often imbued with a kind of detached optimism, always smiling, always (seeming to be) the master of every occasion.

He also bears an obvious resemblance to his co-star in *Time to Love*, William Powell. Rather, he resembles what Powell was *later* to become, with his charming, sophisticated roles in the thirties and forties. In 1926, though, Powell was still alternating between comic portrayals (as in *Time to Love*) and villainous ones (*Beau Geste*). Did Griffith play any part in helping to shape Powell's witty, laconic persona? Maybe, maybe not. But there is no doubt the two mined similar fields of character, gesture, and timing.

In fact, Griffith might even have carried on in the talkies as a star like Powell or an urbane supporting player like Adolphe Menjou if not for the fact that he had no voice—at least not much of one. He spoke in a raspy whisper (probably the result of bronchial pneumonia) that apparantly proved unsuitable for sound films (although he appeared in two Christie Paramount Talking Plays in 1929). Ironically, most movie buffs are familiar with Griffith only through the one sound feature in which he appeared: *All Quiet on the Western Front* (1930). He played a French soldier, dying in a foxhole while Lew Ayres looks on helplessly. It was a memorable—nonspeaking—role for Griffith. It was also his last screen appearance. He continued working for several years in the movie busi-

Alfred Sabato (in turban) Vera Voronina, Josef Swickard, and William Powell

ness as a producer on films like *Under Two Flags* (1936), *Heidi* (1937), and *Drums Along the Mohawk* (1939).

Since nearly all of Griffith's work as a star is gone, it is impossible to decide which of his films is most representative of his output as a whole. *Time to Love* didn't receive particularly glowing notices upon its original release, but it seems to have been agreeably silly, with a dizzyingly complex plot filled with outrageous situations. Too, it was directed by the always interesting, and seriously underrated, Frank Tuttle, a filmmaker with a singularly fertile imagination for offbeat sight gags.

Little is known about the production of *Time to Love*. Alfred Savoir's original story was purchased by Paramount for $26,500 in the late fall of 1926. Pierre Collings was assigned to turn the story into a script and was paid $13,589 for the job. The interiors were constructed at Paramount's Astoria Studios while the exteriors were filmed on Long Island at Hollenbeck Park and the Brunswick Estate. The entire production cost $250,318.77.

Variety's reviewer suggested that *Time to Love* had been banished to an out-of-the-way theater, the Hippodrome, when the film opened in New York in June 1927. "Papa Par[amount] was evidently displeased with this one, for it's hiding over on 6th Avenue this week sans any title of credit for direction, story, etc."[2]

The *New York Times* found the film "utterly incoherent but occasionally humorous" and complained that Tuttle and Griffith were guilty of dragging "in stunts that seem to have little or nothing to do with the slender thread of a narrative . . . [Y]ou go from a waterfall to a lot of door-slamming scenes, then to an endless series of dueling episodes, and finally to glimpses of the silk-hatted hero and the fair heroine up on a captive balloon."[3]

The *New York Times* critic poses something of a riddle regarding the names of the characters. In the review, Griffith's character is called "Raymond Casanova," and William Powell is said to play "the Marquis de Daddo." However, all the documents — scripts, synopses, treatments, etcetera — in *Time to Love*'s file in the Paramount Collection at the Margaret Herrick Library give the character names as they are listed in this chapter's credits and synopsis. Since the *Times* critic was obviously making notes during a screening, it is probable that the character names were

Raymond Griffith between William Powell and Josef Swickard

changed just prior to release. What other changes were also made? We will probably never know.

Of course, the *Times* review also names Alfred Savoir as a member of the cast. He wrote the original story and is named in no other cast list. This is probably just a mistake but, of course, there's no way of knowing. Even this is complicated by the fact that Griffith's original character name is "Alfred Sava-Goiu," which is quite close to the author's name.

Time to Love was not supported by Paramount and disappeared from theater screens quickly. Sometime later, it disappeared from everywhere—for good. At least one print seems to have survived until 1941. That year, Paramount reviewed all of the properties owned by the studio to determine which of them had remake potential. *Time to Love* was one of the films screened with this in mind, but a reader's report put the kibosh on that plan: "The implausibility of this old time comedy," said the reader, "makes it nonsensical rather than funny."[4]

So, if everyone disliked *Time to Love*, why should we mourn its passing? Because too many comedies of daring and complexity have been damned for being "incoherent" and "implausible." Because the plot seems so rich both with silly episodes and with hilarious morbidity. Because Griffith's sly, implacable gaze, staring at us from surviving stills, is enough to convince me, at least, that this odd Beau Brummell would be worth watching in any vehicle, no matter how seemingly unworthy.

And, finally, because Raymond Griffith will never receive his due, not as long as his work exists only in fragment.

"It is difficult to develop a new audience for a man who is more than half invisible," wrote Walter Kerr in his peerless book *The Silent Clowns;* "and critical judgements must be somewhat reserved, given such piecemeal evidence. I feel no reserve of my own: Griffith seems to me to occupy a handsome fifth place — after Chaplin, Keaton, Lloyd, and Langdon — in the silent comedy pantheon, a place that is his by right of his refusal to ape his contemporaries and his insistence on following the devious curve of an entirely idiosyncratic eye."[5]

Robert E. Sherwood, writing a half century before Kerr, saw Griffith's unique qualities, too: "Raymond Griffith deserves enthusiastic encouragement. He is flying in the face of movie tradition and getting away with it beautifully."[6]

20

GENTLEMEN PREFER BLONDES

....

Paramount/Famous Players–Lasky Corporation. Production number 679. First
shown November 16, 1927. Released January 18, 1928. Seven reels;
6,871 feet (75 minutes).

C R E D I T S

Director: Malcolm St. Clair; *Scenario:* Anita Loos and John Emerson; Based on the book
Gentlemen Prefer Blondes: The Illuminating Diary of a Professional Lady (1925) by Anita
Loos; *Titles:* Anita Loos and Herman Mankiewicz; *Camera:* Hal Rosson; *Second Camera-
man:* A. Clark; *Editor-in-Chief:* Hector Turnbull; *Film Editors:* Jane Loring and William Shea;
Assistant Director: George Hippard; *Second Assistant Director:* Joe Dill; *Unit Manager:*
Richard Blaydon; *Clerk:* Gertrude May; *Assistant Cameramen:* Leonard Eilers and Arthur
La Shelle; *Property Man:* John Leonard; *Assistant Prop Man:* George Sherman; *Grip:* Roy
Watson; *Assistant Grip:* Kenneth DeLand.

C A S T

Ruth Taylor (*Lorelei Lee*); Alice White (*Dorothy Shaw*); Ford Sterling (*Gus Eisman*); Holmes
Herbert (*Henry Spoffard*); Mack Swain (*Francis Beekman*); Emily Fitzroy (*Lady Beekman*);
Trixie Friganza (*Mrs. Spoffard*); Blanche Frederici (*Miss Chapman*); Ed Faust (*Robert*); Eugene Borden (*Louis*); Margaret Seddon (*Lorelei's mother*); Luke Cosgrave (*Lorelei's Grandfather*); Chester Conklin (*Judge*); Yorke Sherwood (*Mr. Jennings*); Mildred Boyd (*Lulu*).

....

SYNOPSIS

F I R S T   T I T L E

"Two generations ago, led by the spirit of the pioneers, there wandered
into the hills of Arkansas a man of dreams—dreams of gold."

C U T   T O   A   M I N E R

"But as time went on, gold finally did crop out in those hills, and the spirit of that old pioneer lived on in his grandchild."

C U T   T O   L O R E L E I

An Arkansas miner and his wife and cave girl are living in their primitive surroundings. The girl is playing outside on a dilapidated guitar. Even in the shabby surroundings of an Arkansas farm, Lorelei shows her propensities as a gold digger: At the broken-down gate appears a young man, one of the many who visit. He advances, and they sit down at the porch steps.

In the parlor, father and mother hear talking [and] go to the window and look out. On the porch, the girl sees the scarf pin the youth has, wants it, and without further ado appropriates it. The youth goes, and another—a long and lanky one—enters and sits down on the steps, opens his handkerchief, and displays a pretty bracelet.

Her family decides she should have a larger field for her activities and sends her to business college in Little Rock. In the classroom, the girls are all seated at their desks. Mr. Jennings, the big Rotarian, a corpulent individual, enters the classroom in search of a stenographer, and all he sees at first is legs. Then he switches higher and sees knees. Finally he sees a girl at a typewriter, who seems to touch his fancy; all she types is dollar signs. Jennings steps closer and tells her he will be here only a week, says he needs a girl in the office, and boastfully flashes a grand diamond ring in the sunlight. He asks her for her address, and she asks for a pencil. He hands her his golden pencil, tells her to keep it, and pets and caresses her, to which she is not at all averse. Jennings picks Lorelei for his secretary, and Lorelei, eyes on Mr. Jennings's diamond ring, picks on Mr. Jennings.

Mr. Jennings and Lorelei become great little pals, but after a year Lorelei learns that Mr. Jennings is not confining his attentions to her. In his apartment, Jennings is seen kissing a lady. Lorelei enters, shouts and scolds, and, a revolver being handy, she shoots him. She stands there, dazed, while the police investigate.

Lorelei goes on trial but relates a tale so convincing that the jury promptly turns in a verdict of Not Guilty. Lorelei is very happy, hugs the lawyer, and kisses the judge. Then she turns to the jurors and thanks them warmly. The judge tells her he wants to see her in his chambers. There he has a few fatherly words with Lorelei and, much to his surprise, finds himself staking her to the price of a ticket to Hollywood.

On the train, a man sits down beside Lorelei and at once wants to be familiar with her [and] taps her foot meaningfully. She ignores him and he leaves. Shortly thereafter, Lorelei meets benevolent old Gus Eisman, the Button King, who warns her not to make friends with everybody that talks nice to her.

In the Pullman sleeper Lorelei, after a hard time, finds her berth, but she cannot sleep. She gets down and meets Eisman, who also cannot sleep, and insists that she avail herself of his compartment while he takes her lower berth.

Lorelei has broken down the gates to Hollywood and is standing in the yard talking with a director when Eisman's car drives up. She says this movie business is hard work; she has to get up so early!

Good old Gus decides that a swell old girl like Lorelei shouldn't be an extra in the movies but should go to New York to be educated.

In New York, Eisman and Lorelei arrive at the hotel. In the big hall a dance is going on. Eisman and Lorelei arrive in the corridor and are met by a maid. He steps out for a minute while Lorelei waits. In another room, Eisman meets his girlfriend, Dorothy Shaw. At first, Lorelei looks dumb to the effervescent Dorothy but a couple of minutes' conversation changes this impression, and Dorothy sits back to watch the fun.

In the manicure shop, Dorothy is at work. Enter dressmaker with dress for Dorothy, and Eisman says, "Put plenty of buttons on." Lorelei spies a fur coat. Eisman sees the price tag and says he feels sick, but Lorelei pets and cajoles him.

At the breakfast table, an old maid is reading the paper, and Lorelei reads on the outside page about Henry Spoffard, America's richest bachelor. Lorelei is eager to know more about that and asks the old maid for that part of the paper. The old maid tears off the page and hands it to

Lorelei, who then and there makes up her mind to take a trip to Europe to meet this wonderful Mr. Spoffard.

In the corridor, Eisman appears with a bunch of flowers. The maid receives him and bids him enter. In her bedroom, Lorelei is getting up and starts to dress. Dorothy invites Eisman in.

In the parlor, Eisman chats with Dorothy, when Lorelei enters, happy as a lark, and at once tells Eisman that she wants to go to Europe; she has seen and knows enough about New York. But Eisman protests that to go to Europe alone is no job for a single girl. This objection is easily met. Lorelei points to Dorothy and says, "She would make a fine chaperon." Eisman laughs, and this angers Dorothy. After much hesitation, and with a resigned heart, he consents and before he knows it is waving goodbye to Lorelei and Dorothy on an outbound liner.

On the ocean liner deck Dorothy and Lorelei are sitting, reading. Without their knowing it, Spoffard is sitting alongside Lorelei, and he is a dry, sober-looking chap. Lorelei is rather free and tries to hook up a conversation, but he is pre-engaged [and] picks up his briefcase and takes out a . . . magazine with many girls' pictures in it. Seeing she cannot make an impression on him, she finally asks what makes the ocean blue. He merely looks at her and thinks her silly question unworthy of an answer. On the other side of Spoffard is his mother, an old lady, with ear trumpet. Again and again, Lorelei [attempts] a conversation, but it all falls flat. He is still staring at a picture in the magazine, then looks at Lorelei and sees she is the same party. She then asks if the ocean is not quite rough this day; he is disgusted, gets up, and leaves the scene. Seeing the space vacant, Lorelei moves over to the old lady with the ear trumpet and tries to have a conversation with her. The old lady admires the orchids Lorelei has on her dress, and Lorelei gives them to her. Then Lorelei flatters the old lady about her good looks and at once makes a hit. Just when the two are at the height of their joy, a Miss Chapman comes in, a sort of private nurse to Mrs. Spoffard, and takes her away, much to the [latter's] discomfort. After Miss Chapman has taken Mrs. Spoffard away, Dorothy has much to say to Lorelei about her maneuvers. They are still talking together when a corpulent, wealthy-looking gentleman, Sir Francis Beekman, enters the scene, passes, looks at the two, and, being an ardent admirer of beauty despite being . . . old and married, returns and bumps into them. Lorelei tells Dorothy she will educate him good and plenty.

At the railing, Beekman and his wife are looking out over the water when Dorothy and Lorelei enter the scene. He turns and looks after them. Dorothy first, then Lorelei, turns and gives him the high sign. They halt the steward and ask him a question, and he directs them.

In his cabin, Spoffard is really sick, and the doctor is attending him.

In the flower store, Dorothy and Lorelei are buying flowers, go out again, hunt up the steward, and tell him to go and tell Mr. Francis Beekman that Lorelei wants to see him in her stateroom.

On deck, the steward finds Beekman alone and tells him to go and see Miss Lorelei. He goes at once.

Arrived in front of her door, he knocks and enters.

In the stateroom, Lorelei receives Beekman. Beekman, the tightest man in England, fills his own cigarette case with Lorelei's cigarettes. A waiter brings drinks and presents the check. Lorelei has no pencil so Beekman hands her his own golden pencil. She signs the check and keeps the pencil. They drink and chat. After a little while, per arrangement, a lad brings in a bouquet of flowers. Lorelei looks and looks but cannot find any card and wonders who could have been so generous and unselfish to send her such beautiful flowers. She looks accusingly at Beekman and says he must have been the guilty one, and flatters him. He laughs. She raves over the flowers and kisses Beekman all over his face. Dorothy stands aside and takes in the show and grins to herself. Beekman is not slow; he hugs up closer and closer.

To pass the time and make herself useful, Lorelei has started a drive for the seamen's widows and pension fund, and she goes around with her box to take [up] the collection. When she comes to Mrs. Beekman, who wears a magnificent tiara, Lorelei lets fall a slip and asks if anyone would lend her $2,000. Just then, Beekman enters in his uniform as a Captain, and Lorelei flatters him. Amid the crowd, they are lost and sneak upstairs by themselves.

On the top deck, Beekman and Lorelei are sitting, looking out over the ocean. Lorelei says she has never seen such a wonderful tiara on a lady during a ball, and she wished she had one like that—but it would have to be a bargain. She keeps on telling him how much she would like to have it and flatters and kids and coaxes Beekman.

The ship arrives at Cherbourg.

At the hotel, Beekman knocks on the door, and when Lorelei opens it, he hands her the tiara and tells her she need not pay it back. He leaves and she goes back into her room, but he thinks of something else and knocks again and again, but the girls are inside, laughing to themselves. Beekman, seeing that his knocks are unheeded, walks down the corridor. The girls then start to dress to go out.

In Paris, the girls do a lot of sight-seeing around Cartier's and Coty's but they give a wide berth to a certain restaurant, Poissons, where Dorothy once ate bad fish and was sick for a week.

In his room, Spoffard is sitting up in bed, reading Lorelei's letter.

Having arrived home from their walk, Lorelei is alone in her apartment when there is a knock at the door. Lorelei opens and in comes Mrs. Spoffard in retiring attire [pajamas?], sucking at a fruit. They have scarcely had a chance to speak a word when there is another knock. Lorelei thrusts the old woman into the bathroom, then opens the door. There stands Miss Chapman, asking if Lorelei has seen anything of Mrs. Spoffard, for the old patient needs watching as she is not quite right in the head. Lorelei shakes her head, whereat Miss Chapman, with a suspicious look around the room, leaves. Mrs. Spoffard has issued again from the bathroom, and Lorelei shoves her back again and goes to the door to let Beekman in, followed by Dorothy. Dorothy makes a pretense to mail a C.O.D. package and asks him to go with her. Reluctantly, he follows.

In the hallway, Spoffard is standing in front of Lorelei's door, in answer to her letter. He knocks and enters. Dorothy also slips back in again and busies herself.

Lorelei introduces Spoffard to Dorothy. Then Spoffard and Lorelei sit on the sofa and talk. He tells her of his endeavors at social reform, and Lorelei says she is also much in favor of social reforms; thus, in their mutual interests, their friendship becomes doubly strong.

In the bathroom, Mrs. Spoffard acts like a kid, turning everything upside down, opening the medicine chest and taking things out, sampling this bottle and that.

Someone knocks on the door. Lorelei whisks Spoffard into the clothes closet while Dorothy opens the door and admits Mrs. Beekman, who proudly demands her tiara back. Lorelei looks very innocent and says she doesn't know anything about a diamond tiara, and Dorothy laughs. Mrs. Beekman threatens to call the police, and Lorelei becomes somewhat worried.

In the hall stands Beekman, a big smile on his face, a huge bouquet in his hand. He knocks on the door. Mrs. Beekman seems to recognize the knock, and when Dorothy wants to open the door, she thrusts the girl aside and opens the door herself. Her husband is thunderstruck at seeing his wife there. She wants to know if this is as far as he got on his trip to Scotland, then demands that he get her tiara from that young woman over there. Beekman looks surprised and says he doesn't know anything about the tiara. With an angry look and threatening gesture at the girls, Mrs. Beekman yanks her husband out of the room.

When they are gone, Dorothy warns Lorelei that they may soon be in the hands of a solicitor.

In the bathroom, Mrs. Spoffard is still enjoying herself.

Hearing that the visitors have left, Spoffard leaves his hiding place in the clothes closet and says he must be going.

In the hallway, a solicitor and a gendarme knock on the door, again and again.

Lorelei again whisks Spoffard into the closet and opens the door, and the bewhiskered, officious-looking gentleman, accompanied by the gendarme, enters and makes a deep bow. He asked to be excused for the intrusion and talks excitedly, in French fashion. He tells of Mrs. Beekman's tiara. Dorothy vamps the solicitor to take him off his guard. The solicitor writes something in his notebook.

In the bathroom, Mrs. Spoffard is helping herself to some bottles she has discovered, and the stuff seems to have an exhilarating effect on her.

Dorothy's vamping has the desired effect. The old solicitor turns quite attentively to Dorothy, while the gendarme asks Lorelei to accompany him to the theater, followed by supper. He tells the solicitor to charge the whole thing to Mrs. Beekman. While the young and old gentlemen are conferring on the matter, Lorelei opens the closet and leads Spoffard out. There is a general greeting all around, after which the two officers leave. Outside, they chuckle and laugh to each other as they walk down the hall.

Lorelei explains to Spoffard the meaning of the visit; then they go back to the sofa and start to discuss social reforms again. Seeing that Lorelei is in sympathy with his schemes, Spoffard asks her if she would join him, as he is about to purify Paris, and she is delighted to do so.

In the bathroom, Mrs. Spoffard is acting quite wobbly under the affect of some stimulant. Dorothy enters and helps her out by a side door.

In the parlor, Spoffard tells Lorelei that he has a list of all the disreputable places in Paris which they are going to visit.

Dorothy has managed to lead Mrs. Spoffard into the bedroom, and there, not being able to hold up the old lady any longer, both tumble to the floor. Dorothy picks her up again and leads her out into the hall.

Spoffard then outlines to Lorelei a two weeks' program, after which Spoffard leaves the room. In the hall, he hesitates a moment and thinks, then walks on to his room.

And then who should show up but Gus Eisman? It looks as though Lorelei's whole plan is going to be spoiled. When she hears that Eisman is on their trail, she is frantic. Dorothy wants to know why Lorelei has neglected her mail; she points to the unopened telegrams. Lorelei opens one and finds that she has been warned of Gus's coming. Lorelei wonders how they can get rid of Gus for a week. Dorothy gets the brilliant idea of taking Gus to lunch at the poisoned fish place. That's a good idea! They are dancing around with glee when Eisman enters. They greet and kiss each other, and Lorelei at once suggests that they have a bite to eat, and suggests a swell fish dinner that she knows about.

At the restaurant, the three are eating. Eisman, upon Lorelei's recommendation, has ordered lobster salad, while the girls order something less poisonous. He eats ravenously and says it is goody-good. He happens to look up at a sign, the suddenly stops eating. Lorelei asks what the matter is and he says the thing tastes funny. He points to the word POISSONS, grows dizzy and says he better go home and call a doctor. Dorothy winks at Lorelei and smiles: It worked!

And this effectively removes him from the scene for a week. In his room, Eisman is in bed, a very sick man, and a nurse is in attendance. Lorelei looks at her wristwatch and says she must be going; she has to keep an appointment with Mr. Spoffard. Eisman is very angry at that, but Lorelei gets up and goes out.

In the hall, Spoffard has been waiting for Lorelei, and when she comes out they chat a while, leaving the door open. Spoffard looks in, sees the man in bed, and asks Lorelei about him.

In the bedroom, as sick as he is, Eisman is determined to meet this man Spoffard face to face. He leaps out of bed, goes to the door, and there confronts Spoffard. Eisman lifts a cigar, and when Spoffard wants to explain, Eisman blows the smoke in Spoffard's face. He angrily accuses Spoffard of having smirched Lorelei's good name by taking her to questionable resorts. Lorelei immediately begins to weep with such a depth of ruined innocence that what could a gentleman such as Mr. Spoffard do except propose marriage in order to make an honest woman out of her?

On the return to New York, the wedding is celebrated with all conceivable magnificence. There is one hectic moment when the preacher asks the question about anyone having objections and Lorelei, looking furtively around, catches sight of Gus. But good old Gus just swallows hard and holds his tongue, a gentleman to the bitter end.

Outside the church a big curious crowd is waiting—newsboys, also, with extra editions carrying front-page pictures of the newlyweds. When the wedding party comes out of the church and lands at the curbing, Lorelei looks at their pictures and Spoffard buys the whole stack the newsboy has.

Amid the cheers of the crowd, the newlyweds drive away.

Gus Eisman has lost Lorelei, but he has his reward after all, for on leaving the church whom should he see but another swell little blonde, waiting for a streetcar or something. He picks her up—and another Lorelei has been launched upon her delightful career.

> —Paramount Story Department and the Silent
> Synopsis Collection, Margaret Herrick
> Library, AMPAS (see *The Last Moment*
> synopsis note for more information on the
> latter collection). The Silent Synopsis was
> made from a screening at The Casino Theater
> on Sunday, May 20, 1928.

....

THE PRODUCTION

By 1925, when Anita Loos wrote *Gentlemen Prefer Blondes,* she had already been a successful motion picture scenarist for thirteen years. In 1912, at the age of nineteen, she sold a story called "The New York Hat" to D. W. Griffith. The resulting film, which starred Mary Pickford, was successful and Loos began writing regularly for Griffith and Biograph. By her own count, she submitted 105 scenarios, and Biograph bought all but four.

In the early days of American film, title cards were utilitarian and used sparingly, only when needed to help viewers follow the plot. Loos was among the first writers to compose witty title cards that were entertaining on their own terms. Griffith warned her that "people don't go to the movies to read," but she continued to embellish her scenarios with snappy dialogue.

Loos met director John Emerson while working with him on several Douglas Fairbanks films, like *His Picture in the Papers* (1916). She married him in 1919.

In 1925, she began writing the diary of a gold digger named Lorelei Lee and began serializing it in *Harper's Bazaar* Magazine. When the hilarious adventures of Lorelei became popular, Loos gathered them into book form and called the result *Gentlemen Prefer Blondes.* Within months the book sold over a million copies and was eventually translated into fourteen languages.

Author Anita Loos

Obviously, that kind of success needed a little augmentation. First stop, Broadway. Loos and Emerson turned *Gentlemen Prefer Blondes* into a play, which opened at the Times Square Theater in New York on September 28, 1926.

Next stop, Hollywood. Paramount Pictures purchased the screen rights to Loos's story in June 1927 for $88,649.33 and paid Loos and Emerson $51,154.07 to turn the novel and play into a motion picture. The translation from medium to medium apparently didn't tax the team too badly. They turned in their script—with the rather risqué subtitle *The Lay of a Modern Lorelei*—on September 9, 1927, and the film went into production less than a week later.

The director of *Gentlemen Prefer Blondes* was Malcolm St. Clair, a brilliant director of silent film comedy whose brilliance would quickly disappear with the introduction of sound to movies. At his best, St. Clair could imbue his films with a beguiling mixture of sophistication and silliness, both qualities that *Gentlemen Prefer Blondes* called for in spades.

After a widely publicized search, Ruth Taylor was cast as Lorelei

Mack Swain and Ruth Taylor

and Alice White (a brunette for the occasion) as her more pragmatic friend, Dorothy. Ruth Taylor's career in the movies only extended to four feature films, none of which is available for viewing today. However, many of Alice White's films survive and, because she specialized in comic portrayals of dizzy-but-calculating blondes, the casting of Taylor and White in *Gentlemen Prefer Blondes* seems backward.

The supporting cast, on the other hand, seems just right; it's composed of some of the great comic actors of the silent era: Holmes Herbert, Ford Sterling, Mack Swain, and Chester Conklin, among them.

Production, at Paramount's Astoria Studios on Long Island, was completed on October 15, 1927, less than a month before the first previews. The final cost of the production was $351,137.92. *Gentlemen Prefer Blondes* opened to the public at New York's Rivoli Theater on January 18, 1928. *Variety* felt that the screen version lacked the "sophistication of the play and the demand upon the imagination created by Anita Loos's diary. Miss Loos has 'adapted down' and 'sapped up' to the film public.

Ruth Taylor and Trixie Friganza

Malcolm St. Clair directed likewise, undoubtedly from the basic knowledge that it had to be done."[1]

Mordaunt Hall of the *New York Times* was always an easier touch
than *Variety*'s critics. He found the film to be "an infectious treat. Malcolm St. Clair has given it just the right touch."[2]

Motion Picture News also felt that "the sparkle of the book and the
play was unable to be captured. The wisecracks are there, the story is
adapted faithfully enough, but somewhere something is lacking."[3]

The "something" that was "lacking" must have been Loos's verbal
snap, so effective on the page and the stage, but rather lifeless when
nailed down to a title card. Reading through the shooting script, in the

Paramount Collection at the Margaret Herrick Library of the Academy of Motion Picture Arts and Sciences, one is hard-pressed to find much humor in any of the dialogue cards. That's a bigger problem with a film like this than for a motion picture that was *conceived* as a silent movie. In Howard Hawks's uproarious remake of *Gentlemen Prefer Blondes* (1953), the dialogue is fine, but it's the delivery of those lines by Marilyn Monroe, Jane Russell, Charles Coburn, and the rest of the cast that really makes the film hilarious. If this lost version was also hilarious, it must have been because of other reasons—pace, performance, sight gags—than verbal wit and sophistication.

All that means, however, is that the *Gentlemen Prefer Blondes* of 1928 was a different experience from the *Gentlemen Prefer Blondes* of 1953 and from the book and various stage productions. But different doesn't mean worse, and there is plenty of reason to regret that we can never truly

Miss Taylor as Lorelei Lee, predating Carol Channing and Marilyn Monroe

compare the various versions to each other again. There are very few Mal St. Clair films of the period that aren't worth the price of admission, and the rest of the cast were proven laugh getters. The only unknown quantity is Ruth Taylor, and with few exceptions, every one of the critics thought she was a real find.

Even *Variety*'s critic, who didn't care for the picture as a whole, thought Ruth Taylor (although "merely a copy of June Walker's stage performance") had made an impressive debut. "It's a sweet picture for Ruth Taylor and as produced probably consummates one of the greatest 'breaks' any girl has ever gotten in pictures. If she gets as much attention in her next release, and can follow up on the ability shown here, the girl is an odds-on choice to land somewhere."[4]

She may, indeed, have "landed somewhere," but not in much of a movie career. She made only three more pictures and then left the business. That's no reflection on her acting ability or screen presence, though—we may never know just how great either of those qualities was. Instead, Ruth Taylor left the screen for pretty much the same reason Lorelei Lee would have.

"She was very pretty and very dainty and delectable," said Anita Loos, "and so much the real character that she married a multimillionaire and quit work!"[5]

21

BEAU SABREUR

Paramount/Famous Players–Lasky Corporation. Released January 7, 1928.
Seven reels; 6, 704 feet.

C R E D I T S

Presented by: Adolph Zukor and Jesse L. Lasky. *Director:* John Waters; *Titles:* Julian Johnson; *Adaptation:* Tom Geraghty; based on the novel by Percival Christopher Wren (New York, 1926); *Camera:* C. Edgar Schoenbaum; *Second Cameraman:* Harry Hollenberger; *Aikley Cameraman:* James Knot; *Assistant Cameraman:* Ralph Burdick, Lloyd Ahearn and Martin Cornica, Paul Lockwood; *Editor:* Rose Lowenger; *Assistant Directors:* Charles Barton and R. L. Johnson; *Unit Managers:* Arthur Koch and Sidney Street; *Clerk:* Alma Macrorie; *Property Men:* Al Tuck, Johnny Richmond; *Auditor:* Sam Dunham.

C A S T

Gary Cooper (*Major Henri de Beaujolais*); Evelyn Brent (*Mary Vanbrough*); Noah Beery (*Sheikh El Hammel*); William Powell (*Becque*); Roscoe Karns (*Buddy*); Mitchell Lewis (*Suleman the Strong*); Arnold Kent (*Raoul de Redon*); Raoul Paoli (*Dufour*); Joan Standing (*Maudie*); Frank Reicher (*General de Beaujolais*); Oscar Smith (*Djikki*); H. J. Uttenhore.

SYNOPSIS

[The film began with a painting of the skyline of Algiers with this superimposed title: "In Algiers . . . port of missing men . . . where romantic or unfortunate souls go for adventure, or to forget . . ."]

The uncle of Henri de Beaujolais is a marshall of France whose dream is to maintain peace and amity in France's possessions in North Africa. Though Henri has exhibited tendencies toward devil-may-care youthful rashness, the uncle is aware that he is made of the right stuff and entrusts him with a delicate and important mission. Before this, Henri had been in military prison for some infraction and there had occasion to fight a duel with Becque, a traitor who plots against his country.

In Africa, Henri is once more pitted against Becque. Henri's mission is to negotiate a treaty of peace and friendship with Sheikh El Hammel. At the same time, Becque is organizing a band of marauding Arabs with the aim of doing as much damage as possible.

In a garrison town, Henri meets a lovely American girl, Mary Vanbrough, and her companion, Maude. Henri and Mary fall in love, but he fights his emotion, realizing that there is no room for sentiment in carrying out his grave mission. Becque's Arabs murderously attack the town, but Henri and the girls manage to slip out in a caravan, and thus they are thrown together in spite of Henri's better judgment. It is inevitable that during the course of the journey, they thaw out considerably and admit to themselves that they have fallen.

Becque's men, after slaughtering the garrison, race after the caravan, catch up with it, and there is a pitched battle. Henri manages to get away with the girls and to reach El Hammel's oasis safely. Sheikh El Hammel and his Vizier are actually two adventurous Americans, Hank and Bud. They had deserted from the Foreign Legion and wandered to this Arab tribe and had made great friends with the old Sheikh. The Arab thought them natives, and after he died, he left the mantle of leadership on the two Americans' shoulders. The boys are having a whale of a time and are tickled silly when not even Europeans, such as Henri and the girls, see through their masquerade.

Sheikh Hank and Vizier Bud fall for the girls and tell Henri that they will sign the treaty he wants provided the girls are left behind. Henri struggles between duty and love, and love triumphs. He refuses to leave his beloved Mary behind for Vizier Bud.

Meanwhile, the villainous Becque arrives with a counter offer of a treaty unfavorable to France. Not only that, but Becque tries to murder Henri, who is only saved by Mary. Sheikh Hank arranges a duel between

Henri and Becque, the result of which Becque—though he tries every foul trick in the book—is killed.

Now Hank and Bud decide to put Henri to the test. They tell him that if he will sacrifice himself and drink poison, then the girls will be set off free and the treaty signed. Henri sees this as the only way out, drinks what he thinks is poison, and passes out. Mary is frantic, and now the boys know that this is real love. Since the poison was a fake, Henri recovers pronto, and there is general revelation [*sic*] by the boys and a happy ending—Sheikh Hank getting Maude, Henri pairing off with Mary.

—Paramount Story Department

THE PRODUCTION

Paramount's *Beau Geste*, directed by Herbert Brenon, was one of the finest, most popular films of the twenties. By combining the stirring adventure of the French Foreign Legion with an intriguing mystery, Brenon—by way of Percival Christopher Wren's 1924 novel—dazzled audiences and critics alike.

In those days, as in our own, that kind of box office success called out for a sequel. Since Wren had been thoughtful enough to provide a follow-up novel called *Beau Sabreur,* Paramount's course was clear: Purchase the film rights to the book and get to work.

Sequels in the twenties had something else in common with present-day sequels: They were never given the same level of budget or production value that helped make the original so memorable. *Beau Sabreur* would have a budget roughly half that of *Beau Geste*. To make sure the sequel possessed the requisite pictorial grandeur, Paramount decided to fill out *Beau Sabreur* with desert scenes filmed for, but never used in, *Beau Geste*.

In March 1927, the trade papers reported that production on *Beau Sabreur* would begin on June 6. The film was to be directed by James

Roscoe Karns and Noah Beery

Cruze,[1] and the female lead would be Esther Ralston,[2] both of whom had made a splash in the studio's *Old Ironsides* (1926). The male lead would be rising star Gary Cooper. A couple of cast members from *Beau Geste* were brought on board, too. However, both Noah Beery and William Powell had to play different characters, since they were killed off in the original film.

Almost immediately, plans changed. Evelyn Brent, the sultry moll of *Underworld* (1927), replaced Ralston, and William A. Wellman, who

Gary Cooper in desert garb

had helmed Paramount's Academy Award-winning *Wings* (1927), would direct. But Wellman balked at making what he considered a cut-rate film after his epic success with *Wings* and persuaded Paramount head B. P. Schulberg to release him from the obligation. Ironically, he then went on to direct *Legion of the Condemned* (1928), which was padded out with stock footage from *Wings* in precisely the same fashion that *Beau Sabreur* cannibalized *Beau Geste*.

(There is another slightly complex irony here, too: Wellman would

Evelyn Brent and Gary Cooper

direct Gary Cooper in the 1939 remake of *Beau Geste*. Had the two worked together on *Beau Sabreur*, it would have constituted a rare case where a star and director made the sequel to a film over a decade before filming the original. Sort of.)

Finally, John Waters was given the assignment. Virtually forgotten today (having been eclipsed by the flamboyant director of bad-taste clas-

William Powell as a renegade

sics like *Pink Flamingos* (1973) who shares his name), Waters worked as
an assistant director from 1916 before becoming a director with *Born to
the West* (1926). Information on his career is sketchy, but it appears that
he was a director until 1929's *Sioux Blood* and then was back to assistant
director on *Just a Gigolo* (1931). He must have been a better assistant
than he was a director, for he served in that function (or as second unit
director) on some of the most prestigious M-G-M films of the thirties:
Viva Villa (1934), *David Copperfield* (1935), *Mutiny on the Bounty* (1935),
and *Ninotchka* (1939) among them. His talent as a filmmaker remains
nearly impossible to assess today, except to take the word of one of *Beau
Sabreur*'s critics who called Waters's direction, "splendid."[3]

    Beau Geste recreated a convincing Sahara Desert atmosphere in But-
tercup Valley, the sand dunes just outside Yuma, Arizona. Waters chose

locations in Red Rock, California, and Guadalupe, a desert area just north of Santa Barbara. A glance through the studio records gives an idea of how complex a task it is to shoot even a rather modest motion picture: In advance of the actors' arrival, nine carpenters and assorted technicians were sent to Guadalupe to construct a prop tent, a hospital tent, a large tent with seats, a film room with loading dock, a water pipeline, water tank, pump, and tank platform.

A projection room was constructed and fitted out with projector and editing equipment. In all, one hundred fifty people were housed in the desert for fifteen days, which called for 1,590 lunches that cost Paramount $1.10 apiece.

When completed, *Beau Sabreur* apparently did not inspire the same compelling interest and admiration as did its forebear. This could have been due to the fact that John Waters was no Herbert Brenon. Or it could be simply because Wren's source novel is not nearly as well-written or involving as *Beau Geste*. Wren had a fatal love for coincidence. Two bumptious American Legionnaires, Hank and Buddy (played by Victor McLaglen and Donald Stuart in *Beau Geste*) who disappeared at the end of *Beau Geste* show up as phony sheikhs in *Beau Sabreur* (here played by Noah Beery, the evil commandant in *Beau Geste*, and Roscoe Karns, who was quickly becoming Paramount's resident wiseacre). Though Hank and Buddy are supposed to be comic characters, it is difficult to see how audiences were supposed to find a situation amusing in which the hero is convinced to kill himself with poison. That Cooper doesn't in fact die doesn't make the outcome any funnier; it just makes these "lovable" Americans look like sadistic cretins.

Also, the character that Cooper plays, Henri de Beaujolais, is a character in *Beau Geste*, but the two seem to have absolutely nothing in common; Cooper is even about twenty years younger than Norman Trevor, who played the role in the first film — and *Beau Sabreur* takes place *after Beau Geste*.

However, Mordaunt Hall, at least, found much in *Beau Sabreur* to admire. "So magnificent are some of the desert scenes," he wrote, "that yesterday afternoon an audience in the Paramount Theater was stirred to applause. The loveliness of these glimpses of rippled, undulating, and hilly tracts of sand was not more pronounced in Rex Ingram's film *The Garden of Allah,* but this current offering has the additional asset of being both beautiful and intelligent. Excellent direction, thoughtful casting, and fine acting are contained in this offering."[4]

While, *Photoplay* admitted, *Beau Sabreur* was "not built with the same suspense as [*Beau Geste,*] this is a story of adventure and romance that is most intriguing."[5] The critic was also enthusiastic about "such a battle with swords as you have never seen" and "the suspense" that "is terrific."[6]

Film Daily praised the film's "fine action scenes with galloping white-robed natives across the desert, fights galore—thrills, love scenes, and all that goes to make colorful entertainment."[7]

Laurence Reid, writing for *Motion Picture News,* was not so positive, however. "Those who have been waiting in expectation of seeing a fitting sequel to *Beau Geste* are sure to be disappointed here," he wrote. "The intention may have been good to equal or surpass it, but the story simply isn't *there*. It turns out to be another sheik and desert romance—with the emphasis placed upon the sheik and his romance. There is some skirmishing over the hot sands, and a villain bobs up to annoy the heroine, a flapper novelist who's been out in the East in search of local color. *Beau Geste* had a real background and spirit and charm besides. It touched deep wells of pathos, too."[8]

Beau Sabreur was moderately successful at the box office, though how well it succeeded artistically, or simply as a movie, we shall probably never know. This much is certain, though: It didn't do any harm to the careers of Gary Cooper, Evelyn Brent, or William Powell.

It also didn't slow up author P. C. Wren. He wrote another novel, *Beau Ideal,* a year later, which served as the final third of the "Beau" trilogy. Herbert Brenon made a sound film of it at RKO in 1930 starring Ralph Forbes (reprising his role from *Beau Geste*) and Loretta Young as Isobel, the part originally played by Mary Brian. *Beau Ideal* is a dreadful film, stilted and dull. It may be an indication that Brenon's particular genius lay behind him, in the silent cinema. Or it may simply suggest that the unique chemistry that made *Beau Geste* such a stirring and beloved classic—both book and film—just couldn't be repeated, by anyone.

22

THE DIVINE WOMAN

••

Metro-Goldwyn-Mayer Pictures〈Released January 14, 1928.〉
Eight reels. 7,300 feet.

C R E D I T S

Director: Victor Seastrom; *Scenario:* Dorothy Farnum; Based on the play *Starlight* (1925) by Gladys Unger; *Titles:* John Colton; *Treatment:* Gladys Unger; *Photography:* Oliver Marsh; *Sets:* Cedric Gibbons and Arnold Gillespie; *Film Editor:* Conrad A. Nervig.

C A S T

Greta Garbo (*Marianne*); Lars Hanson (*Lucien*); Lowell Sherman (*Monsieur Legrande*); Polly Moran (*Madame Pigonier*); Dorothy Cumming (*Madame Zizi Rouck*); John Mack Brown (*Jean Lery*); Cesare Gravina (*Gigi*); Paulette Duval (*Paulette*); Jean de Briac (*Stage Director*).

••

SYNOPSIS

Marianne has been placed by her mother on an Auvergne farm, whence she is brought to Paris by one of her mother's admirers, Legrande of the Theatre Legrande. The pretty peasant is coldly received by her mother. Legrande makes love to her, and she knocks him senseless with her umbrella. Thinking she has killed him, the girl rushes away and runs into the arms of a merry group of soldiers.

With one of these, Lucien, she has supper in a quaint old Montmartre mill, and the two fall in love at first sight. Lucien takes Marianne to his friend Mme. Pigonier, a laundress, who offers Marianne a home in exchange for her services. In Marianne's little room over the laundry she receives Lucien and serves him a little feast. But Lucien is sad, for he must leave at nine; his regiment entrains that night for Algiers. Nine o'clock finds the lovers in passionate embrace. Lucien realizes that Marianne is ready to be his and he cannot tear himself away. He yields to temptation and morning finds him a deserter.

Marianne, carrying laundry to the theatre, meets Legrande again and begs him to give her a chance to show that she can act. He consents, hinting that he expects a reward, and dresses her up in the rich furs and velvets from the wardrobe. Meanwhile, Lucien is bargaining with a shopkeeper for a simple dress for Marianne. He has not money enough and in a moment of temptation steals the dress when the man is occupied with another customer. He waits joyfully for Marianne, but his face darkens when she enters in her rich attire. They quarrel bitterly when he tells her she will become Legrande's mistress but are clasped in an embrace of reconciliation when the shopkeeper brings a gendarme to the house in search of the thief of his goods. The arrest is disastrous for Lucien as the fact that he is a deserter is revealed, and he is sent to prison for five years.

Meanwhile Marianne, grieving but weak and tempted, becomes Legrande's mistress and rises to stardom. Lucien sees her pictured in intimate and laughing conversation with Legrande on the Riviera in a periodical that comes by chance into his hands and realizes that she has been unfaithful. When he is released he finds her at Legrande's theatre.

He arrives on the night of her greatest triumph. Royalty is present and expected to visit her in her dressing room. But Lucien finds her alone and threatens to kill her. She begs poignantly for forgiveness and understanding, tells him she is willing to give up everything and come with him. They are interrupted by the arrival of the royal party. Watching Marianne receive the king, from his hiding place behind a curtain, Lucien realizes that she would never be content deprived of the admiration and luxury to which she has become accustomed. He cannot take her back to Montmartre, cannot live on her earnings. When the royal party have left, he bids her goodbye.

Trade ad

Marianne is called to the stage for the third act after he has gone and breaks down completely. The curtain has to be run down. Legrande, furious, breaks her contract and withdraws his protection.

Gradually, she is reduced to poverty, sells all her jewels, her personal effects, [and] is obliged to return to Mme. Pigonier's little room in Montmartre. And here Lucien rejoins her. He has a ranch in South America, where they can be together and happy once more.

—M-G-M press release

THE PRODUCTION

Clarence Brown, one of Greta Garbo's favorite and most frequent directors, once said that she had "something behind the eyes that you couldn't see until you had photographed it in close-up. You could see thought. If she had to look at one person with jealousy and another with love, she didn't have to change her expression. You could see it in her eyes as she looked from one to the other. And nobody else has been able to do that on the screen."[1]

Such rare ability found its true home in the silent film where faces, gestures, eyes were so much more eloquent than words could ever be. You can indeed see thought in Garbo's eyes; more astonishing, you can see soul. She may not have been the greatest actress who ever graced the screen, but her face is perhaps the cinema's most indelible image. Garbo was extraordinarily beautiful, of course, but beauty is common coin in Hollywood. She had something else, an indefinable quality that suggests the ethereal, the spiritual. She repeatedly played courtesans, prostitutes, adulteresses—creatures of the flesh. It was her peculiar genius to imbue these "fallen women" with an angelic aura, implying that the purity of their souls transcended the weaknesses of their bodies. Garbo died onscreen more often than any other leading lady in the movies. Those deaths were rarely portrayed as retribution for sins committed but rather as welcome release from stifling conventions and intolerable pressures.

Garbo between Lowell Sherman and Johnny Mack Brown

Garbo is such a towering figure of the cinema that the American Film Institute placed *The Divine Woman* on its Ten Most Wanted list even though virtually every other of her films still exists. Of personalities whose careers spanned both the silent and sound eras, Garbo and Chaplin were the luckiest in terms of film survival; today we can see nearly everything they ever made. Therefore, if one could choose only a handful of films from this book to bring back from the dead, *The Divine Woman* probably wouldn't make the cut. It seems far more important to see more of Theda Bara, for instance, or Raymond Griffith or Annette Kellerman.

From the evidence, *The Divine Woman* appears to have been a standard Garbo vehicle in which she falls in love, suffers, descends into moral disgrace, and then is redeemed by her first true love.

But as I have stressed elsewhere in this book, the plot of a film, in cold print, is rarely—if ever—an accurate gauge by which to judge the film itself. Even in the most standard vehicle, Garbo is always a force to be reckoned with, and her costars in *The Divine Woman,* Lars Hanson and Lowell Sherman, were also excellent, skillful actors.

One of the best reasons to imagine how great *The Divine Woman* might have been is that it was directed by Victor Seastrom. Seastrom (an Americanization of his real name, Sjostrom) began directing films in his native Sweden in 1912. He came to Hollywood in 1924, where he directed the powerful *He Who Gets Slapped,* starring Lon Chaney. Seastrom made *The Divine Woman* in between two great films with Lillian Gish, *The Scarlet Letter* (1927) and *The Wind* (1928), both of which also costarred Lars Hanson. Since Seastrom's work all around *The Divine Woman* was of great and enduring quality, we must assume he approached the Garbo film with a similar inventiveness.

Since Garbo's obsessive privacy ("I vant to be alone!") became such a monumental element of her personality, it is interesting to note that in

Garbo in an embrace with Lars Hanson

the *Divine Woman* pressbook, M-G-M's publicity people—only two years after Garbo came to Hollywood—are already struggling to put the best face on her need for solitude.

"Greta Garbo, famous for her glittering roles, seldom stirs from her home, except to go to the studio. In fact, Hollywood calls her 'the girl who never goes anywhere,' because she is never seen at parties or any of the social functions of the screen colony.

" 'I'd rather stay at home,' she says. 'It's not that I think it is wrong to go out to social gatherings and have a lot of fun. It's just that I find more contentment in my own home where I can read, study the English language, and try to improve my mind.' "[2]

Although there is no reference to it in any of the press releases or advertising, several reviewers thought *The Divine Woman* was based on a real personality. "Here and there the incidents suggest anecdotes of the life of Sarah Bernhardt, though this thread is not consistently followed."[3] The plot does not suggest such a connection, at least not explicitly enough for anyone today to catch the implication. Could it be, then, that there were visual cues within the film itself that evoked Bernhardt to those who might actually have seen her perform? Or was the title, which hints at Bernhardt's nickname, the Divine Sarah, the only clue?

The Divine Woman opened at New York's Capitol Theater on January 14, 1928, where it played to enthusiastic, standing-room crowds. While many of the reviewers were of the opinion that Garbo and Seastrom overcame a weak story ("fairly interesting but seldom truly absorbing"[4]), most of them believed that the end result was compelling. The *New York Times*'s critic felt the film was "weakened by an absence of spontaneity and also because of a tendency toward hysteria in the more emotional sequences."[5]

But this same reviewer also gives us a few valuable glimpses into Seastrom's directorial approach to the film:

"Mr. Seastrom revels in sharp contrasts. You see Marianne who has won wealth and fame on the stage, wearing a sparkling bracelet, and this ornament fades out into a glimpse of the handcuffed wrist of Lucien, the hero. Mr. Seastrom does a similar thing again when he takes the spectator from a stage banked with flowers to the shafts of light in Lucien's cell. A flash of an increasing pile of silver coins is enough to tell the audience that Marianne is living opulently."[6]

Like many silent films released just at the moment the studios were beginning to adopt sound, *The Divine Woman* didn't have much of a life. It was quite successful at the box office, but M-G-M couldn't imagine the day when it would have any reissue potential. How long prints of the film survived is anybody's guess, but by the fifties, *The Divine Woman* was already considered a lost film.

Was *The Divine Woman* one of the most significant films of the era? Probably not. It probably wasn't even one of the most significant films of 1928, which was a particularly rich year for the dying silent cinema. But it would undoubtedly be a true pleasure to experience it again, both for the cinematic genius of its director and for the beauty and skill of its legendary star.

23

LEGION OF THE CONDEMNED

Paramount/Famous Players–Lasky Corporation. Production number 681.
Released March 10, 1928. Eight reels; 7,415 feet.

CREDITS

Presented by: Adolph Zukor and Jesse L. Lasky. *Produced and Directed by:* William A. Wellman. *Associate Producer:* E. Lloyd Sheldon; *Screenplay:* John Monk Saunders and Jean DeLimur; *Story:* John Monk Saunders and William A. Wellman; *Novelization:* Eustace Hale Ball; *Titles:* George Marion, Jr.; *Camera:* Henry Gerrard; *Second Cameraman:* Cliff Blackstone; *Editor:* Alyson Schaeffer and Carl Pearson; *Editor-in-Chief:* E. Lloyd Sheldon; *Art Direction:* Laurence Hitt, Hans Dreier; *Assistant Director:* Richard Johnston. *Second Assistant Director:* Charles Barton; *Stunt Pilots:* Dick Grace, Frank Clarke, Frank Tomick, Earl H. "Robbie" Robinson; *Costumes:* Travis Banton, Edith Head; *Makeup:* James Collins; *Props:* John Richmond and Joseph Youngerman; *Unit Manager:* Roger Manning; *Assistant Cameramen:* Cliff Schertzer and Loyal Griggs; *Aikley Cameraman Assistant:* Burton Steene; *Grip:* Art Miller; *Men's Wardrobe:* A. MacDonald; *Sound Effects:* Western Electric. *French Title: Les Pilotes de la Morte.*

CAST

Fay Wray (*Christine Charteris*); Gary Cooper (*Gale Price*); Barry Norton (*Byron Dashwood*); Lane Chandler (*Lane Holabird*); Francis MacDonald (*Gonzolo Vasquez*); Albert Conti (*Von Hohendorff*); Charlotte Bird (*Celeste, Tart in Café*); Voya George (*Robert Montagnal, a Gambler*); Freeman Wood (*Richard DeWitt, a Bored Man*); E. H. Calvert (*Commandant*); Toto Guette (*Mechanic*).

SEQUENCE SYNOPSIS

FLYING FIELD
HEADQUARTERS

Introducing various members of the Legion of the Condemned, known along the front as the squadron which no man ever quitted alive. A succession of short sequences introduce the characters: Vasquez is there because he killed a man over a woman in Buenos Aires; Korsi, because he lost all his money gambling at Monte Carlo; Whitehill, because even the life of a young millionaire in New York had grown flat and stale for him; Dashwood, the apple-cheeked young Englishman, because in an automobile accident he had killed the girl he loved; Holabird, the lean Texan, because his past was a closed book no one cared to open.

A newcomer is introduced: Gale Price, a young American. As they stand drinking at the bar, an envelope containing a *mission speciale* is cast on the table. The assignment, generally concerned with landing spies in enemy territory, means almost certain death, yet these desperate men fight over it. Dashwood gets the coveted mission.

DASHWOOD'S MISSION

Dashwood lands his spy passenger safely but is caught in an ambush. He and the spy are tied to stakes and shot. Back at headquarters the name of Dashwood is removed from the bulletin board of the Legion.

PRICE'S STORY

One of the cabaret girls is guessing Price's reason for joining the Legion, saying it must have been a girl, and we cut back to: Price, a cub reporter in Washington during the early years of the war, is given an assignment to cover the Embassy Ball. Delighted, he calls up the girl of his choice, Christine Charteris, and asks her to go with him. At the Embassy Ball they meet. Price is madly in love, and the Ball, in its color and magnificence, is intoxicating. In the garden, he makes wild love to Christine and she responds. Then he loses her in the whirl of the Ball, only to find her hours later in a private room, very drunk, being fondled on the knee of a foreign diplomat. That is why Price joined the Legion.

LEGION HEADQUARTERS

Another *mission speciale* is being handed out. This time Price gets it. The next morning at dawn when he comes to pick up his passenger, he finds out that it is Christine. Christine explains all to him: how she was a French spy, how she had tried to find him later that night, to make him understand that the scene in the bedroom was only part of her work. Price breaks down in an agony of remorse and of reawakened tenderness and begs her forgiveness. Then they climb into the plane and set off on their dangerous adventure.

CHRISTINE'S CAPTURE

Price lands Christine safely and promises to be back in ten days to pick her up. Christine, however, is discovered and court-martialed. She is about to be released for lack of evidence when word comes that Price is planning to return for her. Christine is condemned to act as decoy in the hope that they may attract Price. She manages to send off a note, warning him not to come for her as it will mean death to them both, but Price, full of happiness at the thought of seeing her again, is already winging his way onward when the note reaches camp.

THE RESCUE

The squadron immediately sets out to rescue Price and Christine, but before they can catch up with him, Price, speeding on wings of love as well as of metal, arrives at the rendezvous, sees Christine, mistakes her frantic signals, lands, and is captured. For a moment he has a dreadful doubt that Christine may have double-crossed them, but when the two of them are led out in front of a firing squad, his doubts are dissolved in the dreadful certainty that she will pay the price along with him. Before the black muzzles of the rifles, they promise each other undying love beyond the grave. But the squadron arrives in time to rescue them, even though Vasquez and Holabird are shot down.

Christine and Price leave for Paris on leave, and the commandant, knowing that a woman is more dangerous to a warrior than bullets, sadly removes the name of Gale Price from the bulletin board of the Legion of the Condemned.

—Paramount Story Department

THE PRODUCTION

William Augustus Wellman had been a flyer with the Lafayette Flying Corps during World War I. The corps, an offshoot of the famous Lafayette Escadrille, was composed of Americans who had joined the French Foreign Legion to get into the fighting before America entered the war. Young "Wild Bill" Wellman was a brave, apparently reckless, flyer who is credited with at least two German kills. He was shot down in 1918 and invalided home with an injured back. While convalescing he wrote (or had ghost-written for him) an autobiographical account of his thrilling days in the skies above France called *Go Get 'Em!* (Boston: Page Company Publishing, 1918).

Wellman came to Hollywood in 1919 and began directing films in 1923. It was his experience as a flyer that, despite his youth, won him the plum assignment of directing *Wings*, Paramount's biggest production of 1927. The epic film not only broke box office records, it won the very first Academy Award as Best Production.

Wings was written by John Monk Saunders, also an ex-flyer. When Paramount wanted to rush a follow-up to *Wings* into production, reteaming Saunders and Wellman seemed the obvious move.

But *Legion of the Condemned* was no *Wings*. Given only a moderate budget of just over $295,000 (about $12,000 of which was paid for the story), Wellman was encouraged to use as much as possible of the spectacular stock footage accumulated during the filming of *Wings*. However, those interested in the significant autobiographical element of Wellman's career must particularly mourn the loss of *Legion of the Condemned* for — beyond its improbable, melodramatic plot — it seems to relate much more directly to Wellman's experience in the war.

Indeed, many reviews specifically refer to the "legion of the condemned" as the Lafayette Escadrille. Although Eustace Hale Ball's novelization of Saunders's script never names it so, the fictional air squadron has the multinational quality of both the French Foreign Legion in general and the Lafayette Flying Corps in particular.

One atmospheric element that strikes an authentic note is the way in which the Legion's planes are decorated. Every plane, according to the script, is marked with "the insignias of death" — a skeleton with a scythe, a sable vulture, a headstone over a grave, a skull and crossbones, a hooded cobra, a gallows tree. "Each of the designs bears the same ominous import: Death." This wry fatalism has always been part of the character of both aviators and soldiers of the Foreign Legion; the characters in *Legion of the Condemned* are both.

Although *Wings* was a big, sprawling, sometimes overwhelming screen epic, *Legion of the Condemned* may have been a more intriguing film cinematically. Producer David O. Selznick, who came to Paramount at about this time and often worked with Wellman later on, told film historian Kevin Brownlow, "The opening sequence of [Wellman's] *Legion of the Condemned* I've many times quoted as one of the most brilliant uses of film to tell a story that I've ever seen. He told the whole story of four individual men in, I think, less than one minute each. He was really a remarkable talent."[1]

The critic for the *New York Times* also singled out this sequence for praise. "The best chapter in the film is the first one," he wrote. "Here are given the reasons why some of the fliers don't care a rap about living. There is an Argentinean who is depicted on his native heath in a pistol duel over a girl. From there you turn to London where a young Britisher, through reckless driving, is the cause of a girl's death. There is the gambler in Monte Carlo who, after throwing away bills and gold on the green baize tables, walks out to the balcony to put a bullet through his brain. A laugh, supposedly cruel, stays the trigger, and the gambler turns his eyes on his mistress who, according to George Marion, Jr., the title writer, says: " 'Don't try to blow out what you haven't got.' "[2]

The script is peppered with laconic wit as well as a fair taste of hyperbole; in one title card the Legion of the Condemned is described as: "The rarin', tearin', galoots who aim to die in their tall boots." Credit for specific lines is difficult to assign in nearly any motion picture. In this case, for instance, Wellman and Saunders wrote the original story, Saunders and Jean DeLimur (formerly, he claimed, a pilot with the Lafayette Escadrille and later a director) wrote the script, and George Marion, Jr. wrote the title cards. But there is an element in the script that strongly suggests the voice of Wellman.

Wellman had a fondness for assigning catchphrases to characters; it is a consistent element in his films, no matter who the screenwriter is. Sometimes these were little more than running gags, but often they were recurring points of character punctuation. In *Wings*, Buddy Rogers and Richard Arlen establish a ritual of saying, "All set?" "Okay" before each takeoff. When Arlen says, "All set?" and gets no reply, we sense he will not return from this flight. In *Legion of the Condemned*, Holabird (Lane Chandler), a happy-go-lucky Texan, is constantly singing an obscure fragment from an unknown song: "She had her boots on when she fell. So what the hell, Bill, what the hell." In the climactic air attack in which hero and heroine are rescued, Holabird is killed. His death is followed by a title card reading, "He had his boots on when he fell . . ." This peculiar little motif could have originated from any one of the film's writers, of course, but it is definitely an identifiable Wellman ingredient.

Legion of the Condemned teamed relative newcomers Gary Cooper and Fay Wray. Cooper had made an immediate impression on moviegoers with his single scene in *Wings*, and he followed it with increasingly larger roles in *Nevada* and *The Last Outlaw* (both 1927). He played the lead in *Beau Sabreur* (also discussed in this book) and then was cast in *Legion of the Condemned*. From that point on, Cooper established himself as one of Hollywood's greatest stars.

Fay Wray had been in movies since 1923 when, at the age of sixteen, she began playing bit parts. 1928 was a banner year for her, including

Gary Cooper and Fay Wray

not only her starring role in *Legion of the Condemned* but her striking appearance in Erich von Stroheim's *The Wedding March*. It was not until 1933, of course, that Fay Wray became a permanent part of American culture by screaming away in a certain gigantic hairy paw.

"*Legion of the Condemned* was the first of four films I made with Gary Cooper," Miss Wray told film historian John Andrew Gallagher. [The other three are *The First Kiss* (1928), *The Texan* (1930), and *One Sunday Afternoon* (1933).] "He was extraordinary, but you couldn't tell right away. You'd see him on the set, and then you'd look at him on film, and there was this wonderful face making the slightest change of expression seem terribly important. So he had magic for the camera."[3]

Wray and Cooper shared a terrific onscreen chemistry that led the studio to publicize the pair as "Paramount's Glorious Young Lovers." But Miss Wray's offscreen chemistry was directed at an altogether different glorious young lover: John Monk Saunders. When filming of *Legion of the Condemned* was completed, she and Saunders were married.

About her director, Miss Wray recalls that "Wellman's reputation as 'Wild Bill' wasn't apparent on the set. There were rumors of his wild behavior, but that made him kind of an exciting personality, I think. He was almost a belligerent director. He was going to get this wonderful scene, you know, and he was like a whole rooting section himself. He was a vital director with strong emotions, but he didn't ever have the

Fay Wray being rescued

delicacy or the nuances that were possible for a director like Von Stroheim to realize."[4]

Legion of the Condemned was filmed between October 10 and November 9, 1927, at the Paramount Studio on Melrose Avenue in Hollywood, at the Burbank Airport, and in the open countryside of Canoga Park (where open countryside is, these days, at a premium). After spending months on location in San Antonio while filming *Wings*, this was down-and-dirty shooting of the kind that Wellman was always noted for. The speed of production did, however, drive some of the crew to distraction. An anonymous hand-scrawled note in the AMPAS Library's Paramount Files reads: "In order to accomplish the above amount of work in 27 days, it has been necessary to work a great many nights. Whether or not this pace can be maintained remains to be seen — if not, we will fall behind schedule."[5]

Although it isn't certain who wrote the note (Wellman? Assistant director Richard Johnston?), one thing is known: The company did not fall behind schedule. The final inserts and model shots were completed on November 11.

Critical response to *Legion of the Condemned* was surprisingly positive. "This picture has been heralded as the companion to *Wings*," wrote *Photoplay*'s critic. "Emotionally, it is above *Wings*. There are some tremendous aerial combat scenes, and when the heroine stands before a firing squad of Germans, the suspense is terrific. Because William Wellman flew over the lines ten years ago he knew just how to direct this picture."[6]

The *Film Daily* called it "one of the best of the new year. In entertainment value, this ranks high, one of the chief reasons being the excellent and plausible story that has been developed."[7] The reviewer mistakenly calls *Legion of the Condemned* Fay Wray's film debut. "You'll see more of her and deservedly so."[8]

Apparently, the first screenings of *Legion of the Condemned* had far more stock footage from *Wings* than did the general release prints. Paramount officials became concerned that they were tipping their hand; *Wings*, still in roadshow engagements when *Legion of the Condemned* was released, had not been seen nationwide yet. However, one action cen-

Fay Wray and Gary Cooper in the romantic conclusion

terpiece remained: a solo raid on a German troop train that had been filmed for *Wings* and never used.

Wings is one of the masterpieces of the silent cinema, but it seems probable that *Legion of the Condemned*, a smaller, less pretentious production, just might have been closer to its director's heart and might have more accurately portrayed the reality of war in the skies in those early days of aviation. Besides all that, *Legion of the Condemned* just sounds like a good *movie,* one with "a fine lot of good action material set off with much pictorial beauty. With all the war pictures ahead of it, there wouldn't be much argument if it was accepted as the *hottest* war film of them all. . . . It is shot full of suspense and a creditable line of romance, and builds to a climax which carries a fine thrill. William Wellman, who handled *Wings,* was the boss here and succeeds in getting everything out of the story and out of his players."[9]

24

LADIES OF THE MOB

Paramount/Famous Players–Lasky. Production number 696.
June 30, 1928. New York premiere: May 17, 1928, at the Paramount.
Seven reels; 6,792 feet.

CREDITS

Presented by: Adolph Zukor and Jesse L. Lasky. *Produced and directed by:* William A. Wellman. *Screenplay:* John Farrow; *Adaptation:* Oliver H. P. Garrett; *Based on:* a story in *The American Mercury* (December 1927) by Ernest Booth; *Titles:* George Marion, Jr.; *Camera:* Henry Gerrard; *Editorial Supervisor:* E. Lloyd Sheldon; *Editor:* Alyson Schaefer, Edgar Adams; *Art Direction:* Hans Dreier; *Costumes:* Travis Banton, Edith Head; *Makeup:* James Collins; *Assistant Directors:* Otto Brower and Charles Barton; *Technical Advisor:* Captain Peoples; *Unit Managers:* R. L. Johnston and Frank L. Newman, Jr.; *Clerk:* Elsworth Hoagland; *Second Cameraman:* Cliff Blackstone; *Assistant Cameramen:* C. Shirpser and Loyal Gregg; *Property Man:* John Richmond; *Grip:* Art Miller; *Assistant Grip:* Jack Haring.

CAST

Clara Bow (*Yvonne*); Richard Arlen (*Red*); Helen Lunch (*Marie*); Mary Alden (*Soft Annie*); Carl Gerrard (*Joe*); Bodil Rosing (*The Mother*); Lorraine Rivero (*Little Yvonne*); James Pierce (*The Officer*).

SYNOPSIS

In the office of the prison sits a grief-stricken woman, her small daughter asleep on her lap. Near her is the warden's wife. A man is about to be electrocuted for murder and, as the lights flicker and almost go out, leaving the room in half darkness, the woman roughly clutches the child to her in agony. Waking, the child screams in fright. The warden returns and, going to her mother, tries to soothe the little girl. Holding her child close to her, the mother bitterly tells him that someday, through their daughter, the father's death will be avenged. As she comforts the little girl, on her left hand is seen, instead of a wedding ring, a coiled golden serpent, head raised as if to strike.

Years later, the child, Yvonne, is living in a little bungalow in a quiet neighborhood. Red, her man, and Joe, who works with them, are seated at the breakfast table, discussing the details of a bank robbery to be pulled off that morning. The shades are drawn, and the electric lights are turned on. A noise is heard outside. It is only the morning paper flung against the milk bottles on the porch, but both men start to their feet, tense, gun ready. Yvonne enters, and a few minutes later, fully armed, the three leave the house. As they are leaving, Yvonne draws Red back for a minute and pleads with him to avoid using the guns. She cannot bear that he shall risk the fate that ended her father's life. Softened by her pleading and the knowledge of her love for him, he promises.

At their car, a Buick, Red finds a summons for illegal parking near a hydrant. Crumpling the paper into a ball, he tosses it carelessly away. It rolls to the base of the hydrant and stops. The Buick drives away. Meeting three others of their gang in a Lincoln touring car, Joe is left with the Buick, and Yvonne takes the wheel of the Lincoln. As she holds out her hand in signalling, Red speaks of the serpent ring which she always wears. She tells him that it has always brought them luck.

Arrived at the bank, Yvonne waits in the car, ready to start at a moment's notice. A bank clerk hurries into the scene, but as he unlocks and throws open the door of the bank, Red is at his elbow. A little gun persuasion and they enter together. Outside in the car, Yvonne is getting anxious. An old blind beggar shuffles along by her, his cane tapping the running board of her car. She draws back as he peers up at her, then hastily drops a coin in the extended cup. A banker enters and goes up the bank steps. An arm is thrust out and he is quickly drawn inside. A few minutes later, Red and the three men come out and cross to the

Lincoln. As it draws away from the curb, the robbery is discovered, and the alarm given. But as a crowd gathers, Yvonne is speeding around the corner to safety.

A policeman stops the old beggar and asks if he was at the bank at 8:30 as usual. Quickly, the beggar describes the car and Yvonne. A message is flashed to the police of the city, warning them to be on the lookout for a red-haired girl wearing a snake ring on her left hand.

Back at the bungalow, Yvonne, Red, and Joe are dividing the plunder. Yvonne is happy at the thought that, now they have got their stake, they can quit and live honestly, as Red has promised.

Outside, the policeman who tagged their car finds the summons in the gutter and the Buick again parked near the hydrant. He goes over to the bungalow. Cautiously, Yvonne goes to the door and, drawing the drapes a little aside, peeks out. She signals to the others that it is a policeman. Half drunk, Joe hastily leaves his share of the booty on the table and makes his escape via the back door. Opening the front door a little way, Yvonne takes the crumpled paper from the officer. She is puzzled, and as she reads it through again, his attention is suddenly riveted on the serpent ring she wears. He grabs her hand. Panic-stricken, she tries to close the door, but the officer's foot prevents [it]. As he tries to force his way in, Red, in the darkened dining room, raises his gun to shoot. Yvonne deliberately gets in front of the officer. She has him covered. Red enters and grabs him, and the two force him to enter a closet. Then the door is locked. Hurriedly, Red and Yvonne leave the house and drive away.

After endless driving, Yvonne and Red evade their pursuers and reach California. At last Yvonne can have the home she has always wanted. But the quiet of the new life is not to Red's liking. He longs for the excitement of former days. When Yvonne is busy out in the yard he goes to the phone and calls up Soft Annie, whose home is a crook's refuge. With Annie is Marie, a former sweetheart of Red. As Marie hears Red's name, her face lights, and when Annie tells Red she has a letter for him, Marie begs Annie to let her deliver it.

A taxi drives up and Marie alights. Going to the porch where Red is sitting in the hammock, she throws her arms around him and kisses him enthusiastically. Looking up toward the house, Yvonne sees this and, furious, crosses over to them. When Marie learns that this girl is Red's wife, she starts to go, telling Red he can go to Annie's himself and get his letter. She then waits outside, hoping he will come after her. But Yvonne has gone into the house, and Red follows her.

That night, Annie phones Red to come to her house. Yvonne begs him not to get mixed up with the gang again. But he is determined to go, and, feeling to change his mind, Yvonne goes with him. Red gets his letter. It is from Joe, asking for his share of the bank plunder. He writes that he was caught and needs the money for bail. As Red draws some bills from his pocket, Yvonne remonstrates. It is all they have left and Joe was a quitter. Marie taunts Red, telling him she never asked him to hold out on his pals. Yvonne starts for Marie and the fight is on. He separates them. As Yvonne and Marie sit slumped in their chairs, three men enter and urge Red to join them in a bank robbery. Desperate, Yvonne attempts to dissuade Red, but he pays no heed. Marie is triumphant at Yvonne's defeat.

As they leave, the men are questioned by an officer, who orders them to be on their way, then, looking up at Annie's house, crosses over and enters. Marie is looking out of the window and turns, about to warn Red, when the thought comes to her that here is her opportunity to get square with Yvonne. She says nothing. The officer knocks and Marie admits him. Red draws his gun, but Yvonne throws herself in front of him. The officer fires, and the bullet enters Yvonne's shoulder. As she falls, Annie puts the chandelier out of commission and, in the darkness, Yvonne and Red make their escape.

Red tells Yvonne he will get that cop for shooting her. Almost fainting as the wound is being dressed, she says she can bear anything but that. If he kills the officer, they will be separated forever. Finally, he agrees to forego his vengeance.

The next evening they are to leave for San Francisco. Yvonne is determined to get Red away from the gang at Annie's. He tells her that she is in no condition to travel and promises they will leave the next day and he will get an honest job. She goes to bed, only half convinced, and pretends to sleep. Red tiptoes over to his revolver and fondles it lovingly. Then, remembering his promise, he throws it from him and sits staring into space.

The telephone rings. Red answers. Yvonne is listening, tense. It is Marie. She asks him to ditch the redhead and come over. They are going to do the bank job at midnight and will wait for him. He tells her that he is not coming and that, moreover, he is through with her as well. As she hears this, Yvonne relaxes.

Driven by her hatred of Yvonne, Marie goes to the police station and tips off the detectives as to Red's whereabouts. Just before midnight, Red goes to the door to call his dog. A searchlight is thrown on him, and he rolls back into the house. Yvonne rushes from the bedroom. A stone, with note attached, is thrown through the window. The police give them three minutes to come out. Yvonne begs Red to surrender. It will only mean a few years, and they will then be free. But Red angrily refuses. He tries to induce Yvonne to leave him, but she will not. She goes to the window in the glare of the lights and fires at the officers. There is a sharp battle. Fearful that Red will kill someone and put his life in jeopardy, she urges him to come with her. She knows a way of escape. Hurriedly she lights the gas burners in the stove, turning them to different heights, and then empties a box of cartridges on them. As Red enters with some groceries, they leave the house by the cellar stairs.

A little distance from the house they are stopped by a policeman. Only half convinced by their story, he yet lets them go unmolested.

Back in the house, the cartridges are exploding. Suddenly, Red tells Yvonne he is going to join the gang in the bank robbery. She begs him to stay with her and keep his promise. He refuses, and as he starts to leave her, she threatens to shoot him. Unbelieving, he goes on. A moment later he falls to the ground; she has made good her threat. The police enter and the two are arrested. But before they are led away, Yvonne has made Red understand that she only shot him so that after they have served their time, they can be together always.

—Paramount Story Department

THE PRODUCTION

"Despite the good acting on the part of Miss Bow and of the thrilling action, it is a gloomy affair at best, and one that neither edifies nor pleases. On the contrary, it leaves one in the frame of mind one finds himself after returning from a funeral or after surviving a great calamity."
— *Harrison's Reports,* June 23, 1928

Ladies of the Mob was intended only as a Paramount programmer, but it represented an important career move for at least two of its participants. For director William A. Wellman, after scoring solidly with *Wings* (1927) and slightly less solidly with *Legion of the Condemned* (1928), the film was a harbinger of things to come. Set in a seedy underworld of violence and betrayal, *Ladies of the Mob* seems to relate more directly to the *essential* Wellman to come than does the epic *Wings.* It looks forward to his fast, tough, unpretentious melodramas of the early thirties: *Woman Trap* (1930), *The Public Enemy, Night Nurse, The Star Witness* (all 1931), *The Hatchet Man, Love Is a Racket* (both 1932), and *Midnight Mary* (1933), to name just a few.

For star Clara Bow it was an important opportunity to take on a starkly dramatic role after a long string of what seemed to her inconsequential comedies and racy dramas that emphasized her considerable sex appeal far more than her acting ability: *It, Hula, Rosie* (all 1927), *Red Hair* (1928). Paramount head B. P. Schulberg purchased Ernest Booth's magazine story expressly for Bow, but it was clear that the studio did not want to see their biggest star change her frivolous, sexy image. *Ladies of the Mob* was a bone tossed to Bow, not a significant new direction in her career. "Clara was making money doing the hula," said one friend. "Why not keep on making millions with her doing just the same thing?"[1]

There was definitely no hula dancing in *Ladies of the Mob,* an unrelentingly dramatic—even grim—story from the very first frame. Author Ernest Booth, who was serving a life sentence for bank robbery at Folsom Prison, insisted that he had drawn the characters in his story from gangsters and molls he had known professionally. In his first synopsis of the story, Booth describes various ladies of the mob that he has known:

Clara Bow

"There are girls who make their livelihood off thieves without ever entering crime. Their prey is the egotistical thief upon whose susceptibilities they play and whom they eventually devour. Others steal from thieves, and still others practice a polite, subtle form of blackmail, delicately eliciting clothes and jewelry from the men who cannot afford to ditch them, because they know too much. But there are girls who are fascinatingly beautiful, ardently loyal and infinitely clever."[2]

Paramount contract writer Oliver H. P. Garrett wrote a treatment for the screen in December 1927. Garrett was then replaced by John Farrow, an Australian sailor, poet, and novelist who was still a newcomer to the field of writing movies; *Ladies of the Mob* was only Farrow's fifth screenplay. His four drafts of the script (dated January 23, February 5,

Helen Lynch, Richard Arlen, and Clara Bow

March 12, and April 3, 1928) didn't change the basic plot much, but each version became darker, more uncompromising.

The first title set the tone: "A man is about to be killed."

In the moody opening scenes, a hearse approaches the prison gates. The script calls for the camera to be constantly moving, slowly dissolving to a corridor inside the prison walls.

"Six pair of feet are marching firmly, slowly, and rhythmically down the corridor. The feet marching with heavy precision . . . the camera gathers speed and goes through the feet of the marching men down the corridor ahead of it . . . it stops at a cell at the end which is facing the corridor."

A man is being taken to the electric chair. (It is worth noting that all scenes in the script describing the death chamber are X'd out, suggesting that they were never filmed.) A mother and her five-year-old daughter wait in the warden's office. Suddenly, the lights dim from the surge of power needed by the Chair. The sleeping child awakes and "screams loudly . . . terrifically . . . horribly."

The constant camera movement noted in the script may have originated with Wellman or Farrow or some combination of the two. From the few surviving Wellman silents, it is obvious he loved to keep his camera on the move. The crane shot through the Folies-Bergère in *Wings* is one of the most famous examples, but Wellman's restless camera is similarly in evidence in *Big Dan* (1923), *You Never Know Women* (1926), and, particularly, *Beggars of Life* (1928). "He had the eye of an aviator," David O. Selznick said of Wellman, "who was used to constant movement."[3]

Farrow, who became a stylish, if idiosyncratic, director himself, was also a master of camera movement, with a fondness for long, long takes that sometimes encompassed several sets (see *China* (1943), *Two Years Before the Mast* (1946), *The Big Clock* (1948), among many others). Perhaps he caught that particular bug while working on films like *Ladies of the Mob*.

Ladies of the Mob was filmed from April 10 to May 7, 1928, at Paramount Studios on Marathon Street in Hollywood at a cost of $220,148.27 ($7297.07 for the script) and released just over a month

later. The shooting schedule seems brief, but it was not exactly uneventful. In 1928, special effects "squibs" hadn't yet been developed to
simulate bullet hits. So when some scenes featuring gunfire were shot,
real machine guns, using real bullets were used. Years later, in a letter
to costar Richard Arlen, Clara Bow remembered one such incident. "The
live ammunition he (Wellman) insisted on using with marksmen just
behind our heads and in front of said heads was only too real for us,"
she said. "Even my shotgun and your machine gun were filled with real
bullets. I believe one of the bullets ricocheted and hit you, I think, in
your leg, right? I was hit, too, but slightly, in my arm. But did we stop
work? No! Wild Bill just yelled, 'Keep your heads down, damn it!' "[4]

Richard Arlen, who had made a hit in Wellman's *Wings*, is the film's
leading man, but, concentrating on Bow as they were, few of the critics
had much to say about him. One typical response to his performance:
"Richard Arlen is a trifle too refined for the part of the gangster, but he
comes through with flying colors."[5] But while Arlen didn't make much
of an impression, most of the critics applauded this change of pace for
Clara Bow.

"Clara Bow steps right into stark melodrama with a fistful of fire-
arms and proves by her fine handling of this tense role that she has been
'holding out' on us," wrote one. "You will scold yourself a long time if
you fail to see Clara in this."[6]

Motion Picture News's Laurence Reid agreed. "They've taken Clara
Bow out of the 'it' roles to bask her under the emotional flame of drama —
and she does very well. Indeed, she does so well by the role that provision
should be made toward giving her a chance to do a Bernhardt occasionally."[7]

Mordaunt Hall of the *New York Times*, however, found *Ladies of the
Mob* to be "gloomy and artificial. . . . Miss Bow's acting is fairly good,
but her characterization of Yvonne is on the whole disappointing."[8]

Bow biographer David Stenn points out that although many critics
appreciated Bow's change of pace, her fans didn't. "We don't want to
see you suffer," wrote one. "You stand for happiness to us. Keep on
laughing and dancing."[9] An exhibitor complained that Bow "didn't flap
enough to suit her followers."[10] Her next film was "an inane trifle"[11]

called *The Fleet's In*. Clara Bow never strayed so far from type again. Her career ended a scant five years later, when Bow was only twenty-eight years old.

In 1932, Paramount considered remaking *Ladies of the Mob* as a possible follow-up to *Ladies of the Big House* (1931), which starred Sylvia Sidney and Gene Raymond. The plans were eventually scrapped.

In 1941, the Paramount story files were scoured for anything the studio owned that might have remake potential. Presumably, the studio still had a print of *Ladies of the Mob* on hand. However, a studio reader didn't see much in this violent tale: "Glorifying crooks isn't an apt subject for 1941. The story has little to recommend it, either in subject or dramatic values, and isn't remake material."[12]

25

THE PATRIOT

Paramount/Famous Players–Lasky Corporation. Released in New York on
August 17, 1928. Generally released on September 1, 1928. Sound version
10,172 feet. Silent version 9,819 feet. Working Title: *High Treason.*

CREDITS

Presented by: Adolph Zukor and Jesse L. Lasky; *Directed and Edited by:* Ernst Lubitsch; *From
the play:* "Der Patriot; Drama in 5 Akten" (1927) by Alfred Neumann; *Titles:* Julian Johnson;
Adaptation: Hans Kraly; *Photography:* Bert Glennon; Second Cameraman: William Rand;
Assistant Cameramen: William Clothier, Ralph Burdick; *Set Design:* Hans Dreier; *Musical
Direction:* Nathaniel Finston; *Musical Score:* Domenico Savino and Gerard Carbonaro;
Costumes: Ali Hupert; *Technical Advisor:* Nicholas Koliansky; *Assistant Directors:* George
Hippard, George Yohalem; *Technical Directors:* Eugene Hager, Alexander Arkatov; *Unit
Manager:* Eric Locke; *Secretary:* Barbara Bridgeford; *Cutter and Clerk:* Hans Blanche;
Props: Bob Margolis. *Talking Sequences, Sound Effects, and Musical Score:* Movietone.

CAST

Emil Jannings (*Czar Paul I*); Florence Vidor (*Countess Ostermann*); Lewis Stone (*Count Pahlen*); Vera Voronina (*Mademoiselle Lapoukhine*); Neil Hamilton (*Crown Prince Alexander*);
Harry Cording (*Stefan*); Carmenetti (*Count Ostermann*).

AWARDS

Writer Hans Kraly won the 1928–29 Academy Award for adapting *The Patriot.* The film
was also nominated in the following categories: Production [Best Picture]; Actor (Lewis
Stone); Director; Interior Decoration [Set Design].
   The Patriot was named one of the Ten Best Films of 1928 by the *New York Times.*

SYNOPSIS

Emperor of All the Russias, Paul the First, is a strange combination of tyrant, coward, weakling, and mad man. He is feared and hated by his subjects whose resentment and bitterness are inward and without visible protest. But even as Paul creates terror and woe in the hearts of his subjects, so does Paul himself live in constant dread and fear of these subjects. He is harassed by suspicion and doubt, afraid even to eat, drink, or sleep. He fears he will meet the end that had been the fate of some of his ancestors.

There is only one living soul in whom Paul places any trust, and that only at intervals. He is the Prime Minister, Count Pahlen, who has won a powerful influence in the Empire by virtue of this trust. He can handle the Czar like a child. His position is unapproachable save only by the Czar himself.

Count Pahlen is in love with the Countess Ostermann, wife of an Army officer. They are surprised by the husband. He picks up one of Pahlen's boots to throw out a window but is the victim of a Cossack bullet. One of the Czar's edicts is that no one shall present himself at a window when he rides by. The Czar and his Cossack guard had just passed.

THE CONSPIRACY

Pahlen—"The Patriot"—pitying the Czar, is at the same time bleeding for his suffering country. He determines to use his love, the Countess, as a pawn to lure the Czar into a game of death.

At St. Michael, built as a murder-proof castle by Paul, the Czar is more concerned with the number of buttons on the gaiters of Stephan, than with matters of international importance. He whips Stephan for not having enough buttons. Stephan suffers in silence.

Pahlen arrives and, after an audience with the Czar, sees Stephan. He presses the solider into service as his personal bodyguard, promising Stephan revenge. He also outlines plans of dethroning of the Monarch to court attachés.

Alexander, the Crown Prince, is an idealist with a yearning towards his father, and Pahlen's proposition shocks and horrifies him. When Pahlen realizes that his plea to the young man has been in vain, he determines to take drastic steps and warn the Czar against Alexander. The Czar has no love for his son, for he knows the attitude of his subjects towards the Crown Prince. They love him. Paul therefore immediately places his son under arrest.

THE PLANS ARE OUTLINED

Pahlen's next step is to surround himself with his faithful followers and outline his plan minutely, whereby the Czar will be pressed for his abdication, and failing in this, he is to be assassinated, thus clearing the way for Alexander's being placed on the throne.

On the day of the night the plan is to materialize, Paul suddenly decides to leave the city with Lapoukhine, his mistress. This will upset the plans, and in desperation Pahlen manages to put the Czar in contact with a snuff box which he, Pahlen, owns. In this snuff box, hidden by a secret lid, there is an alluring likeness of Countess Ostermann, Pahlen's love.

The Czar becomes excited and calls off the trip. He must meet the Countess. Pahlen arranges this and ingeniously manages to leave the Countess alone with the Czar. He clumsily makes love to her. The Countess, outraged with her betrayal by Pahlen, discloses the minister's plans to the Czar.

THE CZAR IS SATISFIED

The Count is summoned and he explains that he has been in the service of the conspirators to learn of their plans. He pledges his life for the Czar's life. Paul is satisfied and retires to his quarters.

Later that night while the Czar sleeps fitfully, his officers appear. They gain entrance to his bedroom. He shrieks in fear and calls for Pahlen. The Count waits outside weeping. The officers are subdued for the moment by the Czar's dramatic plea: "I am the Czar by Divine Right!" Then from behind appears Stephan. He rushes up to the Czar, and presently the Czar is dead.

While the bells toll ominously outside, and the peasants hail their new Czar, Pahlen and Stephan face each other in Pahlen's home. Stephan holds a pistol. As the clock strikes the hour a shot rings out. Pahlen is mortally wounded.

At this moment the Countess appears. She embraces Pahlen. He turns to her and says: "I have been a bad friend and lover—but I have been a 'Patriot.'"

With these words "The Patriot" falls dead.

—Paramount Press Book

THE PRODUCTION

Ernst Lubitsch's *The Patriot* had one of the shortest lives of any comparable film of its time. Widely praised in reviews as a masterpiece, the recipient of five Academy Award nominations—and one Oscar—there were no known surviving prints of *The Patriot* a scant twenty years after it was produced.

At its original release, however, it seemed to be a movie for all time. "There can be no other opinion," wrote one critic, "than that *The Patriot* is a masterpiece."[1] All of the considerable resources of Paramount were put at the service of this powerful epic: director Ernst Lubitsch; Emil Jannings, who had won an Academy Award a year earlier for his roles in *The Last Command* (1927) and *The Way of All Flesh* (1927); and popular supporting players Florence Vidor, Lewis Stone, and Neil Hamilton. At nearly a million dollars, *The Patriot*'s budget was one of the highest of the year.

Everything about the production was epic. Twelve huge interior sets were designed by Hans Dreier, including the Czar's study, bedroom and antechamber, a military prison, a full-scale art gallery, and a magnificent

Emil Jannings as Tsar Paul

grand staircase. The exterior sets included a church, street, palace square, and courtyard. Surviving photographs show these sets to be strikingly beautiful; they combine the eccentric angles and dramatic lighting of German Expressionism with the scale of craftsmanship that defined Hollywood films of the era.

"One of the sets," wrote a reviewer, "is the vast palace courtyard and long shots of soldiers moving through its intricate vistas, columns of foot soldiers with galloping horsemen weaving around dim corners and streaking across the snow-covered spaces, are stunning effects. Sleighs dashing through the snow-covered streets; a lone horseman streaking across the palace yard in the moonlight, vague shots of the mad

Florence Vidor and Emil Jannings

emperor's soldiery committing pillage on oppressed villages, and a hundred other deft suggestions go to build fine atmosphere."[2]

Costumer Ali Hupert, with whom Lubitsch had worked often in the past, was imported to Hollywood from Berlin for the film, bringing with him scores of period costumes. A glance at the costuming budget ($49,057.30) reveals the irony that while costume rental cost Paramount $11,900, simply paying duty on them cost $12,240.15. The money seems to have been well spent, however; the uniforms, peasant clothes, dresses, and furs have the air of authenticity. *The Patriot* must have been a spectacularly attractive film.

Production began on *The Patriot* on January 3, 1928, after a three week delay in getting sets completed. The first scene shot was Pahlen's tryst with Lady Ostermann in her boudoir (scene #66). We know little about the day-to-day working methods of the *Patriot* crew, but the magnitude of the production was such that it attracted attention beyond the

Czar Paul plans troop movements

studio walls. A reporter for the *New York Times* wrote: "Quite recently, when Ernst Lubitsch was directing night scenes for *The Patriot,* Emil Janning's new film, he used more than a thousand extra players and an enormous outdoor set which represented a snowy square in Petrograd. The interest and excitement on this set, which was increased by the crowd, communicated itself to the surrounding city. During the course of the night, thousands of would-be spectators who could see nothing but the lights in the sky gathered outside the lot and waited patiently for the lights to fade. They could see nothing—there was nothing to be heard—they knew from experience that their vigil would go unrewarded. But such is the fascination of motion pictures that they came, stood long hours in the street, talked motion pictures, and went home."[3]

After sixty-four days in production, on March 6, 1928, filming completed with the burning of a miniature cottage (scene #10).

At some point during production it was decided to add sound to the film, a practice thatParamount—and most of the major studios—was

Emil Jannings with director Ernst Lubitsch

turning to with ever-greater frequency. William Wellman's *Wings* (1927) and *Beggars of Life* (1928) and Erich von Stroheim's *The Wedding March* (1928) were similarly equipped with recorded musical score and sound effects and, in a few cases, a line or two of dialogue. An advertisement touting Paramount's sound releases in the September 1928 issue of *Photoplay* invited audiences to: "Hear the thunderous Russian marches, the charge of the wild Cossacks, the pistol shots, the cries of the innocent!" Interestingly, many critics did not even mention *The Patriot*'s sound. *Variety*'s reviewer, however, gives us this valuable record:

> Sound effects are managed inconspicuously. There is no dialog. In one sequence the Emperor awakes from a nightmare to call in frightened frenzy for his Pahlen, and his cries for "Pahlen" are recorded, but they supplement the titles. While the cry is heard, the screen also carries the word "Pahlen" done in letters that shiver on the screen.
>
> In other sequences the sound merely supplements the action. In the sequence where the conspirators are awaiting 1 o'clock as the time to strike, screen shows a man striking a huge bell with a hammer. The stroke sounds, but the meaning would be quite as plain without the audible effect. Jubilant cries of the mob before the palace when they receive news that the dreaded tyrant is no more also are conveyed by sound, but the camera flashes of the huge crowd expresses the meaning amply.
>
> Musical accompaniment throughout is splendid, merging into the picture so that the auditor forgets it is a mechanical effect and not a functioning orchestra.[4]

Harrison's Reports had a different opinion of *The Patriot*'s sound quality: "The synchronization of this picture is 'atrocious.'"[5]

The Patriot was both Lubitsch's next-to-last silent film (*Eternal Love*, released in May 1929, had a recorded music and effects track but no dialogue) and his first sound film. While many other filmmakers during this chaotic period grappled unsuccessfully with sound, Lubitsch found dialogue and music to be perfect tools for getting his brilliantly witty vision onto the screen. In this sense *The Patriot* can be seen as the first tentative step toward the wonderful dialogue and music of Lubitsch's later masterworks such as *Trouble in Paradise* (1932), *The Merry Widow* (1934), *Ninotchka* (1939), and *To Be or Not To Be* (1942).

Star Emil Jannings was not so fortunate. Wildly, even extravagantly, praised for his bravura performance in *The Patriot* (Richard Watts: "It is impossible to deny that he is infinitely the greatest actor yet produced by the motion picture"[6]), his heavily accented voice ruined his chances for continued success in American films. He returned to Germany with one masterpiece—(von Sternberg's *Der Blaue Engel* (1929)—and many Nazi propaganda films ahead of him. After the Second World War he was blacklisted by Allied authorities and never worked again. He died at 65 in 1950.

We may never know just how effective Janning's portrayal of Paul the First was and must rely on the opinions of contemporary observers. If we accept the critics' view, it was a remarkable performance. *Variety* insisted, "If Jannings were unknown instead of an international screen figure, this picture would make him overnight."[7] *Photoplay* agreed: "[Janning's] uncanny ability to get the intimate nuances of a character makes his portrayal both technically and psychologically accurate."[8]

To many, however, the real star of the piece was Lewis Stone, who portrayed Pahlen "The Patriot." Stone had acted in movies since 1915 without achieving any real stardom. His role in *The Patriot*, however, garnered an Academy Award nomination and an offer of a contract by M-G-M. Stone accepted the contract and stayed at the studio until his death in 1953, one of Metro's most dependable and accomplished actors.

Florence Vidor, like Jannings, found her career in jeopardy with the arrival of talkies. A star throughout the twenties, her flat Texas accent proved unsuitable to sound recording, and after appearing in William Wellman's peculiar part-talkie *Chinatown Nights* (1929), she retired from the screen.

The Patriot, filled with intrigue, betrayal, darkness and death—does not seem typical of the American films of Ernst Lubitsch, who is better known for his remarkable comedies and musicals of the thirties. While still in Germany, however, he often specialized in historical melodramas such as *Carmen* (1918), *Madame Dubarry* (1919), and *Anne Boleyn* (1920). But it may not be true that *The Patriot* was devoid of the famous "Lubitsch touch"; Richard Watts Jr., writing in the *Film Mercury* notes, "Ernst Lubitsch has impressed his individual qualities on it so strikingly that what is essentially a moving tragedy for the moment [turns] into sly and brilliant sex comedy."[9]

Elsewhere in the same review, Watts describes a scene "in which the Czar, having been roguishly slapped on the cheek several times by his mistress, suddenly awakens to the importance of his position and socks the lady in the jaw with considerable violence. So far as I know this admiration arises from no particular suppressed desire, but only from the pleasure of watching an amusing and unexpected incident perfectly played. Then, too, every time Jannings put the lady's dog out of his room, I found high comedy prevailing."[10]

Despite high praise from most quarters, *The Patriot* was not uniformly considered one of the great films of all time. Historian Paul Rotha in his book *The Film Till Now* never lost an opportunity to badmouth the production. He called Janning's performance "very banal, in nauseating bad taste."[11] The film itself was, Rotha said, "mishandled, highly theatrical, over-acted [and] rather pathetic . . . [lacking] not only unity, but sincerity, purpose, style, and dignity."[12] Of course, in the same book, Rotha calls F. W. Murnau's brilliant *Sunrise* (1927) "a masterpiece of bluff, insincerity, unsubstantial nonsense," so we may perhaps be forgiven if we take his comments about *The Patriot* with a grain of salt.[13]

Was *The Patriot* one of the masterpieces of the twenties or, perhaps, of all time? Very sadly, we will probably never know. A thorough search through film archives and private collections over the past five decades has turned up nothing, and it is extremely unlikely that a print will ever resurface. However, miracles do happen, and perhaps we will one day get a chance to evaluate for ourselves this honored, and sorely missed, motion picture.

26

THE CASE OF LENA SMITH

••

Paramount/Famous Players–Lasky. Released January 19, 1929.
Eight reels; 7,229 feet.

C R E D I T S

Director: Josef von Sternberg; *Screenplay:* Jules Furthman; *Titles:* Julian Johnson; *Story:* Samuel Ornitz; *Photography:* Harold Rosson; *Second Cameraman:* Bill Rand; *Assistant Cameramen:* Ed Pyle and Paul Lockwood; *Technical Directors:* Hans Dreier and Martin Porkay; *Film Editor:* Helen Lewis; *Assistant Directors:* Bob Lee and Martin Porkay; *Unit Manager:* J. W. Schleif; *Clerk:* Eleanor McCary; *Property Man:* Lew Asher.

C A S T

Esther Ralston (*Lena Smith*); James Hall (*Franz Hofrat*); Gustav von Seyffertitz (*Herr Hofrat*); Emily Fitzroy (*Frau Hofrat*); Fred Kohler (*Stefan*); Betty Aho (*Stefan's Sister*); Lawrence Grant (*Commissioner*); Leone Lane (*Pepi*); Kay Deslys (*Poldi*); Alex Woloshin (*Janitor*); Ann Brody (*Janitor's Wife*); Wally Albright Jr. (*Franz, age 3*); Warner Klinger (*Franz, age 18*).

••

SYNOPSIS

P R O L O G U E

This story is framed between a prologue and an epilogue. The prologue opens on a little Hungarian village in August 1914. War has been declared. Lena, the woman whom the story chiefly concerns, is introduced with her husband, Stefan. Franz, the son of Lena's first husband and the child of our story, has been called to the colors. Then we show what Lena has undergone for the sake of this child.

S E Q U E N C E   A

Stefan (Fred Kohler), a Hungarian farmer, is working in his fields when he notices three peasant girls coming down the road. He calls to the first one, Lena (Esther Ralston), and again brings up the question of their marriage. Lena kids him along. Stefan becomes insistent. He seizes Lena and starts to drag her behind a haymow, but the husky girl fights him off, boxes his ears, and tells him that she is going to Vienna in company with her two friends. Stefan tells her that he will be waiting for her when she comes back. If she doesn't come back, he will go and get her. Lena laughs and flounces on down the road.

S E Q U E N C E   B

The three girls are on their way to Vienna on foot. They discuss what they are planning to do in Vienna. A carter passes and offers them a ride—with reservations. One of the girls accepts but Lena and the other girl prefer to walk. However, they are rather intrigued by the encounter.

S E Q U E N C E   C

Night in the Prater. Lena and her two friends are thoroughly enjoying the various exhibits and sideshows. One of the girls takes up with a soldier and leaves. Lena and her friend are picked up by a couple of officers, one of them being Franz (James Hall), who show them a good time and work on the simple country girls with complete success. At the end of the sequence, Franz is assuring Lena that he will take good care of her. Lena has implicit faith in her handsome cavalier.

S E Q U E N C E   D

Four years later. Lena is working as housemaid for [Herr] Hofrat (Gustav von Seyffertitz), and she and several other wenches are busy with their week's washing. They discuss their sweethearts. The other girls kid Lena about hers. Nobody has ever seen her in public with a

Gustave Von Severitz with Esther Ralston as Lena Smith

man, yet they know that she slips out every night on some mysterious assignment. Lena only laughs.

Their conversation is interrupted by a call from Frau Hofrat (Emily Fitzroy), who calls Lena back to prepare lunch for her spouse. Downstairs, Lena gets a letter about which her mistress is very suspicious. Lena tells her that it is from Stefan, an old friend of hers, and explains that Stefan only writes to get news of his sister in Vienna. Her mistress seems satisfied for the moment. [Herr] Hofrat enters, and lunch is served with all the pomposity of a petty bureaucrat's establishment.

The meal is interrupted by the arrival of Franz, who is introduced as the son of the household. Franz comes to get money for a gambling debt. His father is extremely angry, but when Franz nonchalantly reminds him of the penalty that will be his unless he pays this debt of honor, [Herr] Hofrat relents and gives him the money. Franz then sits down to lunch, and Lena waits on him without any particular sign of recognition. After lunch, Franz leaves while his father and mother turn in for their afternoon nap, assisted by Lena.

DISSOLVE TO Franz at a coffeehouse, paying his debt. In response to a request as to what he is doing that evening, Franz smiles and responds that he has an appointment with a lady.

S E Q U E N C E   E

Punctually at ten o'clock that night, [Herr] Hofrat dismisses Lena and prepares to retire. As Lena leaves, he notices that her glance lingers on the portrait of Franz hanging on the wall. His suspicions are aroused and he ponders. Meanwhile, Lena goes upstairs, puts on her hat and coat, and slips out of the house. Her master hears this and investigates. When he discovers the empty bedroom, he indignantly calls to his wife and they go through Lena's belongings. In addition to the letter from Stefan, they find a portrait of Franz. [Herr] Hofrat determines to get to the bottom of the matter and, putting on his coat and hat, he departs after Lena.

DISSOLVE TO him arriving at Franz's apartment and being admitted. In the apartment a lightly clad blonde jumps out of bed and disappears into the clothes closet as Franz admits his father. [Herr] Hofrat makes a survey of the apartment under the guise of a friendly visit but finds nothing and leaves much relieved. So is Franz. As he closes the door, the blonde returns from the balcony where she has been hiding, and it is revealed that she is not Lena.

DISSOLVE TO Lena in the apartment of Stefan's sister, where she is cuddling her three-year-old baby. The sister announces that Stefan is coming to Vienna. Their subtitles establish that this is the only time of day that Lena has in which to visit her child.

S E Q U E N C E   F

Next morning at breakfast, [Herr] Hofrat takes Lena to task. She lies about the object of her nocturnal trip, saying that she wanted to get some fresh air. [Herr] Hofrat warns her, as the head of the Bureau of Morals, that good girls don't take the air after dark. She must behave accordingly in future.

S E Q U E N C E   G

On Lena's day off she takes Baby Franz on an airing in the Prater, where she goes through the same routine with the baby that she had gone through with Franz four years before. She comes face to face with the janitor (of the Hofrats' apartment house) and his wife, who are thrown into a flurry of excitement at the sight of Lena with the baby.

S E Q U E N C E   H

That night, when Lena returns, the janitor grins at her queerly. She understands this better when she is met by [Herr] Hofrat, who proceeds to fire her without giving her a chance to defend herself. Lena's temper flares up at this unfair treatment. She talks back to [Herr] Hofrat and, on the way out, boxes the ears of the grinning janitor, precipitating a brawl from which she is rescued by the police.

DISSOLVE TO Lena arriving at the house of Stefan's sister. When she gets there she learns to her horror that the police have just left, taking with them Baby Franz.

S E Q U E N C E   J

Lena appears next at the Bureau of Morals, forces her way in on the official in charge, and demands the return of her child. The official tells her that she is charged by [Herr] Hofrat with being an immoral woman, unfit for the care of her child; but promises to look into the matter. He changes her long Hungarian name to Lena Smith.

A poignant moment with Lena and her son

S E Q U E N C E   J

Franz is seated in an outdoor café when Lena walks by and drops him a note saying that she wants to speak to him. She tells him about their child being taken away and put in a public asylum and that she will have to put up a bond of 1,000 crowns to get the baby back. Franz assures her that he hasn't got any such sum. Then Lena reminds him that she can get the child back very easily by announcing the fact that she and Franz are really married. Franz admits this but reminds her very nonchalantly that, in that case, he would be obliged to commit suicide in order to escape the disgrace. This stumps Lena, and they part without coming to any decision.

DISSOLVE TO Lena returning to the apartment of Stefan's sister. Here she finds a surprise in the person of Stefan himself come to pay a visit. He knows of her trouble. Stefan demands the name of the child's father. Lena refuses to give it. Stefan produces 700 crowns, the savings of years, and tells her to try to get the balance from Franz with the understanding that if he gets the child back, she is to return with Stefan to the farm. Lena hurries out. Stefan follows her at a distance.

DISSOLVE TO Lena again passing by Franz's table and signalling to him. She tells him about the 700 crowns and demands that he get her the remaining 300. Franz's face lights up at the thought of 700 crowns within his reach. He tells Lena that if she will entrust the money to him, he will win her many times that amount at the gambling table. He finally convinces her, and she turns over the money to him.

LAP DISSOLVE TO Franz returning to his table on the sidewalk where he finds his place occupied by Stefan. Stefan now knows Franz to be the man he is looking for. He proceeds to insult Franz very skill-fully, taking advantage of the difference of their stations and of the fact that an officer cannot very well challenge a peasant to a duel. The furious Franz has to be rescued by a policeman.

DISSOLVE TO Franz that evening at home. He is writing a letter. Lena comes, eager to get the money he had promised her. Franz puts her off with the remark that his money troubles are now over, [then] goes into the bedroom and shoots himself. The police are called and find the stupefied Lena looking down at his dead body.

S E Q U E N C E   K

Lena has been called to testify at Franz's inquest. The verdict is suicide, but [Herr] Hofrat insists that Lena be examined. At first, Lena declines to answer out of loyalty to Franz. Finally, however, [Herr] Hofrat scares her by further threats against her baby into telling about her marriage to Franz. Instead of softening [Herr] Hofrat, this news makes him harsher than ever. He now insists on taking his grandson into his own home, away from Lena forever. Lena frantically threatens to announce her marriage publicly and becomes so obstreperous that she is given six months in the workhouse for contempt of court.

S E Q U E N C E   L

Lena, in the workhouse, is kicking and screaming and refusing to be incarcerated. She is finally thrown into her cell and beaten by the matron.

DISSOLVE TO the women prisoners being taken to the fields for the daily work. Lena manages to escape. The alarm is given, but Lena hides in a ditch until night, climbs over the barbed wire fence, and, in spite of the guards, gets away.

DISSOLVE TO Lena breaking into the asylum and kidnapping Baby Franz. She finally escapes out of town, turns her face to the open country, and marches along happily.

E P I L O G U E

We return to the scene of the prologue. Lena's son bids farewell to his mother and marches away with his comrades. There is no patriotic exaltation in Lena's heart. All her struggles—all her sufferings—all her hopes—have been for nothing. She has lost her son after all.

—Paramount Story Department

. . . .

THE PRODUCTION

Samuel Ornitz's first story treatment of *The Case of Lena Smith* (which, for the first two drafts, was known simply as "Ralston Mother Story") bore virtually no resemblance to the film as it would eventually be made by Josef von Sternberg. Ornitz's first Lena was a hardened New York prostitute whose son is taken away from her by ultramoral hypocrites. After she makes her neighbors confront their own biased attitudes, they support her and her son is returned to her.

This version of the story went through several treatments, gradually transforming into quite a different tale altogether. Lena has changed from a tough-talking prostitute to a naive peasant girl who comes to Vienna and is seduced by, then marries, a good-for-nothing cavalry officer. She bears his child, then becomes a servant in his father's home, all the while keeping their marriage a secret. When the father learns the truth, he tries to take the child away from her, but she escapes back to the country and marries the man who has truly loved her all along.

The story as it evolved was obviously a more personal one for Sternberg, being set in 1894, the period of his childhood in old Vienna. "*The Case of Lena Smith*," Andrew Sarris writes, "in both mood and milieu may well be Sternberg's one overt memory film."[1]

In his autobiography, Sternberg admits as much, describing "the vast amusement park" that Vienna seemed to him at the age of three and stating how the memories of that time and place later entered into his work, specifically, *The Case of Lena Smith*. "This was the air that filled my lungs," he wrote of the sights and sounds of *Alt Vien*, "and some of it I was able to exhale when the time was ripe."[2]

The changes in the story also allowed for some satirical — often quite angry — swipes at the unhealthy upper class of the decaying Viennese empire and gave the film's director some promising visual material with which to work. From the earliest points of his career, Sternberg was noted for his brilliant use of lighting for mood and effect. For him, the control of the studio environment was always preferable to location work; Sternberg had no use for "realism."

Consequently, virtually every scene in *The Case of Lena Smith* was shot on the Paramount lot in Hollywood. The only location excursions were to a cornfield in Van Nuys, for the early scenes in which Lena is going to Vienna, and the Selig Zoo for the scene in which the characters visit a monkey cage.

Lena Smith was to be played by Esther Ralston, a beautiful and talented actress, twenty-six years old, who had already been acting in films for a dozen years. Ralston had appeared in such excellent films as Herbert Brenon's *Peter Pan* (1924) and *A Kiss for Cinderella* (1925) and James Cruze's *Old Ironsides* (1926) but the Paramount executives didn't believe that she was capable enough as an actress to play such a dark and complex role as Lena. According to Ralston, Sternberg disagreed with the studio brass.

"He believed that I was an actress, and I was being wasted as a comedienne," she said. "He said, 'Let me have her in this really great role, and I think I can show you. I think I can make an actress of her.' Well, by golly, he had mud dumped all over me, I climbed barbed-wire fences, and I went from a young girl to an old lady. I got marvelous notices. As a director, Mr. von Sternberg was very, very subtle and very sensitive. He would bring out exactly what he wanted. He just worked very sensitively and quietly until you felt you could do anything that he wanted."[3]

"Mr. von Sternberg was so patient and understanding that he helped me do far better than even I could have hoped."[4]

Sternberg didn't remember things quite that way.

He wrote, "Blue-pencilling, rearranging, and dominating another human being, investing it with an alien personality, is hard work, not only for the one who does this, but even more so for the one so maneuvered. But very often, perhaps more often than not, the performer does not know what is going on, and accepts everything that is done to him and is even flattered by all this attention. One such lady was Esther Ralston (*The Case of Lena Smith*, 1929), who sailed through the film unruffled. No one but her husband, who was present at all times, noticed the change in her personality."[5]

Ralston never made another film for Sternberg, so it is impossible to know what kind of performance she gave. Even the reviews offer a toss-up. One critic wrote that Ralston "manages to give one of the best performances of her career to date"[6] and another said that she "holds the interest throughout."[7]

But the *New York Times* wrote that although Ralston was "charming and graceful," she was "miscast" in the role. "For while Miss Ralston is able to rise to the occasion in a lighter type of story, she does not succeed in expressing the emotions. . . . [She] is pretty enough to be a handicap to the plot, for her very looks preclude the possibility of many of the happenings in this blue melodrama."[8]

Variety never mentioned Ralston at all but praises *The Case of Lena*

Smith as "a picture that departs from all commercial lines. The story is fine, theme full of meaning, acting and production are of the best. But it holds nothing to captivate the frivolous fan mass. The picture hasn't a spark of light to relieve its shadow."[9]

Dwight Macdonald's praise was even more fulsome:

"Lena's flight is expressed by the camera following her like a watchful eye as she moves along a wall, hiding behind water pipes and shrinking into dark corners. . . . Von Sternberg does not use his skill in handling the camera to avoid coming to grips with his story. His attack is direct, aggressive, bringing out all the power of his theme, the love, nay, urge, of a mother for her child. . . . I regard it as the most completely satisfying American film I have seen."[10]

Years later, Herman G. Weinberg, in his book *Josef von Sternberg,* recalled, "The desperate terror of Lena's flight from the orphanage with her child—dirty, torn, and bloody, a fugitive from the law, making her way back to her village in the country—is one of the great searing passages in the cinema."[11]

High praise, indeed. Photographs confirm that *The Case of Lena Smith* must have been a masterpiece of moody, baroque visuals. Judging from Sternberg's surviving work of the period, particularly *The Docks of New York* (1928), which just precedes *The Case of Lena Smith,* the director had all the creative tools necessary to bring such a bitterly dramatic story to life.

The Case of Lena Smith was a failure at the box office. This may have been partly for the reason predicted by *Variety*'s critic—that "the frivolous fan mass" just didn't have much patience for so serious and demanding a film. But a bigger reason for the film's poor commercial performance was sound. By January 1929, when *The Case of Lena Smith* opened at New York's Paramount Theater, talkies were beginning to flood the marketplace, and audiences were less and less interested in silent films. Paramount responded by rushing films like *The Case of Lena Smith* through its distribution system and then forgetting about them. There is no way of telling how long prints survived of the film, but the original negative was probably gone in no time, to clear valuable shelf space for new talking pictures. Ironically, the period closest to the sound era is the period from which most silent films have been obliterated.

Esther Ralston keenly regretted the unfortunate circumstances surrounding the release of *The Case of Lena Smith*. It came out, she said decades later, "just as talkies hit. That would have been my greatest role. Although sound didn't hurt my career, it hurt *The Case of Lena Smith*, because it was a great picture, but it was ill timed, you know. It certainly was my best role in silents."[12]

27

4 DEVILS

Fox Film Corporation. Twelve reels. Silent version released October 3, 1928; 9,295 feet. Dialogue version released June 15, 1929; 8,800 feet.

CREDITS

Presented by: William Fox; *Director:* F. W. Murnau; *Screenplay:* Carl Mayer; *Adaptation:* Berthold Viertel and Marion Orth, based on *De Fire Djaevle: excentrisk novelle* (Kristiania, 1895) by Herman Joachim Bang; *Photography:* Ernest Palmer [Academy Award Nomination] and L. W. O'Connell; *Second Unit Photography:* Paul Ivano; *Film Editor:* Harold Schuster; *Sets:* William Darling, from designs by Robert Herlth and Walter Rohrig; *Assistant Art Direction:* Edgar Ulmer; *Assistant Director:* A. F. Erickson; *Second Assistant Directors:* Frank Hansen and Herman Bing.

ADDITIONAL SOUND VERSION CREDITS

Staged by: A. H. Van Buren and A. F. Erickson; *Dialogue:* John Hunter Booth; *Additional Dialogue:* George Middleton; *Musical Score:* S. L. Rothafel; *Song "Marion" by:* Erno Rappé and Lew Pollack; *Recording Engineer:* Harold Hobson; *Sound Effects, Musical Score, and Talking Sequences by:* Movietone.

CAST

First Sequence: J. Farrell MacDonald (*The Clown*); Anders Randolf (*Cecchi*); Claire McDowell (*Mother*); Jack Parker (*Charles, as a boy*); Philippe De Lacy (*Adolf, as a boy*); Dawn O'Day [later known as Anne Shirley] (*Marion, as a girl*); Anita Fremault [later known as Anita Louise] (*Louise, as a girl*); Wesley Lake (*Old Clown*).

Second Sequence: Janet Gaynor (*Marion*); Charles Morton (*Charles*); Nancy Drexel (*Louise*); Barry Norton (*Adolf*); Mary Duncan (*the Lady*); Michael Visaroff (*Circus Director*); George Davis (*Mean Clown*); Andre Cheron (*Old Roué*); Trapeze Stunt Doubles: The Four Cordonas.

SYNOPSIS

A white horse, two little girls, an old clown, and a poodle dog make up the personnel of "Cecchi's Circus," itinerant troupers who eke out a meager existence by entertaining at countryside villages.

An unnourished woman appears with two small boys, whom she begs the circus master to take, as she can no longer feed them. They are the children of two world-renowned trapeze performers who fell to death in the circus.

Yes, Cecchi will take them—and train them. The lads, in panic at being given to this cruel man, find a friend in the old clown and sisters in the little girls.

In the circus ring, Charles, the older of the boys, is being taught to ride horseback. He falls off many times and is cruelly beaten by Cecchi. Marion tries to soothe the sobbing boy and presses into his hand the little watch she had cherished as the sole remembrance of her mother.

In the circus wagon at night, Cecchi, in drunken fury, threatens the sleeping children. The old clown, aroused by this cruel treatment, leaps upon Cecchi and in a terrific fight, beats him insensible.

Into the rising sun just breaking over the hills we see the old clown leading a donkey cart with the four children and the poodle dog away to a new life.

• •

In a larger circus, fifteen years later, we find the old clown with his four fledglings, now grown circus performers. The friendly clown is aged, weary, bent by years of toil training his protégés, but the youngsters assure him they will soon lift the burden.

Adolf and Louise are in love with each other, while Marion is deeply in love with Charles. He loves her as a sister, cherishing the little watch she gave him so many years ago.

At rehearsal, the old clown is gripped with fear and anxiety, for his daring young troupers are about to attempt the great aerialistic feat that will bring them fame—"The Leap of Death."

Success! Charles and Marion both accomplish the death-defying leap. The great burden has been lifted from the old clown ... he is a happy man. More rehearsals—the feat is accomplished successfully again and again. The old man lays aside his clown trappings.

....

We find ourselves gazing in wonder at the sight of a modern-day hippodrome circus. All the first nighters of a great continental city are there. Outside, blazing electric lights proclaim "4 Devils" ... "Breathtaking" ... "Thrilling" ... "The Leap of Death!!!"

Seated in the audience, we watch the Four Devils. Each one, standing astride two white horses, bounds into the ring, grasps swinging bars, and is drawn to the dome of the amphitheater.

A gorgeously dressed woman of the aristocracy occupies a box. Charles swings deftly overhead, and the woman is fascinated. As Charles takes his bow with Marion, a rose falls at his feet, tossed by the jeweled hands of the infatuated woman. Later, they meet. At subsequent performances more roses are thrown ... then notes ... love notes, breathing passion.

In a modest café, the old clown is giving a party for the four devils. Adolf and Louise announce their engagement, but Marion waits in vain for her adored Charles, who is visiting the woman.

The clandestine visits continue, and the old clown in despair attempts to dissuade Charles, who throws him roughly aside. Marion follows Charles to the woman's apartment, gains entrance, and pleads with the woman to save him from ruin. Finally, Marion leaves.

Remorse overcomes Charles, who has been waiting in another room. A scene follows in which he breaks with the woman, and as he leaves, he sees a figure huddled in the snow. It is Marion, who is nearly frozen. Charles takes her into the car, revives her, and explains that he has broken off with the woman. He declares that he only loves Marion.

In the meantime, Charles has told the manager of the theater that he will make the leap of death WITHOUT the net. Everything is set for the final performance, a record house being assured to witness the super-sensational feat.

That morning at rehearsal, Charles discovers that Marion is attempting to conceal something from him. She finally gives in and tells Charles that she has a little surprise for him in his dressing room. (She has bought him a handsome new wristwatch to take the place of the little old one she gave him years before.)

Charles rushes to his dressing room. He opens the door and finds the woman waiting for him. In his excitement he forgets the watch. Her wiles finally overcome him, and he goes with the woman to her apartment, where an orgy of drinking and lovemaking follow. Later, he realizes that it is the night of the final performance featuring the leap of death without the net.

He staggers out and rushes to the circus. The old clown and his associates are nearly distracted. It is time for the act when Charles eventually shows up. He is so shaky he can hardly stand upright, and Marion works in frenzied despair, striving to revive him for the terrible leap.

In the cupola of the circus: Charles is on one pedestal, Marion on another opposite. They plunge in their "leap of death" just as the woman appears in her box. Charles almost misses his grip—but succeeds in saving himself. The temptress tosses the symbolic rose. To Marion, it means that Charles has finally thrown aside her love for the charms of the siren. Her heart is breaking . . . her strength is going . . . her hold weakens . . . she is slipping . . . SHE FALLS!

Charles stares at the crumpled little form in the sawdust ring. He swings down madly, hoping against hope that Marion may be spared. Will she live? A love so strong cannot—*must not*—end this way! As he gathers her in his strong arms, she looks up and whispers to him, "We're always going to be happy . . . aren't we?" And Charles answers, "Always happy . . . you and I!"

ABOUT THE TITLE

The title of this film usually appears in print as *Four Devils* or *The Four Devils*. However, the Fox campaign book for the film is quite clear on the point: "Most newspapers, if not all of them, would spell out the word 'four,' but in the film, '4 Devils' flashes off and on from a huge electric sign, with the figure '4' prominent, and as the name of the picture was taken from that, it was decided to copy it exactly and use the numeral."[1]

—Fox press book

THE PRODUCTION

When the brilliant German director F. W. Murnau came to America in 1927, he put his best foot forward. The first motion picture he made in Hollywood, *Sunrise,* starring Janet Gaynor and George O'Brien, is, not to put too fine a point on it, one of the greatest films ever made—anywhere. It was overwhelmingly praised by contemporary critics and is today regarded as a masterpiece, not only of the silent period, but of all time.

Sunrise was not, however, a financial success. And in Hollywood, then as now, prestige is only desirable when accompanied by cold cash. William Fox, the head of Fox Studios, made sure that Murnau's follow-up film would be produced with an eye toward both budget and box office.

According to Murnau's biographer, Lotte Eisner, the director wrote to Fox on December 22, 1927, stating he intended to begin filming *4 Devils* on January 3, 1928. "He said he was delighted with Hermann Bang's story," Eisner writes, "because it was about young, beautiful, wholesome people, which enabled him to introduce and train a group of new talents who hadn't yet had their heads turned by stardom. He would be able to make the film for a reasonable sum because he wouldn't need 'exorbitant' sets as in *Sunrise.* Moreover, because of the uncertainty of the California weather, all the shooting would be done in the studio."[2]

After completing *Sunrise,* Murnau returned to Germany for a visit. Upon his return, he began researching *4 Devils* by accompanying Ringling Bros.–Barnum and Bailey Circus on a tour through Virginia. Back in Hollywood, Robert Herlth began making storyboard sketches and set designs. Many of these dramatic drawings are in the collection of the Cinemathèque Français in Paris. Drawn with a swift, bold stroke in a style of exaggerated perspective (a favorite Murnau visual device), Herlth's sketches have a texture and immediacy that the surviving stills from *4 Devils* lack. We can look to the photographs for documentary evidence of what the film looked like, but Herlth's sketches help us know what it *felt* like.

To adapt Hermann Bang's original story into script form, Murnau turned to his favorite collaborator, Carl Mayer, who had written the screenplays for *The Last Laugh* (1924), *Tartuffe* (1925), and *Sunrise*. The work had to be conducted by long distance, though: Mayer had never left Germany. Berthold Viertel and Marion Orth were also assigned to the *4 Devils* script. A Fox campaign book for the film explained why Orth was brought on board:

"Marion Orth furnished the feminine reaction to certain phases of *4 Devils* from Hermann Bang's novel. Mayer and Viertel prepared most of the script, but Murnau felt that certain parts needed the viewpoint and handling that a woman would give them. He selected Miss Orth."[3]

Orth was a veteran writer who worked frequently at Fox. She worked on the scripts for some of John Ford's earlier films, like *Hangman's House* (1928) and *Cameo Kirby* (1930). In 1929 she and Viertel would again collaborate (without Carl Mayer this time) on *City Girl,* from which Murnau was removed as director toward the end of production.

The first actor to be cast in *4 Devils* was Janet Gaynor, who had delivered a performance of heartbreaking simplicity in *Sunrise* as George O'Brien's wronged wife. Gaynor had been acting in motion pictures for only two years but was steadily building the faithful audience that would make her Hollywood's top box-office attraction in the early thirties. The rest of the young cast included Mary Duncan, Barry Norton and Nancy Drexel. Dawn O'Day, who played Gaynor's character, Marion, as a child, later starred in RKO's *Anne of Green Gables* (1934) and took the character's name for herself: Anne Shirley.

A very young Dawn O'Day (later to act under the name
of Anne Shirley) with Phillipe De Lacy

Although Murnau was working as a Fox employee, with all the
restrictions that implied, he was still determined that *4 Devils* would be
a worthy follow-up to *Sunrise*. To capture the trapeze acts with dynamic
fluidity, he developed an apparatus called the "go-devil."

"This consisted of a large steel upright, from which swung a big
steel boom, on the end of which was a car carrying batteries of lights
and cameras, capable of revolving at various heights and at dizzy speeds.

"This framework, which weighed twenty tons, was designed by the
director to shoot the young players as they whirled through the air in
their acrobatic feats. As the singular 'go-devil' spun about, it tickled the

spines of the most blasé atmosphere people [extras] quite as much as the stunts of the stars."[4]

For the climactic scene in which Marion falls from the trapeze, assistant cinematographer Paul Ivano built rails high above the set that curved down to the ground. He placed the camera in a triangular carriage to which a remote control motor was fixed. The camera operator could control the speed and movement of the camera so that Marion's point of view could be expressed in one thrilling swoop.

Up to thirteen hundred extras were used as spectators in the circus tent sequences. Most of them were frustrated actors, and when asked to register startled reactions to some tragedy in the circus ring, they began hamming it up to a distressing degree. Murnau hit upon a plan to get a more sincere reaction. He called them to the set one morning and then began shooting close-ups of the stars, ignoring the extras. The crowd

The four devils: Charles Morton, Barry Norton, Mary Drexel, and Janet Gaynor

was left to its own devices for several hours, growing more and more bored.

Suddenly, late in the afternoon, a trapeze artist swung out over the crowd and shrieked as if in fear. All thirteen hundred faces jerked upward, genuinely startled and concerned. Murnau, having trained six cameras on the crowd, got all the reaction shots he needed.

Released both as a silent film and with a recorded musical score by S. L. Rothafel, *Variety* found *4 Devils* to be "an elegantly produced, photographed, and directed picture" but thought the slim story did not justify the film's two-hour running time.[5] However, William Fox must have been pleased (and a bit relieved) to read that *Variety* found Murnau to have "turned out a commercial proposition in this expensive production. Murnau's indoor circus is superb; his entire circus arrangement never falters and no circus on the screen under canvas or roof has approached the semblance of bigness Murnau has given here."[6]

Film Daily thought Murnau's direction was "excellent, but too repetitious," the cinematography "magnificent," and the entire production "rich with directorial niceties and evidencing high intelligence."[7]

Photoplay wrote that the first episode, showing the characters as children, was "so beautifully and tenderly filmed that it is worth seeing the picture for. And the work of little Dawn O'Day deserves special tribute. . . . Janet Gaynor gives a sympathetic, sincere and touching performance. She has remarkable personality and persuasive charm. Charles Morton and Barry Norton are extraordinarily fine, and you'll like Nancy Drexel. The weakness of the film is Mary Duncan's old-fashioned vampire. In dress and direction, the role is exaggerated, a flashback to the days of Theda Bara."[8]

The film was reasonably successful at the box office (more successful than *Sunrise,* certainly) but even a synchronized recorded musical score wasn't quite the draw it once was. Audiences demanded talkies, and so Fox pulled *4 Devils* back in for reshoots in sound. The last two reels of the film were now to include dialogue.

A "legit" playwright, John Hunter Booth, was hired to write the dialogue. A. H. Van Buren, a stage director, and veteran assistant director A. F. Erickson were brought on to supervise the talking sequences. It is not clear how much Murnau was involved in the reshoots, although

Charles Morton, Mary Duncan, and director F. W. Murnau

the Fox campaign book gives the impression that Van Buren and Erickson were entirely in charge.

Variety wasn't much impressed with the talking sequences, finding the actors too strident and uncomfortable and the recording "harsh."[9] However, the trade paper saw the commercial angle in a more positive light: "The addition of dialogue for the two [reels] should add to [the film's] impression. General theme of the picture is of the type apparently constructed to unleash the tear ducts and make the sad-eyed sisters pull out their handkerchiefs in unison."[10]

Variety—and William Fox—was right. The revamped *4 Devils* was a box-office success. That the grafting-on of sound might have marred Murnau's carefully executed visual style was irrelevant. Fox proved that he could keep those artistic guys in their place.

Murnau's next film, *Our Daily Bread,* was also taken out of his hands. Although sound was added to the film, it survives today only in a silent version entitled *City Girl* (1930). While the film retains flashes of Murnau's genius, it barely resembles his original conception.

After teaming with documentarian Robert Flaherty on the sumptuous *Tabu* (1931), Murnau was about to sign with Paramount when he was killed in an automobile accident. He was only forty-two years old.

Though his career as a filmmaker spanned only a decade, F. W. Murnau is indisputably one of the giants of the cinema. Because we know what towering achievements he was capable of, the loss of *4 Devils* seems doubly tragic. Although he was somewhat hampered by studio-imposed limitations during the film's production, Murnau was working at the peak of his creative powers, and, whatever compromises may have occurred, it is a certainty that *4 Devils* was at least interesting; it may in fact have been a masterpiece.

However, according to Hollywood legend, *4 Devils* star Mary Duncan didn't think so. The story goes that she asked Fox for a print of the film sometime in the thirties. She was apparently not pleased with what she saw. After her viewing of the film, she took the rare print out on a boat and dumped it into the Pacific.

This tale might be apocryphal, but at least it supplies a more colorful reason for the demise of *4 Devils* than we can come up with for most lost films.

Anyway, quality seems never to have been a factor in whether a film survived or disappeared. If it were, the majority of the films discussed in *Lost Movies* would still be here, amusing us, moving us, giving us privileged glimpses into other eras and different sensibilities. Chances are, on seeing some of them, we might be tempted, like Mary Duncan, to throw the prints into the sea. But I believe it's far more likely that even the least of these films would prove to be treasures in some way and that we would welcome the opportunity to have just one more look.

How sad that we will never get that chance.

NOTES

···

Introduction

1. Jean Firstenberg, interview with the author, April 1991.

2. Robert Gitt, interview with the author, March 1991.

3. Eileen Bowser, interview with the author, April 1991.

4. Susan Dalton, interview with the author, April 1991.

5. Bowser interview.

6. *Motion Picture News*, November 3, 1917.

7. *Photoplay*, September, 1921, p. 55.

8. Ibid.

9. *Photoplay*, September, 1921, p. 105.

1. The Immortal Alamo

1. Gaston Méliès, *Complete Catalog of Genuine and Original Star Films* (New York: Méliès Star Film Company, 1903) p. 5.

2. *Moving Picture World*, March 26, 1910.

3. *Film Index*, February 26, 1910, p. 3.

4. *San Antonio Light*, January 8, 1911.

5. *San Antonio Daily Express*, January 8, 1911.

6. *Film Index*, April 29, 1911.

7. *Film Index*, April 22, 1911.

8. *Motography*, June 1911, p. 149.

9. Ibid.

10. *New York Dramatic Mirror*, May 3, 1911.

11. Ibid.

12. *New York Dramatic Mirror*, May 31, 1911.

13. *New York Dramatic Mirror*, May 3, 1911, p. 29.

14. *Moving Picture World*, June 10, 1911, p. 1313.

15. *Motography,* June 1911.

16. *Film Index,* January 22, 1910.

17. *San Antonio Light,* June 2, 1914.

18. If you have any information at all on these last three lost Alamo films, please contact me through the publisher. For a more thorough discussion of them, see: Frank Thompson, *Alamo Movies,* Plano, Texas: Republic of Texas Press, 1994.

2. Saved From the Titanic

1. *New York Dramatic Mirror,* May 15, 1912.

2. *Moving Picture News,* April 27, 1912, p. 7.

3. Ibid.

4. *New York Dramatic Mirror,* May 1, 1912, p. 13.

5. *Moving Picture News,* April 27, 1912, p. 7.

6. *New York Dramatic Mirror,* May 1, 1912, p. 13.

7. *Moving Picture News,* May 11, 1912.

8. *Moving Picture News,* May 4, 1912, p. 27.

9. *Moving Picture World,* May 11, 1912.

3. The Battle of Gettysburg

1. *New York Dramatic Mirror,* June 11, 1913.

2. *Motography,* July 13, 1913.

3. *New York Dramatic Mirror,* June 11, 1913.

4. Interestingly, Thomas Ince's brother Ralph, a fine director as well as actor, was already quite well known for his portrayal of Abraham Lincoln on film. Just a year earlier, Ralph had portrayed the president in *Lincoln's Gettysburg Address* (1912).

5. *New York Dramatic Mirror,* June 4, 1913.

6. *Motography,* July 12, 1913.

4. Damaged Goods

1. *Moving Picture World,* October 2, 1915.

2. Joan Bennett and Lois Kibbee, *The Bennett Playbill,* New York: Holt, Rinehart & Winston, 1970.

3. *New York Dramatic Mirror*, September 30, 1914.

4. *Variety*, October 1, 1915.

5. *Moving Picture World*, October 2, 1915.

6. *Motography*, September 25, 1915.

7. *Motography*, October 9, 1915.

8. *Motography*, October 9, 1915.

9. *Motion Picture News*, October 2, 1915.

10. *Motography*, October 9, 1915.

11. Juliet Benita Colman, *Ronald Colman: A Very Private Person*, New York: William Morrow, 1975.

12. Kevin Brownlow, *Behind the Mask of Innocence*, New York: Alfred A. Knopf, 1990.

5. Purity

1. *Moving Picture World*, July 29, 1916, p. 804.

2. *Moving Picture World*, August 26, 1916, p. 1355.

3. *Variety*, July 7, 1916, p. 25.

4. *Wid's Daily*, July 13, 1916, p. 714.

5. *Moving Picture World*, July 29, 1916, p. 804.

6. *Motion Picture News*, August 5, 1916, p. 789.

7. *Variety*, July 7, 1916, p. 25.

8. *Motion Picture News*, August 5, 1916, p. 789.

9. *New York Times*, July 24, 1916, p. 7:4.

10. Ibid.

11. Kevin Brownlow, *Hollywood: The Pioneers*, London: Collins, 1979, p. 120.

6. A Daughter of the Gods

1. *Moving Picture World*, February 14, 1920, p. 1011.

2. *Photoplay*, August 1916, p. 134.

3. *Moving Picture World*, November 4, 1916, p. 673.

4. *Photoplay*, August 1916, p. 134.

5. *Photoplay*, July 1916, pp. 135-137.

6. *New York Times*, October 18, 1916, p. 9:1.

7. *Motography*, November 4, 1916, p. 1037.

8. *Wid's Daily*, October 19, 1916, p. 1039.

9. *New York Times*, October 18, 1916, p. 9:1.

10. Ibid.

11. *Motion Picture News*, December 23, 1916.

12. *Motion Picture News*, February 14, 1920, p. 1011.

13. *New York Dramatic Mirror*, October 28, 1916, p. 24.

7. The Conqueror

1. *Motion Picture News*, September 29, 1917, p. 2205.

2. Raoul Walsh, *Each Man in His Time*, New York: 1974, p. 155.

3. *New York Dramatic Mirror*, September 22, 1917, p. 25.

4. Raoul Walsh, p. 155.

5. Ibid. p. 157.

6. *Motion Picture News*, September 29, 1917, p. 2205.

7. *Motography*, October 13, 1917, p. 783.

8. *Wid's Daily*, October 25, 1917, p. 678.

9. *Moving Picture World*, September 29, 1917, p. 2006.

10. *Wid's Daily*, October 25, 1917, p. 678.

11. *Variety*, September 21, 1917, p. 44.

8. Cleopatra

1. *Moving Picture World*, January 16, 1926.

2. *Photoplay*, March 1926, p. 34.

3. William M. Drew, *Speaking of Silents: First Ladies of the Screen*. Vestal, N.Y.: Vestal Press, Ltd., 1989.

4. *Cleopatra*, the Fox press book.

5. Ibid.

6. *Motion Picture News*, November 3, 1917.

7. *New York Dramatic Mirror*, October 27, 1917.

8. *Cleopatra*, the Fox press book.

9. *Moving Picture World*, November 3, 1917, p. 708.

10. *Motion Picture News,* January 5, 1918, p. 102.

11. Ibid.

12. *Forum,* July 1919.

13. *Wid's Daily,* October 18, 1917, p. 663.

9. Roped

1. Peter Bogdanovich, *John Ford,* Berkeley: University of California Press, 1970, p. 39.

2. *Motion Picture News,* November 16, 1918, p. 2981.

3. Ibid.

4. Ibid.

5. Ibid.

6. *Variety,* January 31, 1919, p. 54.

7. *Wid's Daily,* January 12, 1919, p. 11.

8. *Motion Picture News,* January 25, 1919, p. 581.

9. Ibid., p. 582.

10. The Knickerbocker Buckaroo

1. *Exhibitor's Trade Review,* May 24, 1919.

2. *Moving Picture World,* June 7, 1919, p. 1475.

3. Ibid.

4. *New York Times,* May 26, 1919.

5. *Exhibitor's Trade Review,* June 7, 1919, p. 55.

6. Ibid.

7. Mike Steen, *Hollywood Speaks: An Oral History,* New York: G. P. Putnam's Sons, 1974, pp. 156–157.

8. *Exhibitor's Trade Review,* June 7, 1919, p. 55.

9. *Moving Picture World,* June 7, 1919, p. 1475.

10. *Wid's Daily,* June 1, 1919, p. 20.

11. *Motion Picture News,* June 7, 1919.

11. *The Miracle Man*

1. *Exhibitors Trade Review*, July 26, 1919, p. 621.
2. *Photoplay*, October 1919, p. 76.
3. *Wid's Daily*, August 31, 1919, p. 3.
4. *Photoplay*, September 1921, p. 55.
5. William K. Everson, *American Silent Film*, New York: Oxford University Press, 1978, p. 63.
6. Kevin Brownlow, *Behind the Mask of Innocence,*. New York: Alfred A. Knopf, 1990, p.71.
7. This part of the story, at least, is in error. *Traffic in Souls* was made while Tucker was with IMP (Independent Motion Picture Company). Because IMP head Carl Laemmle didn't want to make the film, Tucker produced it with funds raised from investors and fellow IMP employees Herbert Brenon, King Baggott, Jack Cohn, and William Robert Daly. For more background on the production of *Traffic in Souls*, see Brownlow, *Behind the Mask of Innocence*, pp. 71–80.
8. *Exhibitor's Trade Review*, July 26, 1919, p. 621.
9. *Variety*, August 29, 1919, p. 66.
10. *Wid's Daily*, August 31, 1919, p. 3.
11. *Exhibitor's Trade Review*, September 6, 1919.
12. *Photoplay*, October 1919, p. 78.
13. *Variety*, August 29, 1919, p. 66.
14. *Exhibitor's Trade Review*, July 26, 1919, p. 621.

12. *Hollywood*

1. Robert E. Sherwood, *The Best Moving Pictures of 1922–1923*, Small, Maynard and Company, 1923, pp. 78–85.
2. Ibid.
3. Ibid.
4. *Harrison's Reports*, August 4, 1923.
5. *New York Times*, July 30, 1923, 11:4.
6. *Hollywood* script file, Paramount Files, Margaret Herrick Library, Academy of Motion Picture Arts and Sciences.

7. *New York Times,* July 30, 1923, 11:4.

8. *Motion Picture News,* July 14, 1923.

9. Sherwood.

10. *Hollywood* script file, Paramount Files, Margaret Herrick Library, Academy of Motion Picture Arts and Sciences.

13. Pied Piper Malone

1. *Photoplay,* August 1924, p. 47.

2. William M. Drew, *Speaking of Silents: First Ladies of the Screen,* Vestal, N.Y.: Vestal Press, 1989, p. 255.

3. *Photoplay,* August 1924, p. 47.

4. *Georgetown (S.C.) Times,* November 9, 1923, p. 1.

5. *American Film Institute Catalog: Feature Films, 1921–1930,* p. 603.

6. *Morning Telegraph,* January 24, 1924.

7. *Georgetown (S.C.) Times,* November 16, 1923, p. 1.

8. *Georgetown (S.C.) Times,* November 23, 1923, p. 1.

9. Ibid.

10. Ibid.

11. *Georgetown (S.C.) Times,* November 30, 1923, p. 1.

12. *Motion Picture Classic,* April 1924, p. 52.

13. *Photoplay,* March 1924, p. 97.

14. Ibid.

15. *Variety,* January 31, 1924.

16. *New York Times,* January 28, 1924.

17. Unidentified review. Chamberlin Scrapbook no. 6, p. 75. Margaret Herrick Library, Academy of Motion Picture Arts and Sciences.

18. *Motion Picture News,* February 9, 1924, p. 657.

19. *Moving Picture World,* February 9, 1924, p. 488.

20. *Harrison's Reports,* February 2, 1924.

14. So Big

1. Colleen Moore, *Silent Star*, Garden City, N.Y.: Doubleday & Company, 1968, p. 141.

2. William M. Drew, *Speaking of Silents: First Ladies of the S creen*, Vestal, N.Y.: Vestal Press, 1989, p. 173.

3. *Motion Picture News*, January 17, 1925, p. 270.

4. *Los Angeles Examiner*, September 9, 1924.

5. *Oakland Tribune*, September 14, 1924.

6. *Chicago Tribune*, October 1, 1924.

7. *New York Times*, January 5, 1925, p. 19:1.

8. *Harrison's Reports*, January 7, 1925.

9. *Variety*, January 7, 1925.

10. Colleen Moore, *Silent Star*, Garden City, N.Y.: Doubleday & Company, 1968, p. 158.

15. The Flaming Frontier

1. For an excellent overview of Custer movies, see Paul Andrew Hutton's "Correct in Every Detail: General Custer in Hollywood" (pp. 488–524) in *The Custer Reader*, edited by Hutton. Lincoln: University of Nebraska Press, 1992. A profusely illustrated version of this essay appeared in *Montana: The Magazine of Western History*, Winter 1991, pp. 28–57.

2. *Exhibitor's Review*, February 20, 1926, p. 12.

3. Unidentified review. Chamberlin scrapbook no. 37, p. 58. Margaret Herrick Library, Academy of Motion Picture Arts and Sciences.

4. *Moving Picture World*, April 17, 1926.

5. Chamberlin Scrapbook no. 37, P. 59.

6. *Variety*, April 7, 1926.

7. *Universal Weekly*, vol 23, no. 10, p. 13.

8. *Variety*, April 7, 1926.

9. *Moving Picture World*, April 17, 1926.

10. *Motion Picture News*, April 17, 1926, p. 1834.

11. *Motion Picture News*, April 10, 1926, p. 1576.

12. *Moving Picture World*, April 17, 1926.

13. Ibid.

14. Ibid.

15. *Universal Weekly*, vol. 23, no. 10, p. 13.

16. Ibid.

17. Ibid.

18. *Moving Picture World*, April 17, 1926.

16. *"That Royle Girl"*

1. *Variety*, January 13, 1926.

2. *Exhibitor's Trade Review*, January 16, 1926, p. 22.

3. *Harrison's Reports*, January 16, 1926.

4. *Exhibitor's Trade Review*, January 16, 1926, p. 22.

5. Ibid.

6. *New York Times*, January 11, 1926, p. 33:1.

7. Ibid.

8. *Exhibitor's Trade Review*, January 16, 1926, p. 22.

9. *Harrison's Reports*, January 16, 1926.

10. *Variety*, January 13, 1926.

11. *New York Times*, January 11, 1926, p. 33:1.

12. *Toronto Daily Star*, date unknown; quoted in Anthony Slide and Edward Wagenknecht's *The Films of D. W. Griffith*. New York: Crown Publishers, 1975, p. 219.

17. *The Last Moment*

1. John W. Dodds, *The Several Lives of Paul Fejos*, United States: The Wenner–Gren Foundation, 1973, p. 27.

2. Dodds, p. 28.

3. Ibid.

4. Ibid.

5. Dodds, p. 33.

6. *Film Spectator*, November 26, 1927, pp. 11–12.

7. Charles Higham, *Hollywood Cameramen*, Bloomington: Indiana University Press, 1970, p. 19.

8. Ibid.

9. Ibid.

10. *Variety,* March 14, 1928.

11. *New York Times,* March 14, 1928.

12. *Film Daily,* March 11, 1928, p. 6.

13. *National Board of Review Magazine,* February 1928, p. 6.

18. The Rough Riders

1. *Motion Picture News,* December 19, 1925, p. 2999.

2. *New York Times,* March 16, 1927, p. 28:2.

3. William A. Wellman, *A Short Time for Insanity,* New York: Hawthorn Books, 1974, pp. 163, 164.

4. *Motion Picture News,* October 16, 1926, p. 1468.

5. *Motion Picture News,* November 6, 1926, p. 1762.

6. Charles Higham, *Hollywood Cameramen,* Bloomington: Indiana University Press, 1970, p. 82.

7. *Motion Picture News,* November 6, 1926, p. 1762.

8. *Variety,* March 30, 1927, p. 14.

9. *Harrison's Reports,* April 9, 1927.

10. *New York Times,* March 16, 1927, p. 28:2.

11. *Motion Picture News,* March 25, 1927, p. 1035.

19. Time to Love

1. *Life,* volume 87, no. 2258, February 11, 1926, p. 6.

2. *Variety,* June 22, 1927, p. 34.

3. *New York Times,* June 22, 1927, p. 33:3.

4. Paramount Collection, *Time to Love* file, Margaret Herrick Library, Academy of Motion Picture Arts and Sciences.

5. Walter Kerr, *The Silent Clowns,* New York: Alfred A. Knopf, 1975, p. 299.

6. *Life,* vol. 87, no. 2258, February 11, 1926, p. 6.

20. *Gentlemen Prefer Blondes*

1. *Variety,* January 18, 1928.

2. *New York Times,* January 18, 1928, p. 16.

3. *Motion Picture News,* January 21, 1928, p. 214.

4. *Variety,* January 18, 1928.

5. John Kobal, *People Will Talk,* New York: Alfred A. Knopf, 1985, pp. 170–171.

21. *Beau Sabreur*

1. *Motion Picture World,* March 4, 1927, p. 797.

2. *Motion Picture World,* March 11, 1927, p. 868.

3. *Film Daily,* January 29, 1928.

4. *New York Times,* January 23, 1928.

5. *Photoplay,* March 1928, p. 53.

6. Ibid.

7. *Film Daily,* January 29, 1928.

8. *Motion Picture News,* January 28, 1928, p. 280.

22. *The Divine Woman*

1. Kevin Brownlow, *The Parade's Gone By,* New York: Alfred A. Knopf, 1969, p. 146.

2. Metro-Goldwyn-Mayer Pressbook, *The Divine Woman,* p. 1.

3. *Variety,* January 18, 1928.

4. *Film Daily,* January 22, 1928.

5. *New York Times,* January 16, 1928, p. 24:1.

6. Ibid.

23. *Legion of the Condemned*

1. Kevin Brownlow, *The Parade's Gone By,* New York: Alfred A. Knopf, 1969.

2. *New York Times,* March 19, 1928.

3. Fay Wray interviews with John Andrew Gallagher, February 22, 1989 and March 2, 1989.

4. Ibid.

5. *Legion of the Condemned* file, Paramount Collection, Margaret Herrick Library, Academy of Motion Picture Arts and Sciences.

6. *Photoplay*, February 1928.

7. *Film Daily*, March 25, 1928.

8. Ibid.

9. Laurence Reid, *Motion Picture News*, March 24, 1928.

24. *Ladies of the Mob*

1. David Stenn, *Clara Bow: Runnin' Wild*, New York: Doubleday, 1988.

2. Ernest Booth, synopsis, *Ladies of the Mob*, Paramount files, Margaret Herrick Library, Academy of Motion Picture Arts and Sciences.

3. Kevin Brownlow, *The Parade's Gone By*, New York: Alfred A. Knopf, 1969.

4. Lee Belser, "Clara Bow Deplores 'Filth' of Modern Books and Films," *Los Angeles Mirror*, March 31, 1961.

5. *Motion Picture News*, June 23, 1928.

6. *Photoplay*, September 1928

7. *Motion Picture News*, June 23, 1928.

8. *New York Times*, June 18, 1928.

9. David Stenn, *Clara Bow: Runnin' Wild*, New York: Doubleday, 1988.

10. Ibid.

11. Ibid.

12. Paramount files, *Ladies of the Mob*, Margaret Herrick Library, Academy of Motion Picture Arts and Sciences.

25. *The Patriot*

1. *Harrison's Reports*, September 1, 1928.

2. *Variety*, August 22, 1928.

3. *New York Times*, April 15, 1928.

4. *Variety*, August 22, 1928.

5. *Harrison's Reports*, September 1, 1928.

6. *Film Mercury*, August 31, 1928.

7. *Variety*, August 22, 1928.

8. *Photoplay*, June 1928.

9. *Film Mercury*, August 31, 1928.

10. Ibid.

11. Paul Rotha, *The Film Till Now*, New York: Funk & Wagnalls, 1930.

12. Ibid.

13. Ibid.

26. The Case of Lena Smith

1. Andrew Sarris, *The Films of Josef von Sternberg*, Garden City, N.Y.: Doubleday, 1966, p. 22.

2. Josef von Sternberg, *Fun in a Chinese Laundry*, New York: Macmillan Publishing Company, 1965.

3. William M. Drew, *Speaking of Silents*, Vestal, N.Y.: Vestal Press, 1989.

4. Esther Ralston, *Some Day We'll Laugh*, Metuchen, N.J.: Scarecrow Press, 1985.

5. Josef von Sternberg, *Fun in a Chinese Laundry*, New York: Macmillan Publishing Company, 1965.

6. *Moving Picture News*, January 19, 1929, p. 195.

7. *Film Daily*, January 10, 1929.

8. *New York Times*, January 15, 1929, p. 22:4.

9. *Variety*, January 16, 1929.

10. Dwight Macdonald, *Miscellany*, March 1931.

11. Herman G. Weinberg, *Josef von Sternberg*, New York: E. P. Dutton, 1967.

12. William M. Drew, *Speaking of Silents*, Vestal, N.Y.: Vestal Press, 1989.

27. 4 Devils

1. Fox Campaign Book, *4 Devils*.

2. Lotte H. Eisner, *Murnau*, Berkeley and Los Angeles: University of California Press, 1973, p. 187.

3. Fox Campaign Book, *4 Devils*.

4. Ibid.

5. *Variety*, October 10, 1928.

6. Ibid.

7. *Film Daily,* October 7, 1928.

8. *Photoplay,* December, 1928, p. 52.

9. *Variety,* June 18, 1929.

10. Ibid.

BIBLIOGRAPHY

The following books contain either additional information on films discussed in *Lost Films* or material on other important lost films that are not included here. Sometimes these films were omitted from *Lost Films* simply for reasons of space, but often the treatment of these titles in other books has been so thorough that, in writing about them here, I would simply be going over ground already sufficiently covered. The books' titles are followed by the lost films discussed.

Brownlow, Kevin. *Behind the Mask of Innocence*. New York: Alfred A. Knopf, 1990. *Damaged Goods* (1914), *Human Wreckage* (1923).

Kerr, Walter. *The Silent Clowns*. New York: Alfred A. Knopf, 1975. Chapter 32, "Missing Film," not only addresses the fragility of motion picture stock but discusses several lost movies including: *A Connecticut Yankee in King Arthur's Court* (1921, starring Harry Myers), *Senorita* (1927, starring Bebe Daniels), *Forty Winks* (1925), *Time to Love* (1927), and *Wedding Bills* (1927)—all three starring Raymond Griffith.

Koszarski, Richard, ed., *The Rivals of D. W. Griffith: Alternate Auteurs 1913–1918*. Minneapolis: Walker Arts Center, 1976. Chapter on Lost Films includes brief discussion of (and terrific photographs from) *Prunella* (1918; Maurice Tourneur), *A Daughter of the Gods* (1916), *The Battle of Gettysburg* (1913), *Cleopatra* (1916), *The Battle Cry of Peace* (1915; J. Stuart Blackton), and *Life's Whirlpool* (1916; Barry O'Neill).

McCabe, John, Al Kilgore, and Richard W. Bann. *Laurel and Hardy*. New York: E. P. Dutton, 1975. *The Rogue Song* (1930).

Sarris, Andrew. *The Films of Josef von Sternberg*. Garden City, N.Y.: Doubleday & Co., 1966. *The Exquisite Sinner* (1925), *The Sea Gull* (1926), *The Drag Net* (1928), *The Case of Lena Smith* (1929).

Skretvedt, Randy. *Laurel and Hardy: The Magic Behind the Movies*. Beverly Hills: Moonstone Press, 1987. *The Rogue Song* (1930).

Thompson, Frank. *Alamo Movies*. Plano, Tex.: Republic of Texas Press: 1994. *The Immortal Alamo* (1911), *The Siege and Fall of the Alamo* (1913), *The Fall of the Alamo* (1914), *The Fall of the Alamo* (1938).

Wagenknecht, Edward, and Anthony Slide, *The Films of D. W. Griffith*. New York: Crown Publishers, 1975. *The Battle of the Sexes* (1914), *The Escape* (1914), *The Great Love* (1918), *The Greatest Thing in Life* (1919), *"That Royle Girl"* (1925).

Weinberg, Herman G. *The Complete Greed*. New York: E. P. Dutton, 1973.

Weinberg, Herman G. *Stroheim: A Pictorial Record of His Nine Films*. New York: Dover Publications, 1975. *The Honeymoon* [Part II of *The Wedding March*] (1928).

Other reference books important to any exploration of the silent cinema:

Brownlow, Kevin. *The Parade's Gone By*. New York: Alfred A. Knopf, 1968.

———. *The War, the West, and the Wilderness*. New York: Alfred A. Knopf, 1979.

———. *Hollywood: The Pioneers*. London: Collins, 1979.

Everson, William K., *American Silent Film*. New York: Oxford University Press, 1978.

Hanson, Patricia King, ed. *The American Film Institute Catalog of Motion Pictures Produced in the United States: Feature Films 1911–1920*. Berkeley: University of California Press, 1988.

Harpole, Charles, ed. *History of the American Cinema*, vol. 1., by Charles Musser, *The Emergence of Cinema: The American Screen to 1907*; vol. 2, by Eileen Bowser, *The Transformation of Cinema 1907–1915*; vol. 3., by Richard Koszarski, *An Evening's Entertainment: The Age of the Silent Feature Picture, 1915–1928*. New York: Charles Scribner's Sons, 1990.

Munden, Kenneth W., ed., *The American Film Institute Catalog of Motion Pictures Produced in the United States: Feature Films 1921–1930*. New York: R. R. Bowker, 1971.

Pratt, George C. *Spellbound in Darkness: A History of the Silent Film*. Greenwich, Conn.: New York Graphic Society, 1966, rev. 1973.

Ramsaye, Terry. *A Million and One Nights: A History of the Motion Picture Through 1925*. New York: Simon & Schuster, 1926, reprinted in 1986.

And, finally, these volumes are invaluable for any study on Lost Movies—indeed, for any study on ways we can keep any more films from disappearing:

Billington, James H. ed. *Film Preservation 1993: A Study of the Current State of American Film Preservation.* vol. 1, Report; vol. 2, Los Angeles, CA, Hearing; vol. 3, Washington, D.C., Hearing; vol. 4, Submissions. Washington, D.C.: Library of Congress, 1993:

Slide, Anthony. *Nitrate Won't Wait: Film Preservation in the United States.* Jefferson, N. C.: McFarland & Co., 1992.

Index